CASEBOOK SERIES

GENERAL EDITOR: A. E. Dyson

PUBLISHED

Jane Austen: *Emma*   DAVID LODGE
Jane Austen: *'Northanger Abbey' and 'Persuasion'*   B.C. SOUTHAM
Jane Austen: *'Sense and Sensibility', 'Pride and Prejudice' and 'Mansfield Park'*
   B. C. SOUTHAM
William Blake: *Songs of Innocence and Experience*   MARGARET BOTTRALL
Charlotte Brontë: *'Jane Eyre' and 'Villette'*   MIRIAM ALLOTT
Emily Brontë: *Wuthering Heights*   MIRIAM ALLOTT
Browning: *'Men and Women' and Other Poems*   J.R. WATSON
Bunyan: *Pilgrim's Progress*   ROGER SHARROCK
Byron: *'Childe Harold's Pilgrimage' and 'Don Juan'*   JOHN JUMP
Chaucer: *Canterbury Tales*   J.J. ANDERSON
Coleridge: *'The Ancient Mariner' and Other Poems*   ALUN R. JONES AND WILLIAM
   TYDEMAN
Conrad: *The Secret Agent*   IAN WATT
Dickens: *Bleak House*   A. E. DYSON
Donne: *Songs and Sonets*   JULIAN LOVELOCK
George Eliot: *Middlemarch*   PATRICK SWINDEN
T. S. Eliot: *Four Quartets*   BERNARD BERGONZI
T. S. Eliot: *The Waste Land*   C. B. COX AND ARNOLD P. HINCHLIFFE
Farquhar: *'The Recruiting Officer' and 'The Beaux' Stratagem'*   RAYMOND A.
   ANSELMENT
Henry Fielding: *Tom Jones*   NEIL COMPTON
E. M. Forster: *A Passage to India*   MALCOLM BRADBURY
Hardy: *The Tragic Novels*   R. P. DRAPER
Gerard Manley Hopkins: *Poems*   MARGARET BOTTRALL
Jonson: *Volpone*   JONAS A. BARISH
James Joyce: *'Dubliners' and 'A Portrait of the Artist as a Young Man'*   MORRIS BEJA
John Keats: *Odes*   G. S. FRASER
D.H. Lawrence: *Sons and Lovers*   GĀMINI SALGĀDO
D. H. Lawrence: *'The Rainbow' and 'Women in Love'*   COLIN CLARKE
Marlowe: *Doctor Faustus*   JOHN JUMP
The Metaphysical Poets   GERALD HAMMOND
Milton: *'Comus' and 'Samson Agonistes'*   JULIAN LOVELOCK
Milton: *Paradise Lost*   A. E. DYSON AND JULIAN LOVELOCK
John Osborne: *Look Back in Anger*   JOHN RUSSELL TAYLOR
Peacock: *The Satirical Novels*   LORNA SAGE
Pope: *The Rape of the Lock*   JOHN DIXON HUNT
Shakespeare: *Antony and Cleopatra*   JOHN RUSSELL BROWN
Shakespeare: *Coriolanus*   B. A. BROCKMAN
Shakespeare: *Hamlet*   JOHN JUMP

Shakespeare: *Henry IV Parts I and II*   G. K. HUNTER
Shakespeare: *Henry V*   MICHAEL QUINN
Shakespeare: *Julius Caesar*   PETER URE
Shakespeare: *King Lear*   FRANK KERMODE
Shakespeare: *Macbeth*   JOHN WAIN
Shakespeare: *Measure for Measure*   C.K. STEAD
Shakespeare: *The Merchant of Venice*   JOHN WILDERS
Shakespeare: *Othello*   JOHN WAIN
Shakespeare: *Richard II*   NICHOLAS BROOKE
Shakespeare: *The Sonnets*   PETER JONES
Shakespeare: *The Tempest*   D. J. PALMER
Shakespeare: *Troilus and Cressida*   PRISCILLA MARTIN
Shakespeare: *Twelfth Night*   D. J. PALMER
Shakespeare: *The Winter's Tale*   KENNETH MUIR
Shelley: *Shorter Poems and Lyrics*   PATRICK SWINDEN
Spenser: *The Faerie Queene*   PETER BAYLEY
Swift: *Gulliver's Travels*   RICHARD GRAVIL
Tennyson: *In Memoriam*   JOHN DIXON HUNT
Webster: *'The White Devil' and 'The Duchess of Malfi'*   R. V. HOLDSWORTH
Virginia Woolf: *To the Lighthouse*   MORRIS BEJA
Wordsworth: *Lyrical Ballads*   ALUN R. JONES AND WILLIAM TYDEMAN
Wordsworth: *The Prelude*   W. J. HARVEY AND RICHARD GRAVIL
Yeats: *Last Poems*   JON STALLWORTHY

The English Novel: Developments in Criticism since Henry James   STEPHEN HAZELL
The Romantic Imagination   JOHN SPENCER HILL

TITLES IN PREPARATION INCLUDE
Dickens: *'Hard Times', 'Great Expectations' and 'Our Mutual Friend'*   NORMAN PAGE
T. S Eliot: *'Prufrock', 'Gerontion', 'Ash Wednesday' and Other Shorter Poems*
    B. C. SOUTHAM
Hardy: *Poems*   JAMES GIBSON AND TREVOR JOHNSON
Jonson: *'Every Man in His Humour' and 'The Alchemist'*   R. V. HOLDSWORTH
Shakespeare: *'Much Ado about Nothing' and 'As You Like It'*   JOHN RUSSELL BROWN
Sheridan: *'The Rivals', 'The School for Scandal' and 'The Critic'*   WILLIAM RUDDICK
Thackeray: *Vanity Fair*   ARTHUR POLLARD

The Development of Drama Criticism   ARNOLD P. HINCHLIFFE
The Development of Poetry Criticism   A. E. DYSON

Dickens
Bleak House

A CASEBOOK

EDITED BY

A. E. DYSON

M

Selection and editorial matter © A. E. Dyson 1969

All rights reserved. No part of this publication
may be reproduced or transmitted, in any form
or by any means, without permission

First edition 1969
Reprinted 1975, 1977

Published by
THE MACMILLAN PRESS LTD
London and Basingstoke
Associated companies in Delhi Dublin
Hong Kong Johannesburg Lagos Melbourne
New York Singapore and Tokyo

ISBN 0 333 05425 3

Printed in Hong Kong by
Shanghai Printing Press Limited

CONTENTS

Part 3: Bleak House *in its Period*

Part 4: *Recent Studies*

ACKNOWLEDGEMENTS

Humphry House, *The Dickens World* (Oxford University Press); John Butt and Kathleen Tillotson, 'The Topicality of *Bleak House*', from *Dickens at Work* (Methuen & Co. Ltd and Oxford University Press, New York; © 1957); *Charles Dickens: His Tragedy and Triumph* (Mr Edgar Johnson, Victor Gollancz Ltd and Little, Brown & Co.; © Edgar Johnson 1952); J. Hillis Miller, *Charles Dickens, The World of His Novels* (Harvard University Press; © the President and Fellows of Harvard College 1959); Monroe Engel, *The Maturity of Dickens* (Oxford University Press and Harvard University Press; © the President and Fellows of Harvard College 1959); Professor C. B. Cox, 'A Dickens Landscape', from *Critical Quarterly*, II i (1960); Mark Spilka, '*Bleak House* and the Trial: Religious Folly', from *Dickens and Kafka* (Indiana University Press); W. J. Harvey, *Character and the Novel* (Mrs M. A. Harvey, Chatto & Windus Ltd and Cornell University Press; © W. J. Harvey 1965); Taylor Stoehr, 'Dickens: The Dreamer's Stance' (Cornell University Press; © Cornell University 1965).

GENERAL EDITOR'S PREFACE

EACH of this series of Casebooks concerns either one well-known and influential work of literature or two or three closely linked works. The main section consists of critical readings, mostly modern, brought together from journals and books. A selection of reviews and comments by the author's contemporaries is also included, and sometimes comments from the author himself. The Editor's Introduction charts the reputation of the work from its first appearance until the present time.

What is the purpose of such a collection? Chiefly, to assist reading. Our first response to literature may be, or seem to be, 'personal'. Certain qualities of vigour, profundity, beauty or 'truth to experience' strike us, and the work gains a foothold in our mind. Later, an isolated phrase or passage may return to haunt or illuminate. Where did we hear that? we wonder – it could scarcely be better put.

In these and similar ways appreciation begins, but major literature prompts to very much more. There are certain facts we need to know if we are to understand properly. Who were the author's original readers, and what assumptions did he share with them? What was his theory of literature? Was he committed to a particular historical situation, or a set of beliefs? We need historians as well as critics to help us with this. But there are also more purely literary factors to take account of: the work's structure and rhetoric; its symbols and archetypes; its tone, genre and texture; its use of language; the words on the page. In all these matters critics can inform and enrich our individual responses by offering imaginative recreations of their own.

For the life of a book is not, after all, merely 'personal'; it is more like a tripartite dialogue, between a writer living 'then', a reader living 'now', and whatever forces of survival and honour link the two. Criticism is the public manifestation of this dialogue, a witness to the continuing power of literature to arouse and excite. It illuminates the possibilities and rewards of the dialogue, pushing 'interpretation' as far forward as it can go.

And here, indeed, is the rub: how far can it go? Where does 'interpretation' end, and nonsense begin? Why is one interpretation superior to another, and why does each age need to interpret for itself? The critic knows that his insights have value only in so far as they serve the text, and that he must take account of views differing sharply from his own. He knows that his own writing will be judged as well as the work he writes about, so that he cannot simply assert inner illumination or a differing taste.

The critical forum is a place of vigorous conflict and disagreement, but there is nothing in this to cause dismay. What is attested is the complexity of human experience and the richness of literature, not any chaos or relativity of taste. A critic is better seen, no doubt, as an explorer than as an 'authority', but explorers ought to be, and usually are, well equipped. The effect of good criticism is to convince us of what C. S. Lewis called 'the enormous extension of our being which we owe to authors'. This Casebook will be justified only if it helps to promote the same end.

A single volume can represent no more than a small selection of critical opinions. Some critics have been excluded for reasons of space, and it is hoped that readers will follow up the further suggestions in the Select Bibliography. Other contributions have been severed from their original context, to which some readers may wish to return. Indeed, if they take a hint from the critics represented here, they certainly will.

A. E. DYSON

INTRODUCTION

I

'I believe I have never had so many readers as in this book', wrote Dickens in his 1853 preface to *Bleak House*. It was not strictly true. The death of Little Nell had attracted nearly three times as many, and the Christmas books sold extremely well. But *Bleak House* did mark an improvement upon recent performances. There had been a falling off from 70,000 to 30,000 copies per issue during the serial publication of *Barnaby Rudge* (1841); and *Martin Chuzzlewit* (1843-4) had slumped to 20,000 at the start. The gradual recovery after this had reached 25,000 with *David Copperfield* (1849-50); and *Bleak House*, with its 35,000, continued the trend. From this time onwards, sales continued to rise for the remainder of Dickens's life. This seems much to the credit of his 'popular' readers, some of whom still hankered after Mr Pickwick and occasionally said so, but – like Mrs Micawber – never deserted, even in seasons of gloom.

Dickens's intellectual readers were less faithful, as the selection of reviews printed here suggests. Many reviewers accepted his great popularity as a fact to be taken for granted, if not actually sneered at, and saw his past novels as so many hurdles for testing and if possible unseating the new. At the same time, the emergent demand for social and moral seriousness in the novel worked against Dickens. While George Eliot catered authentically for this demand in the late 1850s and the 1860s, Dickens's immense vitality was felt to stand in his way. There was also, as so often with reviewers, the problem of snobbery. The *Spectator* reviewer (pp. 56-9) clearly proclaims himself a cut above Dickens, in that tone which is an age-old revenge of moderate intelligence against creative success. The other reviewers, while less determined to scold and re-educate the author, find it hard to see artistic greatness in conjunction with huge popular acclaim.

Shakespeare himself has often been regarded as exceptional in
this respect, or even freakish, with the groundlings as at best a
dubious excuse.

The first complete edition of *Bleak House* was issued in 1853,
and Dickens's preface is characteristically devoted to exonera-
ting his social realism from attack. He brings his deadliest banter
to bear on the Chancery judge who 'once had the kindness to
inform me . . . that the Court of Chancery, though the shining
subject of much popular prejudice (at which point I thought the
judge's eye had a cast in my direction), was almost immaculate'.
He also puts a brave face on Spontaneous Combustion, that crux
where even the most ardent Dickensian turns slightly defensive,
adducing Giuseppe Bianchini and the renowned surgeon Le Cat,
among others, in proof that any one of us might end nauseously
dispersed around the house like Krook. It is of interest to modern
readers that his defence involves no allusion to symbolism, or to
the macabre fitness of Spontaneous Combustion in a novel circling round Chancery and Tom-All-Alone's. No doubt the
powerful undercurrent of linked themes and resonances was an
aspect of the creative process which he did not analyse, and
would have been as unable to talk about, in these pre-symbolist
days, as the reviewers themselves. Certainly he stands at the
opposite pole in this matter to Henry James, and has none of the
later novelist's power to cap the intellectual teasing of creation
with prefaces as irresistible as the novels themselves.

II

The original reviews, which are reprinted here in a representative selection, have a certain historical interest of their own.
Much of what they say remains stimulating and interesting, but
we cannot help noticing the gaps. Indeed, the gaps might strike
us as offering more illumination than the lines surrounding them,
since the greatness of Dickens's art is nowhere made clear. It was
a reviewer in the *Fortnightly Review* many years later (p. 191
below) who sensed that an unsolved critical problem remained.
He hints at certain elusive questions about the power of the novel

which have still to be formulated, and – by implication therefore –
at the limitation of answers given to questions too readily conceived. Most of the early reviewers undeniably split their
response into separate compartments – plot, character, morality,
social realism – and appeared to think that each item could be
pondered on its own. The interrelation of these factors one to
another did not strike them, nor did the presence of images and
allusions delicately running through the whole.

One factor contributing to such simplicities was the low
general repute of the novel as an art form, extending to uncer-
tainty about whether it was an art form at all. Despite Jane Austen
and Scott, novels were still valued chiefly as 'entertainment', in
some lively but ultimately disabling sense. This view was by no
means confined to puritans and the narrowly religious (though
Lucy Snowe found novel-reading a more heinous sin in her
Villette catholic school than lying, while Mr Podsnap would
always think first of the blush on the Young Person's cheek). It
is clear that the novel was felt to lack the same kind of seriousness as poetry, and was not fully accepted either as moral and
social critique or as autonomous art. Matthew Arnold, the only
English critic who might have risen to Dickens's challenge,
largely ignored him, and Bagehot on Dickens is decidedly not at
his best. But, more significantly, the approach needed for novel
criticism was in its infancy, as the excessively fragmented response of these reviewers reveals. There is a great deal about
plot, most of it uncomplimentary, and only occasional puzzle-
ment about why the novel remains so vivid and readable if its
plot is so poor. There is much commentary on 'characters', enthusiastic or derogatory, but little consideration of why these
fifty or so characters should come together, in a common *raison
d'être*, in *Bleak House*. The vividness of characterisation is usually
conceded, but the rarity of the creative gift implied in it is
haltingly praised. Several critics complain of exaggeration and
caricature, as though they had never seen anyone resembling
Esther Summerson or Mr Guppy, Harold Skimpole or old Mr
Turveydrop in their lives. It is not recognised how finely Dickens
observes the eccentric and mad in his fellow men, nor how wide-

spread – back in 'life' again – some degree of eccentricity and
madness is. The word 'daguerreotype' – a voguish word in the
1850s – recurs in an attempt to define one aspect of his vivid
characterisation. Daguerreotyping, dating from the late 1830s
and named after its inventor, was a photographic process in
which the impression was taken on a silver plate sensitised by
iodine, and then developed by vapour of mercury. Dickens's
characters struck several reviewers as daguerreotypes, and Esther
Summerson herself was accredited with the art.

It will be seen that the characters approved of by different
reviewers vary a great deal, with only Jo receiving more or less
general acclaim. For the rest, there is a wide spectrum of praise
and blame, in which diametrically opposite views of the social
realism and artistic integrity of nearly every leading character
are asserted – the Dedlocks, Esther, Jarndyce, the Smallweeds
and the 'satiric' group. Skimpole is especially attacked, obviously
because Dickens was felt to have overstepped the acceptable
bounds of creative tact by making him so recognisably deriva-
tive from Leigh Hunt. Mrs Jellyby, Mrs Pardiggle and the Chadbands strike some reviewers as admirable, others as offensive,
but usually (it seems) in accordance with views about private
philanthropy and nonconformist preachers in actual life. Mrs
Jellyby was particularly resented by such pro-feminists as Lord
Denman (who launched a pamphlet against her) and John Stuart
Mill, though she must have given great pleasure to Carlyle, for
whom she is tailor-made. The Dedlocks seemed to some critics a
sensitive and accurate study of the aristocracy, to others a
further proof that Dickens could succeed only with people from
'low life'. A striking feature is the endless appeal to social realism
for praise or blame of these characters; the appeal to art is made
scarcely at all. In particular, it is not noticed that the characters
are interlinked in certain themes of selfishness and loneliness.
There is little insight into the profound critique of capitalism
which Shaw later seized on, or into the web of analogy which
recent critics all find at the heart of the book. There is little
understanding of Dickens's probing of the problem of identity
in his fluid and brutal society; and little awareness of the poetic

intensity of his language and the endless ground-swell of resonances beneath the plot. Sometimes, reviewers come interest-
ingly to the edge of new discoveries, as if led there by the sheer
spell of Dickens's art. The *Putnam Magazine* reviewer says of
Mr Tulkinghorn that he 'is like a gloomy looking dark passage
in a building that leads nowhere, and puzzles you to guess what
it was intended for', but this extremely sensitive perception is
adduced *against* Tulkinghorn's success. Dickens's extraordinary
sense of the irrationalities and enigmas of human behaviour
remains, therefore, unacknowledged, together with the unifying
and haunting vision of evil in the book. It is not only the profundity of his vision which is overlooked, but even its accuracy;
no one seems to have taken Dickens's temperate and amazingly
good-humoured rebuke in the preface to *Martin Chuzzlewit* to
heart:

What is exaggeration to one class of minds and perceptions, is
plain truth to another. That which is commonly called a long-
sight, perceives in a prospect innumerable features and bearings
non-existent to a short-sighted person. I sometimes ask myself
whether there may occasionally be a difference of this kind
between some writers and some readers; whether it is *always* the
writer who colours highly, or whether it is now and then the
reader whose eye for colour is a little dull?

III

In offering these reservations about the original reviewers I am
by no means claiming intellectual or moral superiority for the
moderns, though they do, in fact, provide more adequate commentary on the work. We are indebted today to the French sym-
bolists, Henry James and many other powerful minds for insights about the nature of literature which were denied to earlier
critics, and there is no particular merit, only very good fortune,
in this. We are indebted, also, with less indisputable good fortune, to insights forced upon us by the twentieth century. Beset
by social and political riddles which are both complex and inescapable, it is comparatively easy to appreciate whatever was

prophetic of such matters in Dickens's art. It could even be argued that modern criticism awakened to Dickens's greatness much later than it might have done, and has earned no right at all to give itself airs. In the 1920s and 1930s, when Baudelaire, Freud, Marx and others had already lent shape to our modern awareness, Shaw's praise was unusual, and Dickens was still an Eminent Victorian, with all the attendant ignominy, to the Bloomsbury élite. It was left to George Orwell and Edmund Wilson to point at last to Dickens's achievement from a distinctively modern viewpoint, and to set signposts for critics in almost unknown terrain. Their essays are too long and too general for this present context, but they are readily available elsewhere. What they offer, perhaps it needs to be added, is not a new and transitory voguishness but original insight; Wilson, for instance, is looking directly, and without any of the older presuppositions, at what is actually there:

Bleak House begins in the London fog, and the whole book is permeated with fog and rain. . . . In *Bleak House* the fog stands for Chancery, and Chancery stands for the whole web of clotted antiquated institutions in which England stifles and decays. All the principal elements in the story . . . are involved in the exasperating Chancery suit, which, with the fog-bank of precedent looming behind it like the Great Boyg in *Peer Gynt*, obscures and impedes at every point the attempts of men and women to live natural lives. Old Krook, with his legal junkshop, is Dickens's symbol for the Lord Chancellor himself; the cat that sits on his shoulder watches like the Chancery lawyers the caged birds in Miss Flite's lodging; Krook's death by spontaneous combustion is Dickens's prophecy of the fate of Chancery and all that it represents.

He goes on to say, with unnecessary modesty, that he goes over this 'old ground of the symbolism' because

the people who like to talk about the symbols of Kafka and Mann and Joyce have been discouraged from looking for anything of the kind in Dickens, and usually have not read him, at least with mature minds. But even when we think we do know

Dickens, we may be surprised to return to him and find in him a symbolism of a more complicated reference and a deeper implication than these metaphors that hang as emblems above the door. The Russians themselves, in this respect, appear to have learned from Dickens.

This reference to a 'deeper implication' opened what Sir Leicester Dedlock would no doubt have identified as floodgates, but it was a seminal point for Dickens criticism, even so.

This brings me to a few specific details about this anthology. The first part collects a few pieces of background information for the two major social themes of *Bleak House* – the plight of Chancery suitors and the plight of the poor; and there is a short piece from the 1890s identifying some of the already-vanishing landmarks of *Bleak House* London. Part 2 includes the selection of early reviews and an extract from Gissing, while Part 3 comprises two celebrated modern pieces of scholarly comment on the novel's topicality. The final part collects a few recent critical articles, written from differing but often converging points of view. Edgar Johnson's analysis forms part of his two-volume biography of Dickens, which is now and for the foreseeable future the standard Life. He sees *Bleak House* as an anatomy of society, and offers us a 'revolutionist' Dickens, while stopping short of the fully Marxist Dickens whom we have also met. J. Hillis Miller confirms Johnson's report on *Bleak House* as a work complexly organised and in the highest degree serious by illustrating some of its many recurring images, allusions and linked themes. Monroe Engel, in a more confined approach, turns a spotlight on the importance of death in the novel as a touchstone for 'reality'; C. B. Cox offers a brief but suggestive analysis of one paragraph of the novel, searching texture and mood. Mark Spilka and Taylor Stoehr both report sensitive psychological reverberations just below the *Bleak House* surface, and – in our reading experience – just below the fully conscious workings of the mind. Spilka draws particular attention to links in technique and sensibility between Dickens and Kafka, while Stoehr invokes the psychoanalytical interpretation of dreams. Whether these two approaches are overschematised will be debated by individual readers, but their illumination of some hitherto hidden power in the novel cannot be denied. The late W. J. Harvey studies the novel by way of its double narration and the implications of this experimental construction. My own piece is from a forthcoming book on Dickens, and is published here for the first time.

Perhaps I can conclude with a reminder of the many quotations about *Bleak House* which are scattered through writings not chiefly concerned with the novel, and not therefore suitable for a collection like this. Conrad confessed on one occasion that he had read *Bleak House* 'innumerable times' and found 'the very weaknesses more precious to me than the strengths of other men's works'. This is not only a handsome compliment, but an acknowledgement that Dickens is a novelist to whom admirers often return. Every reading reveals hitherto unnoticed facets of style and insight, while the perpetual present of the novels never ages or grows stale.

A Casebook cannot represent the *en passant* felicities which flow from a work so huge in its scope and so widely loved, and it cannot fully represent even the Dickens critics when their remarks are in the form of asides. 'His description of our party system,' said Shaw, in his 1912 preface to *Hard Times*, 'with its Coodle, Doodle, Foodle, etc., has never been surpassed for accuracy and for penetration of superficial pretence.' 'The famous analysis of parliamentary government in *Bleak House*', wrote V. S. Pritchett in 'The Comic World of Dickens' (1954, reprinted in *The Dickens Critics*, ed. George H. Ford and Lauriat Lane, Jnr (New York, 1961; London, 1968)), 'is an indignant lark. Dickens understood the art of calling people funny names and his ear for funny sounds is splendid.' We can instance again, as a source of occasional insights, the Smallweeds. Robert Morse, pondering Dickens's many concealed myths and archetypes in his consideration of *Our Mutual Friend*, asks suddenly, 'Who could Mr and Mrs Smallweed be, by the way, other than Punch and Judy?' Dorothy Van Ghent, in her famous essay 'The Dickens World: A View from Todgers's' (in *Sewanee Review*, LVII (1950) iii 419–38), says this:

The animate is treated as if it were a thing. It is as if the life
absorbed by things had been drained out of people who have
become incapable of their humanity. Grandfather Smallweed, in
Bleak House, has to be beaten up periodically like a cushion in
order to be restored to the shape of a man. The ignomy is horri-
fying, suggesting unspeakable deterioration.

This almost H. P. Lovecraft version of Grandfather Smallweed
links, in turn, with a larger insight into the workings of Dickens's
imagination:

... the physical plague that arises out of the slum district of Tom
All Alone's, in *Bleak House*, and that creeps to the houses of the
great, is itself a moral plague, the conditions for it having been
created by moral aquiescence. Its ambiguity is enforced by the
conversion of the slum-dwellers into vermin parasites – 'a crowd
of foul existence that crawls in and out of gaps in walls and
boards; and coils itself to sleep, in maggot numbers, where the
rain drips in; and comes and goes, fetching and carrying fever,
and sowing ... evil in its every footprint'.

For a final quotation, I choose one of T. S. Eliot's typically
gnomic phrases, from his 1927 essay, 'Wilkie Collins and
Dickens': '*Bleak House* is Dickens's finest piece of construction.'
This takes us a very long way, it seems, from the early reviews.

A. E. DYSON

PART ONE

Background to
Bleak House

Report on the Sanitary Condition of the Labouring Population, 1842

... MR BAKER, in his report on the condition of the population, after giving an instance of the contrast presented by the working-people living in better dwellings situated in better cleansed neighbourhoods ... describes the population living in houses – 'With broken panes in every window-frame, and filth and vermin in every nook. With the walls unwhitewashed for years, black with the smoke of foul chimneys, without water, with corded bed-stocks for beds, and sacking for bed-clothing, with floors unwashed from year to year, without out-offices ... while without, there are streets, elevated a foot, sometimes two, above the level of the causeway, by the accumulation of years, and stagnant puddles here and there with their foetid exhalations, causeways broken and dangerous, ash-places choked up with filth, and excrementitious deposits on all sides as a consequence, undrained, unpaved, unventilated, uncared-for by any authority but the landlord, who weekly collects his miserable rents from his miserable tenants.

'Can we wonder that such places are the hot-beds of disease, or that it obtains, upon constitutions thus liberally predisposed to receive it, and forms the mortality which Leeds exhibits. Adult life, exposed to such miasmata, gives way. How much more then infant life, when ushered into, and attempted to be reared in, such obnoxious atmospheres. On the moral habits similar effects are produced. An inattention on the part of the local authorities to the state of the streets diminishes year by year the respectability of their occupiers. None dwell in such localities but those to whom propinquity to employment is absolutely essential. Those who might advocate a better state of things, depart; and of those who remain, the one-half, by repeated exhibitions of indecency and vulgarity, and indeed by the mere fact of neighbourship, sink into the moral degradation which is natural to the other, and vicious habits and criminal propensities precede the death which these combinations prepare.'

No education as yet commonly given appears to have availed against such demoralising circumstances as those described; but the cases of moral improvement of a population, by cleansing, draining, and the improvement of the internal and external conditions of the dwelling . . . are more numerous and decided, though there still occur instances in whom the love of ardent spirits has gained such entire possession as to have withstood all such means of retrieving them. The most experienced public officers acquainted with the condition of the inferior population of the towns would agree in giving the first place in efficiency and importance to the removal of what may be termed the physical barriers to improvement, and that as against such barriers moral agencies have but a remote chance of success. . . .

[*Recapitulations and conclusions* include the following clauses:]

That the various forms of epidemic, endemic, and other disease caused, or aggravated, or propagated chiefly amongst the labouring classes by atmospheric impurities produced by decomposing animal and vegetable substances, by damp and filth, and close and overcrowded dwellings prevail amongst the population in every part of the kingdom, whether dwelling in separate houses, in rural villages, in small towns, in the larger towns – as they have been found to prevail in the lowest districts of the metropolis. . . .

That such disease, wherever its attacks are frequent, is always found in connexion with the physical circumstances above specified, and that where these circumstances are removed by drainage, proper cleansing, better ventilation, and other means of diminishing atmospheric impurity, the frequency and intensity of such disease is abated; and where the removal of the noxious agencies appears to be complete, such disease almost entirely disappears. . . .

That the formation of all habits of cleanliness is obstructed by defective supplies of water. . . .

That the annual loss of life from filth and bad ventilation are greater than the loss from death or wounds in any wars in which the country has been engaged in modern times. . . .

That of the 43,000 cases of widowhood, and 112,000 cases of

destitute orphanage relieved from the poor's rates in England and Wales alone, it appears that the greatest proportion of deaths of the heads of families occurred from the above specified and other removable causes; that their ages were under 45 years; that is to say, 13 years below the natural probabilities of life as shown by the experience of the whole population of Sweden. . . .

That the younger population, bred up under noxious physical agencies, is inferior in physical organisation and general health to a population preserved from the presence of such agencies. . . .

That defective town cleansing fosters habits of the most abject degradation and tends to the demoralisation of large numbers of human beings, who subsist by means of what they can find amidst the noxious filth accumulated in neglected streets and bye-places. . . .

(from *Report on the Sanitary Condition of the Labouring Population*, 1842)

F. Engels: The Working Class in England in 1844

SINCE capital, the direct or indirect control of the means of sub-sistence and production, is the weapon with which this social warfare is carried on, it is clear that all the disadvantages of such a state must fall upon the poor. For him no man has the slightest concern. Cast into the whirlpool, he must struggle through as well as he can. If he is so happy as to find work, i.e., if the bourgeoisie does him the favour to enrich itself by means of him, wages await him which scarcely suffice to keep body and soul together; if he can get no work he may steal, if he is not afraid of the police, or starve, in which case the police will take care that he does so in a quiet and inoffensive manner. During my resi-dence in England, at least twenty or thirty persons have died of simple starvation under the most revolting circumstances, and a jury has rarely been found possessed of the courage to speak the plain truth in the matter. Let the testimony of the witnesses be never so clear and unequivocal, the bourgeoisie, from which the jury is selected, always finds some backdoor through which to escape the frightful verdict, death from starvation. The bourgeoisie dare not speak the truth in these cases, for it would speak its own condemnation. But indirectly, far more than directly, many have died of starvation, where long continued want of proper nourishment has called forth fatal illness, when it has produced such debility that causes which might otherwise have remained inoperative, brought on severe illness and death. The English working-men call this 'social murder', and accuse our whole society of perpetrating this crime perpetually. Are they wrong? . . .

Every great city has one or more slums, where the working class is crowded together. True, poverty often dwells in hidden alleys close to the palaces of the rich; but, in general, a separate territory has been assigned to it, where, removed from the sight of the happier classes, it may struggle along as it can. These slums are pretty equally arranged in all the great towns of England, the worst houses in the worst quarters of the towns; usually one- or two-storied cottages in long rows, perhaps with cellars used as dwellings, almost always irregularly built. These houses of three or four rooms and a kitchen form, throughout England, some parts of London excepted, the general dwellings of the working class. The streets are generally unpaved, rough, dirty, filled with vegetable and animal refuse, without sewers or gutters, but supplied with foul, stagnant pools instead. Moreover, ventilation is impeded by the bad, confused method of building of the whole quarter, and since many human beings here live crowded into a small space, the atmosphere that prevails in these working-men's quarters may readily be imagined. Further, the streets serve as drying grounds in fine weather; lines are stretched across from house to house, and hung with wet clothing.

Let us investigate some of the slums in their order. London comes first, and in London the famous rookery of St Giles which is now, at last, about to be penetrated by a couple of broad streets. St Giles is in the midst of the most populous part of the town,

surrounded by broad, splendid avenues in which the gay world of
London idles about, in the immediate neighbourhood of Oxford
Street, Regent Street, of Trafalgar Square and the Strand. It is
a disorderly collection of tall, three- or four-storied houses, with
narrow, crooked, filthy streets, in which there is quite as much
life as in the great thoroughfares of the town, except that, here,
people of the working class only are to be seen. A vegetable
market is held in the street, baskets with vegetables and fruits,
naturally all bad and hardly fit to use, obstruct the sidewalk still
further, and from these, as well as from the fish-dealers' stalls,
arises a horrible smell. The houses are occupied from cellar to
garret, filthy within and without, and their appearance is such
that no human being could possibly wish to live in them. But all
this is nothing in comparison with the dwellings in the narrow
courts and alleys between the streets, entered by covered passages
between the houses, in which the filth and tottering ruin surpass
all description. Scarcely a whole window-pane can be found, the
walls are crumbling, doorposts and window-frames loose and
broken, doors of old boards nailed together, or altogether wanting in this thieves' quarter, where no doors are needed, there
being nothing to steal. Heaps of garbage and ashes lie in all
directions, and the foul liquids emptied before the doors gather
in stinking pools. Here live the poorest of the poor, the worst-
paid workers with thieves and the victims of prostitution indiscriminately huddled together, the majority Irish, or of Irish
extraction, and those who have not yet sunk in the whirlpool of
moral ruin which surrounds them, sinking daily deeper, losing
daily more and more of their power to resist the demoralising
influence of want, filth, and evil surroundings.

Nor is St Giles the only London slum. In the immense tangle
of streets, there are hundreds and thousands of alleys and courts
lined with houses too bad for anyone to live in who can still
spend anything whatsoever upon a dwelling fit for human beings.
Close to the splendid houses of the rich such a lurking-place of
the bitterest poverty may often be found. So, a short time ago, on
the occasion of a coroner's inquest, a region close to Portman
Square, one of the very respectable squares, was characterised as

an abode 'of a multitude of Irish demoralised by poverty and filth'. So, too, may be found in streets, such as Long Acre and others, which, though not fashionable, are yet 'respectable', a great number of cellar dwellings out of which puny children and half-starved, ragged women emerge into the light of day. In the immediate neighbourhood of Drury Lane Theatre, the second in London, are some of the worst streets of the whole metropolis, Charles, King, and Park Streets, in which the houses are inhabited from cellar to garret exclusively by poor families. In the parishes of St John and St Margaret there lived in 1840, according to the *Journal of the Statistical Society*, 5,366 working-men's families in 5,294 'dwellings' (if they deserve the name!), men, women, and children thrown together without distinction of age or sex, 26,830 persons all told; and of these families three-fourths possessed but one room. In the aristocratic parish of St George, Hanover Square, there lived, according to the same authority, 1,465 working-men's families, nearly 6,000 persons, under similar conditions, and here, too, more than two-thirds of the whole number crowded together at the rate of one family in one room. And how the poverty of these unfortunates, among whom even thieves find nothing to steal, is exploited by the property-holding class in lawful ways! The abominable dwellings in Drury Lane, just mentioned, bring in the following rents: two cellar dwellings, 3s; one room, ground-floor, 4s; second-storey, 4s 6d; third-floor, 4s; garret-room, 3s weekly, so that the starving occupants of Charles Street alone, pay the house-owners a yearly tribute of £2,000, and the 5,336 families above mentioned in Westminster, a yearly rent of £40,000.

The most extensive working-people's district lies east of the Tower in Whitechapel and Bethnal Green, where the greatest masses of London working-people live. Let us hear Mr G. Alston, preacher of St Philip's, Bethnal Green, on the condition of his parish. He says:

It contains 1,400 houses, inhabited by 2,795 families, or about 12,000 persons. The space upon which this large population dwells, is less than 400 yards (1,200 feet) square, and in this overcrowding it is nothing unusual to find a man, his wife, four or five children, and, sometimes, both grandparents, all in one single room, where they eat, sleep, and work. I believe that before the Bishop of London called attention to this most poverty-stricken parish, people at the West End knew as little of it as of the savages of Australia or the South Sea Isles. And if we make ourselves acquainted with these unfortunates, through personal observation, if we watch them at their scanty meal and see them bowed by illness and want of work, we shall find such a mass of helplessness and misery, that a nation like ours must blush that these things can be possible. I was rector near Huddersfield during the three years in which the mills were at their worst, but I have never seen such complete helplessness of the poor as since then in Bethnal Green. Not one father of a family in ten in the whole neighbourhood has other clothing than his working suit, and that is as bad and tattered as possible; many, indeed, have no other covering for the night than these rags, and no bed, save a sack of straw and shavings.

The foregoing description furnishes an idea of the aspect of the interior of the dwellings. But let us follow the English officials, who occasionally stray thither, into one or two of these working-men's homes.

On the occasion of an inquest held 14 November 1843, by Mr Carter, coroner for Surrey, upon the body of Ann Galway, aged 45 years, the newspapers related the following particulars concerning the deceased: She had lived at No. 3 White Lion Court, Bermondsey Street, London, with her husband and a nineteen-year-old son in a little room, in which neither a bedstead nor any other furniture was to be seen. She lay dead beside her son upon a heap of feathers which were scattered over her almost naked body, there being neither sheet nor coverlet. The feathers stuck so fast over the whole body that the physician could not examine the corpse until it was cleansed, and then found it starved and scarred from the bites of vermin. Part of the floor of the room was torn up, and the hole used by the family as a privy.

On Monday, 15 January 1844, two boys were brought before the police magistrate because, being in a starving condition, they had stolen and immediately devoured a half-cooked calf's foot from a shop. The magistrate felt called upon to investigate the case further, and received the following details from the policeman: The mother of the two boys was the widow of an ex-soldier, afterwards policeman, and had had a very hard time since the death of her husband, to provide for her nine children. She lived at No. 2 Pool's Place, Quaker Court, Spitalfields, in the utmost poverty. When the policeman came to her, he found her with six of her children literally huddled together in a little back room, with no furniture but two old rush-bottomed chairs with the seats gone, a small table with two legs broken, a broken cup, and a small dish. On the hearth was scarcely a spark of fire, and in one corner lay as many old rags as would fill a woman's apron, which served the whole family as a bed. For bed clothing they had only their scanty day clothing. The poor woman told him that she had been forced to sell her bedstead the year before to buy food. Her bedding she had pawned with the victualler for food. In short, everything had gone for food. The magistrate ordered the woman a considerable provision from the poor-box.

But in spite of all this, they who have some kind of a shelter are fortunate, fortunate in comparison with the utterly homeless. In London fifty thousand human beings get up every morning, not knowing where they are to lay their heads at night. The luckiest of this multitude, those who succeed in keeping a penny or two until evening, enter a lodging-house, such as abound in every great city, where they find a bed. But what a bed! These houses are filled with beds from cellar to garret, four, five, six beds in a room; as many as can be crowded in. Into every bed four, five, or six human beings are piled, as many as can be packed in, sick and well, young and old, drunk and sober, men and women, just as they come, indiscriminately. Then come strife, blows, wounds, or, if these bed-fellows agree, so much the worse; thefts are arranged and things done which our language, grown more humane than our deeds, refuses to record. And those who cannot pay for such a refuge? They sleep where they find a place, in passages, arcades, in corners where the police and the owners leave them undisturbed. A few individuals find their way to the refuges which are managed, here and there, by private charity, others sleep on the benches in the parks close

under the windows of Queen Victoria. Let us hear the London
Times:

It appears from the report of the proceedings at Marlborough
Street Police Court in our columns of yesterday, that there is an
average number of 50 human beings of all ages, who huddle
together in the parks every night, having no other shelter than
what is supplied by the trees and a few hollows of the embank-
ment. Of these, the majority are young girls who have been
seduced from the country by the soldiers and turned loose on the
world in all the destitution of friendless penury, and all the
recklessness of early vice.

This is truly horrible! Poor there must be everywhere.
Indigence will find its way and set up its hideous state in the
heart of a great and luxurious city. Amid the thousand narrow
lanes and by-streets of a populous metropolis there must always,
we fear, be much suffering – much that offends the eye – much
that lurks unseen.

But that within the precincts of wealth, gaiety, and fashion,
nigh the regal grandeur of St James, close on the palatial splendour of Bayswater, on the confines of the old and new aristocratic
quarters, in a district where the cautious refinement of modern
design has refrained from creating one single tenement for
poverty; which seems, as it were, dedicated to the exclusive
enjoyment of wealth, that *there* want, and famine, and disease, and
vice should stalk in all their kindred horrors, consuming body
by body, soul by soul!

It is indeed a monstrous state of things! Enjoyment the most
absolute, that bodily ease, intellectual excitement, or the more
innocent pleasures of sense can supply to man's craving, brought
in close contact with the most unmitigated misery! Wealth, from
its bright saloons, laughing – an insolently heedless laugh – at
the unknown wounds of want! Pleasure, cruelly but unconsciously mocking the pain that moans below! All contrary things
mocking one another – all contrary, save the vice which tempts
and the vice which is tempted!

But let all men remember this – that within the most courtly
precincts of the richest city of God's earth, there may be found,
night after night, winter after winter, women – young in years –
old in sin and suffering – outcasts from society – ROTTING FROM

FAMINE, FILTH, AND DISEASE. Let them remember this, and learn
not to theorise but to act. God knows, there is much room for
action nowadays.

(from *The Condition of the Working Class in England
in 1844*, 1844)

The Sanitary Condition of the City

The Simon Report

IT is now a matter of everyday notoriety that there are around
us in this city innumerable causes of disease and death, over
which a large, if not an absolute, control has been granted to us.
To remove these causes, and thus to reduce to a *minimum* the
risks incident to life, is the object of sanitary reform. If in one
sense it is true that he who doctors himself has a fool for his
patient, in another sense it is equally true that to every man is
confided the care and guardianship of his own physical existence. Incompetent as men are to deal with the malady which has
already fastened upon them, it is quite within their competence to
foresee and to prevent many conditions of disease. The agencies
which are most powerful on the aggregate health of a community
are those which the ordinary phenomena of existence give birth
to, and which are traceable in them by almost imperceptible
signs. The air we inhale and the fluid we imbibe represent a large
proportion of our probabilities of life. It is not only the direct
and immediate influence of an infected locality or person; it is
not the single breath of tainted air, or the single glass of impure
water, which creates the fatal disorder or the lingering illness; it
is not in the sudden access of disease, or the instance of pre-
mature decline, that the effects of unfavourable circumstances
make themselves visible: they are as plainly and as surely seen in
the depressed vitality, and therefore defective energies of those
who live, in the accelerated ratio with which natural and unavoidable decay invests the human organism, in the total of
mortality as unconnected with immediate and palpable causes.
An admirable exposition of this truth is to be found in the report

just addressed to the Commissioners of Sewers of the city of London by the Medical Officer of Health, Mr Simon. Confined as his researches are to the region technically so called, their bearing upon the general problem which we are now endeavouring to solve is not subject to any such limitation. The *data* which Mr Simon has tabulated, and which refer necessarily to one specific area, are but the introduction to and accessory of a more comprehensive question; and we cannot do better than follow the arrangement which put us first in possession of the statistics of mortality in the city, and then proceed to discuss the causes of endemic disease and the mode of preventing it.

The rate of mortality which during the preceding year averaged over a population of 125,000 about 30 per 1,000, has averaged during the 12 months ending 28 September 21·92 per 1,000; this decrease, due of course in a great degree to the happy absence of cholera, is also in no slight degree referrible to the measures already adopted by the Sanitary Commission. Documents furnished to Mr Simon by the surgeons of the various city unions testify that the improved condition of health has depended very considerably on changes recently wrought in their respective neighbourhoods. That a continuance of the process by which this improvement has been effected may diminish the ratio of mortality to an indefinite extent, may be collected from the fact that there are districts both of town and country where the average is as low as 14 per 1,000. For the whole south-east division of England (comprising more than a million and a half of inhabitants) the death rate is not more than 19; and that the London death rate may be brought down to a level with the most favoured country localities seems established by a case occurring within the City of London Union, where the mortality of one sub-district stood at only 15 per 1,000 during the past year. Mr Simon is therefore of opinion that the traditional threescore years and ten are not a prerogative reserved to rustic life alone. 'I should argue', he says,

that the main conditions which constitute the unhealthiness of towns are definite, palpable, removable evils; that dense overcrowding of a population; that intricate ramification of courts and

alleys, excluding light and air; that defective drainage; that the
products of organic decomposition; that contaminated water and
a stinking atmosphere – are distinct causes of disease and death;
that each admits of being definitely estimated in its numerical
proportion to the total mortality which it contributes to cause;
that each is susceptible of abatement or removal, which will at
once be followed by diminution of its alleged effects upon the
health of the population. . . . Surely, too, above all, I would
maintain this possibility in respect of our capital, the treasury, as
it is, of all means for progress in civilisation, the stronghold of all
applicable knowledge. Let but the wealth, the science, and the
benevolence of the metropolis, deal with removable causes of
death as they have with subjects infinitely more difficult, and few
competent persons will doubt that the mortality of London
might speedily be reduced to the level of any district mortality
yet recorded by the Registrar-General.

One of the strongest proofs that the causes of death are mostly
removable causes is to be found in the circumstance, that more
than one-third of the whole mortality was supplied by the infant
population under five years of age, and that the rate of these
deaths is highest during that early period of life when the child
depends for sustenance upon the mother. Another proof is furnished by the character of the disorders which led to a fatal
issue: 'The high mortality of children', says Mr Simon,

constitutes the readiest and least fallacious evidence of the un-
wholesomeness of the dwellings in which they die; and hence I am
acquainted with no correct material for estimating the sanitary
condition of a district than is afforded by the death rate of its
infant population. . . . Secondly, with regard to particular causes
of death, there are deaths by cholera, epidemic diarrhœa, and
dysentery, of which during the biennial period we have had
nearly 900; by fever, of which we have had 284; by erysipelas and
puerperal fever, of which we have had 84; by smallpox, of which
we have had 50; and cases of this sort partake of the nature of
deaths by violence, not only because they are abrupt and un-
timely, but because they are *avoidable*. . . . The death of a child
by smallpox would, in most instances, call for a verdict of
'homicide by omission' against the parent who had neglected
daily opportunities of giving it immunity by the simple process

of vaccination; the death of an adult by typhus would commonly justify still stronger condemnation against those who ignore the duties of property, and who knowingly let for the occupation of the poor dwellings absolutely incompatible with health.

As an excessive proportion in any given district of such particular forms of disease is a sure key to the presence of some removable causes, so does the diminution already noticed bear witness to the immediate success of sanitary measures. Among the deaths which Mr Simon classes as preventible, those from fever have been fewer by 29 per cent in the past year than in the previous one; those from scarlatina 75 per cent; those from infantile zymotic disorders 40 per cent; those from erysipelas and puerperal fever 9 per cent fewer. It is, therefore, sufficiently plain that the sanitary condition of the city has undergone considerable improvement within the last two years, and that local differences of mortality, ranging from 20 to as much as 40 per 1,000, depend on the operation within certain districts of deleterious causes which are capable of removal. In the case of the cholera, we are told that the habitual sanitary proportions of districts to each were for the most part preserved: in other words, those removable causes which offer an invitation to epidemic diseases in general preserve their relation of pioneers to the most frightful member of the family. We cannot omit the emphatic caution which Mr Simon appends to his remarks upon this disease:

In my last report, when the cholera had scarcely subsided, when men's minds were full of apprehension on the subject, and when there was every human probability (happily since refuted) that with the recurrence of autumn we should again suffer from its invasion, I was unwilling to dwell too pointedly on the wonderful pertinacity with which that disease fixes itself on particular localities, and tends to reappear in them on each new occasion of its rise. Now, however, I think it right to tell you, that the local predilections of this dreadful disease are so marked and so obstinate, that we may almost certainly predict in what parts of the metropolis it would tend to arise on any renewed visitation. We may anticipate that at any such time its latent power of destruction will kindle again in the districts, the streets, the houses, perhaps even in the very rooms, where it previously prevailed, *unless the determining local conditions shall previously have been annulled.*

The conditions which determine this local preference are, in Mr Simon's opinion, a peculiarity of soil, of which dampness is one sure and invariable characteristic, and organic decomposition (promoted by dampness) probably another; from the inspection of a cholera map he tells us these conditions are easily discoverable.

In a line northward from Blackfriars-bridge, in a band of 200 or 300 yards' width – *there*, in the parallelogram which lies along the main road from Stonecutter-street to Bridewell Hospital, were 76 deaths; *there*, in the little clump of houses forming the angle of Farringdon-street and Holborn-hill, were 17 deaths; *there*, in a square space behind 27 shop fronts in Fleet-street, were 57 deaths; *there*, in the small parish of St Anne's, Blackfriars, were deaths at the rate of 25 to every 1,000 of the population. Those who are acquainted with the ancient geography of the city will readily conjecture a reason. They will remember when 'the course of water running at London under Old-bourne-bridge and Fleet-bridge into the Thames was of such breadth and depth that 10 or 12 ships' navies at once, with merchandises, were wont to come to the foresaid bridge of Fleet, and some of them unto Old-bourne-bridge'. Throughout at least a large portion of this district the subsoil consists of black mud – the bed of the ancient river – in which are set the foundations of the modern houses. . . .

Burial Grounds

As the various burial grounds within the limits of the city will fall into disuse now that the Interments Act has become operative, the recommendations which Mr Simon has to make on this head refer less to the provisions of that act than to the means by which the burial grounds, when closed, may become non-injurious, or even beneficial in some degree, to the population. There are three precautions which would tend, in Mr Simon's opinion, to convert the bane into a blessing. The first to plant them with whatever trees or shrubs may be made to flourish in a London atmosphere –

The putrefactive process which must for some years proceed in these saturated soils will be rendered compartively harmless and imperceptible, if at the same time there advance in the ground a sufficiency of vegetation which could gradually appropriate, as fast as they are evolved, the products of animal decay.

The second, to allow no unnecessary disturbance of the soil. The third, in fact a corollary of the second, to keep the respective areas free from any encroachment, so as to subserve the ventilation of the neighbourhoods contiguous to them.

Habitations and Social Condition of the Poor

There are some evils, arising from ignorance, selfishness, and poverty, which under any municipal regulations must be always difficult of cure; such are the aggregations of the indigent and the miserable – some filthy from habit, some from necessity – which form receptacles of every prevalent epidemic and the breeding place of future ones. It is something, however, clearly to comprehend the nature of this evil; it is something more to discover the appearance of a remedy which shall not sink into a hopeless crusade. 'There are', says Mr Simon, 'constructional defects of houses and courts whereby their crowded inhabitants are excluded from a sufficiency of light and air, and constrained, without remission or change, to breathe an atmosphere fœtid with their own stagnant exhalations. . . . It is an incontrovertible fact that subsistence in close courts is an unhealthy and shortlived subsistence in comparison with that of dwellers in the open street. . . . Judge, then, how the mortality of such courts must swell the aggregate death rate when I tell you that their population is in many instances so excessive as in itself, and by its mere density, to breed disease.' What this density is may be gathered approximately from the fact that 'within the City of London Union each human being, on an average, has less than an eighth part of the space he would have if residing in the district of

Islington; and, small as is this pittance, it is more than double what he would enjoy if living in the district of the East and West London Unions'. To remedy this state of things it would be advisable, Mr Simon thinks, in the first place to remove entirely such blocks of building as are in themselves incurably bad and pestilential. In the second place, to empower the corporation to make compulsory purchases of house property, on the ground of its unfitness for human habitation; it being an ascertained fact that no improvement can be wrought while such property remains divided among a variety of owners, and that generally the landlords are deaf to all remonstrance. A third impediment to ventilation consists, as cannot be too universally recognised, in the operation of the window-tax – a tax which, as Mr Simon says, is accurately proportioned to the healthiness of the tenement. Restrictions upon the conduct of lodging houses is one other method by which some amelioration of pauper existence may be effected. A *ragged dormitory* within each union would, Mr Simon thinks, be highly useful in this respect and defray its own cost; and, certainly, our experience of the provisions already made in various parts of the metropolis for the accommodation of the poor tend to show that, while securing something of comfort to them and something of additional security to the universal well-being, we do not supersede those commercial laws which require an ample return upon the expenditure of capital.

(from *The Times*, 31 December 1850 and 2 January 1851)

The Martyrs of Chancery

IN Lambeth Marsh stands a building better known than honoured. The wealthy merchant knows it as the place where an unfortunate friend, who made that ruinous speculation during the recent sugar-panic, is now a denizen: the man-about-town knows it as a spot to which several of his friends have been driven at full gallop, by fleet race horses and dear dog-carts: the lawyer knows it as the 'last scene of all', the catastrophe of a large proportion of law-suits: the father knows it as a bugbear wherewith to warn his scapegrace spendthrift son; but the uncle knows it better as the place whence nephews date protestations of reform and piteous appeals, 'this once', for bail. Few, indeed, are there who has not heard of the Queen's Prison, or, as it is more briefly and emphatically termed, 'The Bench'?

Awful sound! What visions of folly and roguery, of sloth and seediness, of ruin and recklessness, are conjured up to the imagination in these two words! It is the 'Hades' of commerce – the 'Inferno' of fortune. Within its grim walls – surmounted by a *chevaux de frise*, classically termed 'Lord Ellenborough's teeth' – dwell at this moment members of almost every class of society. Debt – the grim incubus riding on the shoulders of his victim, like the hideous old man in the Eastern fable – has here his captives safely under lock and key, and within fifty-feet walls. The church, the army, the navy, the bar, the press, the turf, the trade of England, have each and all their representatives in this 'house'. Every grade, from the ruined man of fortune to the petty tradesman who has been undone by giving credit to others still poorer than himself, sends its members to this Bankrupts' Parliament.

Nineteen-twentieths in this Royal House of Detention owe their misfortunes directly or indirectly to themselves; and, for them, every free and prosperous man has his cut and dry moral, or scrap of pity, or screed of advice; but there is a proportion of prisoners – happily a small one – within those huge brick boundaries, who have committed no crime, broken no law, infringed no commandment. They are the victims of a system which has been bequeathed to us from the dark days of the 'Star Chambers', and 'Courts of High Commission' – we mean the Martyrs of Chancery.

These unhappy persons were formerly confined in the Fleet Prison, but on the demolition of that edifice, were transferred to the Queen's Bench. Unlike prisoners of any other denomination, they are frequently ignorant of the cause of their imprisonment, and more frequently still, are unable to obtain their liberation by any acts or concessions of their own. There is no act of which they are permitted to take the benefit; no door left open for them in the Court of Bankruptcy. A Chancery prisoner is, in fact, a far more hopeless mortal than a convict sentenced to transportation; for the latter knows that, at the expiration of a certain period, he will, in any event, be a free man. The Chancery prisoner has no such certainty; he may, and he frequently does, waste a lifetime in the walls of a gaol, whither he was sent in innocence; because, perchance, he had the ill-luck to be one of the next of kin of some testator who made a will which no one could comprehend or the heir of some intestate who made none. Any other party interested in the estate commences a Chancery suit, which he must defend or be committed to prison for 'contempt'. A prison is his portion, whatever he does; for, if he answers the bill filed against him, and cannot pay the costs, he is also clapped in gaol for 'contempt'. Thus, what in ordinary life is but an irrepressible expression of opinion or a small discourtesy, is, 'in Equity', a high crime punishable with imprisonment – sometimes perpetual. Whoever is pronounced guilty of contempt in a Chancery sense is taken from his family, his profession, or his trade (perhaps his sole means of livelihood), and consigned to a gaol where he must starve, or live on a miserable pittance of three shillings and sixpence a week charitably doled out to him from the county rate.

Disobedience of an order of the Court of Chancery – though that order may command you to pay more money than you ever had, or to hand over property which is not yours and was never in your possession – is contempt of court. No matter how great soever your natural reverence for the time-honoured institutions of your native land: no matter, though you regard the Lord High Chancellor of Great Britain as the most wonderful man upon earth, and his court as the purest fount of Justice, where she sits weighing out justice with a pair of Oertling's balances, you may yet be pronounced to have been guilty of 'contempt'. For this there is no pardon. You are in the catalogue of the doomed, and are doomed accordingly.

A popular fallacy spreads a notion that no one need 'go into Chancery' unless he pleases. Nothing but an utter and happy innocence of the bitter irony of 'Equity' proceedings keeps such an idea current. Men have been imprisoned for many years, some for a lifetime, on account of Chancery proceedings of the very existence of which they were almost in ignorance before they 'somehow or other were found in contempt'.

See yonder slatternly old man in threadbare garments, with pinched features telling of long years of anxiety and privation, and want. He has a weak starved voice that sounds as though years of privation have shrunk it as much as his hollow cheeks. He always looks cold, and (God help him) feels so too; for Liebig tells us that no quantity of clothing will repel cold without the aid of plenty of food – and little of that passes his lips. His eye has an unquiet, timid, half-frightened look, as if he could not look you straight in the face for lack of energy. His step is a hurried shuffle, though he seldom leaves his room; and when he does, he stares at the racket-players as if they were beings of a different race from himself. No one ever sees his hands: they are plunged desperately into his pockets, which never contain anything else. He is like a dried fruit, exhausted, shrunken, and flung aside by the whole world. He is a man without hope – a Chancery prisoner! He has lived in a gaol for twenty-eight weary years! His history has many parallels. It is this:

It was his misfortune to have an uncle, who died leaving him his residuary legatee. The uncle, like most men who make their own wills, forgot an essential part of it – he named no executor. Our poor friend administered, and all parties interested received their dues – he, last of all, taking but a small sum. It was his only fortune, and having received it he looked about for an investment. There were no railways in those days, or he might have speculated in the Diddlesex Junction. But there were Brazilian Mining Companies, and South Sea Fishing Companies, and various other companies, comprehensively termed 'Bubble'. Our friend thought these companies were not safe, and he was quite right in his supposition. So he determined to intrust his money to no bubble speculation; but to invest it in Spanish Bonds. After all, our poor friend had better have tried the Brazilian Mines; for the Bonds proved worth very little more than the paper on which they were written. His most Catholic Majesty did not repudiate (like certain transatlantic States) but buttoned up his pockets and told his creditors he had 'no money'.

Some five years after our friend was startled by being requested to come up to Doctors' Commons, and tell the worthy Civilians there all about his uncle's will – which one of the legatees, after receiving all he was entitled to under it and probably spending the money – suddenly took it into his head to dispute the validity of. Meanwhile the Court of Chancery also stepped in, and ordered him (pending the ecclesiastical suit) to pay over into court 'that little trifle' he had received. What could the poor man do? His Catholic Majesty had got the money – he, the legatee, had not a farthing of it, nor of any other money whatsoever. He was in contempt! An officer tapped him on the shoulder, displayed a little piece of parchment, and he found that he was the victim of an unfortunate 'attachment'. He was walked to the Fleet Prison, where, and in the Queen's Prison, he has remained ever since – a period of twenty-eight years! Yet no less a personage than a Lord Chancellor has pronounced his opinion that the will, after all, was a good and valid will; though the little family party of Doctors' Commons thought otherwise.

There is another miserable-looking object yonder – greasy, dirty, and slovenly. He, too, is a Chancery prisoner. He has been so for twenty years. Why, he has not the slightest idea. He can only tell you that he was found out to be one of the relations of some one who had left 'a good bit of money'. The lawyers 'put the will into Chancery; and at last I was ordered to do something or other, I can't recollect what, which I was also told I couldn't do nohow if I would. So they said I was in contempt, and they took and put me into the Fleet. It's a matter of twenty years I have been in prison: of course I'd like to get out, but I'm told there's no way of doing it anyhow.' He is an artisan, and works at his trade in the prison, by which he gains just enough to keep him, without coming upon the county rate.

In that room over the chapel is the infirmary. There was a death lately. The deceased was an old man of sixty-eight, and nearly blind: he had not been many years in prison, but the confinement, and the anxiety, and the separation from his family had preyed upon his mind and body. He was half-starved, too; for after being used to all the comforts of life, he had to live in gaol on sixpence a day. Yet there was one thousand pounds in the hands of the Accountant-General of the Court of Chancery, which was justly due to him. He was in contempt for not paying some three hundred pounds. But Death purged his contempt, and a decree was afterwards made for paying over the one thousand pounds to his personal representatives; yet himself had died, for want of a twentieth part of it, of slow starvation!

It must not, however, be supposed that Chancery never releases its victims. We must be just to the laws of 'Equity'. There is actually a man now in London whom they have positively let out of prison! They had, however, prolonged his agonies during seventeen years. He was committed for contempt in not paying certain costs, as he had been ordered. He appealed from the order; but until his appeal was heard, he had to remain in durance vile. The Court of Chancery, like all dignified bodies, is never in a hurry; and therefore, from having no great influence, and a very small stock of money to forward his interest, the poor man could only get his cause finally heard and decided on in December 1849 – seventeen years from the date of his imprisonment. And, after all, the Court decided that the original order was wrong; so that he had been committed for seventeen years *by mistake*!

How familiar to him must have been the face of that poor, tottering man, creeping along to rest on the bench under the wall yonder. He is very old, but not so old as he looks. He is a poor prisoner and another victim to Chancery. He has long ago forgotten, if he ever knew, the particulars of his own case, or the order which sent him to a gaol. He can tell you more of the history of this gloomy place and its defunct brother, the Fleet, than any other man. He will relate you stories of the 'palmy days' of the Fleet, when great and renowned men were frequently its denizens; when soldiers and sailors, authors and actors, whose names even then filled England with their renown, were prisoners within its walls; when whistling shops flourished and turnkeys were smugglers; when lodgings in the prison were dearer than rooms at the west-end of the town; and when a young man was

not considered to have finished his education until he had spent
a month or two in the Bench or the Fleet. He knows nothing of
the world outside – it is dead to him. Relations and friends have
long ceased to think of him, or perhaps even to know of his
existence. His thoughts range not beyond the high walls which
surround him, and probably if he had but a little better supply of
food and clothing, he might almost be considered a happy man.
But it is the happiness of apathy, not of the intelligence and the
affections – the painless condition of a trance, rather than the
joyous feeling which has hope for its bright-eyed minister. What
has *he* to do with hope? He has been thirty-eight years a Chancery prisoner. He is another out of twenty-four, still prisoners
here, more than half of whom have been prisoners for above ten
years, and not one of whom has any hope of release! A few have
done something fraudulent in 'contempt' of all law and equity;
but is not even *their* punishment greater than their crime?

(from Household Words, 7 December 1850)

Some Places in *Bleak House*

THERE is absolutely only one such place, that I ever saw, which
would satisfy the claims of the sticklers for absolute accuracy.
This is the horrible little burying ground in which Captain
Hawdon was laid, and on the steps of which Lady Dedlock died
– 'a hemmed-in churchyard, pestiferous and obscene . . . with
houses looking in on every side, save where a reeking little
tunnel of a court gives access to the iron gates'. So runs the
description in the book, and so you will find the place to this day,
on the left-hand side as you go down Russell Court – taking care
of your pockets the while – from Catherine Street to Drury
Lane, the only difference being that the burying ground has been
decently covered over with asphalte and is now used as a play-
ground for the slum children of those parts.

A little farther east is Lincoln's Inn Fields; and No. 58 on the
west side of the square, where John Forster lived, was admittedly
Mr Tulkinghorn's house. But literal exactitude was by no means

observed in the description of its rooms in *Bleak House*. To begin with, Forster's big room was on the ground floor, while Mr Tulkinghorn's was upstairs – mainly, I think, because the staircase was found to be necessary for the working out of the situation on the evening of the murder. I do not clearly remember whether the Roman existed in fact or only in fancy. I do recollect very well that a truculent portrait by Maclise of Macready as Macbeth, in the cauldron scene with the witches, hung on the wall opposite the fireplace, and was constantly present to my very juvenile mind as a kind of nightmare not to be equalled for its power of inspiring terror; but I am inclined to think that the Roman himself only existed in the mind's eye of the writer.

Crossing 'the Fields', we come to New Square, Lincoln's Inn, where Miss Flite had her first interview with Richard, and Ada, and Esther (the Courts in Old Square have long since been pulled down), and close to where, as Esther tells us, 'slipping us out at a little side gate, the old lady stopped most unexpectedly in a narrow back street, part of some courts and lanes immediately outside the wall of the Inn'. Here, at the south-west corner of Chichester Rents, which gives access from Chancery Lane to the side entrance to New Square, is – or was, for when I last saw them, a few weeks ago, 'the Rents' were about to be pulled down – without doubt the house that served as the model for Mr Krook's establishment. There was no difficulty at all about recognising Miss Flite's lodging at the top of the house, a 'pretty large room, from which she had a glimpse of the roof of Lincoln's Inn', while outside the long low garret window was the parapet on which Mr Krook's cat, Lady Jane, crouched with murderous designs on Miss Flite's birds – the only parapet in the neighbourhood available for such a purpose, it may be observed. This is all plain sailing enough so far; but (alas for the photographic accuracy people!) Mr Krook's house is described as having a house to the west of it, while this is at the corner, and the 'Old Ship' Tavern, which unquestionably was the original of the 'Sol's Arms' – it had a large room on the first floor in which the inquest *must* have been held – is opposite, instead of next door. Various houses have been claimed as having been Mr

Snagsby's in Took's Court (Cook's Court), Cursitor Street, and
Mr Jellyby's in Thavies Inn (opened to the world by the Hol-
born Viaduct, and still, apparently, astonished at its sudden
publicity), but not even the smallest evidence exists to support
any of these conjectures.

Out of London also *Bleak House* affords a very conclusive
proof that Charles Dickens very rarely thought it necessary to
actually reproduce the first sketch in the finished picture. Writing
to the Hon. Mrs Richard Watson, he said, 'In some of the
descriptions of Chesney Wold I have taken many bits, chiefly
about trees and shadows, from observations made at Rockingham' and in like manner the great drawing-room and the terrace
walk before its windows were transferred from Rockingham to
Chesney Wold. But Rockingham Castle stands on a breezy hill
in Northamptonshire, and Chesney Wold is placed in a flat,
watery Lincolnshire landscape, and in scarcely any respect
except that which I have mentioned is there any likeness between
the two houses.

(from *Pall Mall Magazine*, July 1896)

PART TWO

Early Reviews and Comment

Athenaeum

(Review of the first number of *Bleak House*)

THOSE of our readers who are yet under the memory of the periodical charm which they derived from the issues of *David Copperfield* – the last, and in our opinion finest of all Mr Dickens's works – may well be congratulated on the re-establishment of their monthly relations with him, of which the number now before us is the pledge and an instalment. Less, however, in the present case than in any other can we help them to anticipate from what has come under our notice of the various actors so far introduced, what are to be their future fortunes – or how Mr Dickens must of necessity conduct them through the intricacies of the action to the goal of the final number. This time we think the *quidnuncs* are thrown out. One broad hint, however, we can give those who have not read the first number of *Bleak House* – and that should be enough, for it is rich in promise of powerful interest and abundant amusement. The leading influence of the piece is to be, a pet Chancery suit – a good, old, orthodox Chancery suit such as the genius of the late Lord Eldon was made to delight in – 'one of the greatest Chancery suits known' – 'itself a monument of Chancery practice' – 'in which, every difficulty, every contingency, every masterly fiction, every form of procedure known in that Court, is represented over and over again' – a suit such as 'could not exist' (as a solicitor in the cause happily expressed it) 'out of this free and great country'. Around this central motive the leading characters and minor motives are apparently to revolve – though in what orbits and relations we do not as yet guess. The principal *dramatis personæ* are to be, we anticipate, 'parties to the suit'; and out of such materials what passionate tragedy and sarcastic force may a pen like Mr Dickens's evoke! Such a work is well timed, too – and may fairly be counted on as a useful contribution to the cause of Chancery Reform. The cause of *Jarndyce and Jarndyce* will doubtless be a famous cause – and take its future place beside the Common

Pleas case of Bardell *v.* Pickwick in the Law Reports of Fiction.
(6 March 1852)

Athenaeum

(Review of *Bleak House* complete)

THIS novel shows progress on the part of its writer in more ways
than one – and thus merits close attention now that it is completed. Ready sympathy has not been denied to it during its
progress – for in the Preface Mr Dickens announces his belief
'that he has never had so many readers as in *Bleak House*'.

There is progress in art to be praised in this book – and there
is progress in exaggeration to be deprecated. At its commencement the impression made is strange. Were its opening pages in
anywise accepted as representing the world we live in, the reader
might be excused for feeling as though he belonged to some orb
where eccentrics, Bedlamites, ill-directed and disproportioned
people were the only inhabitants. Esther Summerson, the narrator, is, in her surpassingly sweet way, little less like ordinary
persons than are Krook and Skimpole. Her own story was of
itself sadly romantic enough – the provident beneficence of Mr
Jarndyce to her was sufficiently unlike Fortune's usual dealings
with those born as she was – to have sufficed for the marvels of
one number. But on her mysterious summons to town to join the
delightful wards in Chancery with whom she makes an instant
and cordial friendship, she is thrown, on the very moment of
arrival, into company with a sharp-witted and coxcombical limb
of the law, in Guppy – with an overweening philanthropist, who
lets everything at home go to rack and ruin for the sake of her
foreign mission, in Mrs Jellyby – with an infuriated madman
who has a mysterious lodger and a demoniacal cat, in Krook –
and with a ruefully fantastic Chancery victim in poor little Miss
Flite. Nay, when she gets to the house of her guardian, he, too,
must needs be marked out as a curiosity by his whimsical manner

of wreaking his vexation at sin, sorrow and meanness, on the weather – while his guest happens to be none other than such a rare specimen of the man of imagination as Mr Harold Skimpole. Here is 'the apple-pie made of quinces' with a vengeance, if there ever was such a thing! Granting the simple heroine of Mr Dickens to possess the immediate power of the daguerreotype in noting at once the minutest singularities of so many exceptional people – granting her, further, in its fullest extent, the instantaneous influence for good in word and in deed which she exercises over every person with whom she is brought into contact – it surely befalls few such angels of experience, simplicity and overflowing kindness to enter Life through the gate of usefulness down a highway lined with figures so strange as the above. The excuse of Esther's creator, we suppose, lies in the supposed necessity of catching his public at the outset, by exhibiting a rare set of figures in readiness for the coming harlequinade. But in *Bleak House* they stand in one another's way; and seeing that, as the narrative advances, they are reinforced by such a cast-iron *Lady Bountiful* as Mrs Pardiggle, with her terrible children – such a horrible *Darby* and *Joan* as the two old Smallweeds – such a greasy, preaching *Mawworm* as Mr Chadband – such a *Boanerges* as Mr Boythorn – such an uxorious admirer of his wife's two former husbands as Mr Bayoam [*sic*] Badger – we must protest against the composition of the company, not merely on the ground of the improbability of such an assemblage, but from the sense of fatigue which the manœuvres of such singular people cannot fail to cause.

This resolution to startle, besides being bad in itself, leads the novelist, even though he have of the richest *cornucopia* of humours at his disposal, into two faults – both of which may be seriously objected against *Bleak House*. First, from noticing mere peculiarities, he is beguiled into a cruel consideration of physical defects – from the unnatural workings of the mind, the step to the painful agonies of the body is a short one. The hideous palsy of Grandfather Smallweed, and the chattering idiocy of his wife, belong to the coarse devices which are losing their hold on the popular taste even at the minor theatres. The death of Krook –

attacked as an impossible catastrophe, and defended by our novelist on medical testimony – would be false and repugnant in point
of Art, even if it were scientifically true. We would not willingly
look into fiction for the phenomena of *elephantiasis*, or for the
hopeless writhings of those who suffer and perish annually in the
slow sharp pains of cancer. Again – in his determination to
exhibit snub minds and pimpled tempers, principles that squint,
and motives that walk on club-feet (analogous to the mis-shapen
figures which ought not to come too frequently even from the
professed caricaturist's pencil) – it is difficult, perhaps, for the
novelist to avoid touching on another forbidden ground, to
abstain from that sharpness of individual portraiture which shall
make certain of his *dramatis personæ* recognizable as reproduc-
tions of living people. This is not a remark, like our former one,
to be substantiated by instances; we will not spread a sore under
pretence of exhibiting it. But the charge has been laid so widely
and so universally against *Bleak House*, that it cannot be wholly
ignored by any faithful analyst. We will assume that Mr Dickens
may not have desired to inflict personal pain on any one – friend
or foe. We will concede that the motion of the hand which
sketched in this or the other known person in *Bleak House* may,
in the first instance, have been involuntary. The more need is
there of strong, grave, friendly protest against devices of style
and manner which may lead kindly-natured men so much further
than they would care to go.

Thus much recorded as regards the progress in exaggerations
which we conceive *Bleak House* to exhibit – we now turn to the
admirable things which this last tale by Mr Dickens contains.
And first, though he has been thereby led away from his great
Chancery case further than may have been his original intention,
we must signalize the whole machinery by which Lady Dedlock's
private history is gradually brought to day – as admirable in
point of fictitious construction – an important advance on anything that we recollect in our author's previous works. Not a
point is missed – not a person left without part or share in the
gradual disclosure – not a pin dropped that is not to be picked
up for help or for harm to somebody. The great catastrophe is,

after all, determined as much by the distant jealousy of Mrs
Snagsby, the fretful law-stationer's wife, as by the more intimate
vengeance of the discarded lady's maid. Capital, too – of an
excellence which no contemporary could reach – is the manner
in which Mr Bucket the detective officer is worked into the very
centre and core of the mystery, until we become almost agreed
with Sir Leicester Dedlock in looking on him as a superior being
in right of his cool resource and wondrous knowledge. Nor has
Mr Dickens wrought up any scene more highly and less melo-
dramatically than those of the night-ride into the country in
which the over-perfect Esther is included – and of the despairing
affectionate, hopeless expectation of the deserted husband in the
town-house. It is curious, however, to observe how completely
our novelist's power has failed him on the threshold of the dank
grave-yard, where the proud and desperate lady lies down to die
of remorse and shame – how despotically he has chosen to forget
that such a catastrophe could not really have been hushed up in
the manner hinted at in his closing chapters. We are not sorry to
be spared a second inquest over the body of the faithless woman,
having assisted at like rites over the corpse of the outcast lover of
her youth – we can dispense with the excitement of the trial of
Mademoiselle Hortense, the murderess, and the horrors of her
execution – but such events there must have been – and to have
overlooked them so completely as Mr Dickens has done in
winding up his story, is an arbitrary exercise of his art, made all
the more striking by the minute painting with which other parts
of the narrative are wrought.

In his own particular walk – apart from the exaggerations
complained of, and the personalities against which many have
protested – Mr Dickens has rarely, if ever, been happier than in
Bleak House. Poor miserable Mr Jellyby, with all hope, life, and
energy washed out of him by the flow of his wife's incessant
zeal – the dancing-school in which the African missionary's
daughter finds her mission – the cousins who cluster round Sir
Leicester Dedlock, giving an air of habitation to the great house,
by filling up its empty corners – could have been hit off by no
one else so well. Then, with all his inanity, pomposity, and

prejudice in favour of his order, the Lincolnshire baronet is a true gentleman – we are not only told this, we are made to feel it. His wife is a comparative failure: a second edition of *Mrs Dombey* – with somewhat of real stateliness superadded. Trooper George is new – and here, again, Mr Dickens is masterly, in preserving (though with some exaggeration) the simplicity, sentimentality, and credulity of the original nature which made the man a roamer – and which have a strong and real life in many a barrack and in many a ship of war. Mr Snagsby 'puts too fine a point' on his intimations concerning the spectre that destroys his home peace, somewhat too ceaselessly. The queerest catch-word may be used too mercilessly, even for a farce – much more for a novel. Perhaps among all the waifs and strays, the beggars and the out-casts, in behalf of whose humanity our author has again and again appealed to a world too apt to forget their existence, he has never produced anything more rueful, more pitiable, more com-plete than poor Jo. The dying scene, with its terrible morals and impetuous protest, Mr Dickens has nowhere in all his works excelled. The book would live on the strength alone of that one sketch from the swarming life around us. Mr Bucket is a jewel among detectives: and the mixture of professional enjoyment and manly, delicate consideration in his great scene with Sir Leicester Dedlock, is marked and carried through with a master's hand. Esther is, as we have hinted, too precociously good, too per-petually self-present, and too helpful to every one around her to carry a sense of reality: nor are her virtues made more probable by the fact that she is the chronicler of her own perfection – though with disclaimers manifold. She does not, it is true, pro-fess less profession than did *Harriet Byron* before her: yet *Har-riet Byron*, as the centre of a galaxy of admiring relations, loving neighbours, and revering domestics, is a 'being of the mind' as clear and as complete as most other fictitious gentlewomen of our acquaintance.

It may be thought, that in the above attempt to sum up the merits and defects of this unequal tale, more account should have been made of what may be called its main argument, the great Chancery suit. But of that we spoke when announcing the publication of its opening number [see p. 49] – and those who, with us, then anticipated scenes which might rival the Pickwick trial, or combinations such as should keep that mighty mystery of Iniquity and Equity perpetually before the reader, must have been disappointed – since at an early period the fortunes of Richard and Ada pass into the place of second interests, while the first concern and sympathy are given to Lady Dedlock's secret: so that the matter has not the importance which Mr Dickens could have given it, had it pleased him so to do. The statements made in his Preface, by way of justification, will make many regret that he should have been fascinated away from his master-purpose, even by such a tempting 'passage of arms', as the silent strife betwixt the haughty woman of fashion and the deep, astute, and ruthless arbiter of her destiny, 'the old man, Tulking-horn'. (17 September 1853)

Spectator

'I BELIEVE I have never had so many readers', says Mr Dickens in the preface to *Bleak House*, 'as in this book.' We have no doubt that he has the pleasantest evidence of the truth of this conviction in the balance-sheet of his publishing-account; and, without any more accurate knowledge of the statistics of his circulation than the indications furnished by limited personal observation, we should not be surprised to find that *Punch* and the *Times* newspaper were his only rivals in this respect. Whatever such a fact may not prove, it does prove incontestably that Mr Dickens has a greater power of amusing the book-buying public of England than any other living writer; and moreover establishes, what we should scarcely have thought probable, that his power of amusing is not weakened now that the novelty of his style has passed away, nor his public wearied by the repetition of effects in which truth of nature and sobriety of thought are largely sacrificed to mannerism and point. Author and public react upon each other; and it is no wonder that a writer, who finds that his peculiar genius and his method of exhibiting it secure him an extensive and sustained popularity, should be deaf to the remonstrances of critics when they warn him of defects that his public does not care for, or urge him to a change of method which might very probably thin his audience for the immediate present, and substitute the quiet approval of the judicious for the noisy and profitable applause of crowded pit and gallery. Intellectual habits, too, become strengthened by use, and a period comes in the life of a man of genius when it is hopeless to expect from him growth of faculty or correction of faults.

Bleak House is, even more than any of its predecessors, charge-able with not simply faults, but absolute want of construction. A novelist may invent an extravagant or an uninteresting plot – may fail to balance his masses, to distribute his light and shade – may prevent his story from marching, by episode and discur-sion: but Mr Dickens discards plot, while he persists in adopting a form for his thoughts to which plot is essential, and where the absence of a coherent story is fatal to continuous interest. In *Bleak House*, the series of incidents which form the outward life of the actors and talkers has no close and necessary connexion; nor have they that higher interest that attaches to circumstances which powerfully aid in modifying and developing the original elements of human character. The great Chancery suit of Jarn-dyce and Jarndyce, which serves to introduce a crowd of persons as suitors, lawyers, law-writers, law-stationers, and general spectators of Chancery business, has positively not the smallest influence on the character of any one person concerned; nor has it any interest of itself. Mr Richard Carstone is not made reckless and unsteady by his interest in the great suit, but simply expends his recklessness and unsteadiness on it, as he would on some-thing else if it were non-existent. This great suit is lugged in by the head and shoulders, and kept prominently before the reader, solely to give Mr Dickens the opportunity of indulging in stale and commonplace satire upon the length and expense of Chan-cery proceedings, and exercises absolutely no influence on the characters and destinies of any one person concerned in it. . . .

The love of strong effect, and the habit of seizing peculiarities and presenting them instead of characters, pervade Mr Dickens's gravest and most amiable portraits, as well as those expressly intended to be ridiculous and grotesque. His heroine in *Bleak House* is a model of unconscious goodness; sowing love and reaping it wherever she goes, diffusing round her an atmosphere of happiness and a sweet perfume of a pure and kindly nature. Her unconsciousness and sweet humility of disposition are so profound that scarcely a page of her autobiography is free from a record of these admirable qualities. With delightful naïveté she writes down the praises that are showered upon her on all hands; and it is impossible to doubt the simplicity of her nature, because she never omits to assert it with emphasis. This is not only coarse portraiture, but utterly untrue and inconsistent. Such a girl would not write her own memoirs, and certainly would not bore one with her goodness till a wicked wish arises that she would either do something very 'spicy', or confine herself to superintending the jam-pots at Bleak House. Old Jarndyce himself, too, is so dreadfully amiable and supernaturally benevolent, that it has been a common opinion during the progress of the book, that he would turn out as great a rascal as Skimpole; and the fox on the symbolical cover with his nose turned to the East wind has been conjectured by subtle intellects to be intended for his double. We rejoice to find that those misanthropical anticipations were unfounded; but there must have been something false to general nature in the portrait that suggested them – some observed peculiarity of an individual presented too exclusively, or an abstract conception of gentleness and forbearance worked out to form a sharp contrast to the loud, self-assertive, vehement, but generous and tender Boythorne [*sic*]. This gentleman is one of the most original and happiest conceptions of the book, a humourist study of the highest merit. Mr Tulkinghorn, the Dedlock confidential solicitor, is an admirable study of mere outward characteristics of a class; but his motives and character are quite incomprehensible, and we strongly suspect that Mr Dickens had him shot out of the way as the only possible method of avoiding an enigma of his own setting which he could not solve. Tulking-

horn's fate excites precisely the same emotion as the death of a
noxious brute. He is a capital instance of an old trick of Mr
Dickens, by which the supposed tendencies and influences of a
trade or profession are made incarnate in a man, and not only is
'the dyer's hand subdued to what it works in', but the dyer is
altogether eliminated, and his powers of motion, his shape,
speech, and bodily functions, are translated into the dye-tub. This
gives the effect of what some critics call marvellous individuality.
It gives distinctness at any rate, and is telling; though it may be
questionable whether it is not a more fatal mistake in art than the
careless and unobservant habit which many writers have of
omitting to mark the effect of occupations upon the development
and exhibition of the universal passions and affections. Conversation Kenge and Vholes, solicitors in the great Jarndyce case,
have each their little characteristic set of phrases, and are well
marked specimens of the genus lawyer; but as they only appear
in their professional capacity, we are not entitled to question
them as to their qualities as men.

The allied families of Jellyby and Turveydrop are in Dickens's
happiest vein, though Mrs Jellyby is a coarse exaggeration of an
existing folly. They may, we think, stand beside the Micawbers.
Mrs Jellyby's daughter Caddy is the only female in the book we
thoroughly relish: there is a blending of pathos and fun in the
description of her under the tyranny of Borrioboola Gha, that is
irresistible; and her rapid transformation from a sulky, morose,
overgrown child, to a graceful and amiable young woman, under
the genial influence of Esther Summerson, is quite Cinderella-
like, and as charming as any fairy-tale. Inspector Bucket, of the
Detective Force, bears evidence of the careful study of this
admirable department of our Police by the editor of *Household
Words*; and, as in the case of Kenge and Vholes, the professional
capacity is here the object, and we do not require a portraiture of
the man and his affections. Poor Joe [*sic*], the street-sweeping
urchin, is drawn with a skill that is never more effectively exercised than when the outcasts of humanity are its subjects; a skill
which seems to depart in proportion as the author rises in the
scale of society depicted. Dickens has never yet succeeded in

catching a tolerable likeness of man or woman whose lot is cast among the high-born and wealthy. Whether it is that the lives of such present less that is outwardly funny or grotesque, less that strikes the eye of a man on the lookout for oddity and point, or that he knows nothing of their lives, certain it is that his people of station are the vilest daubs; and Sir Leicester Dedlock, Baronet, with his wife and family circle, are no exceptions.

If Mr Dickens were now for the first time before the public, we should have found our space fully occupied in drawing attention to his wit, his invention, his eye for common life, for common men and women, for the everyday aspect of streets and houses, his tendency to delineate the affections and the humours rather than the passions of mankind; and his defects would have served but to shade and modify the praises that flow forth willingly at the appearance among us of a true and original genius. And had his genius gone on growing and maturing, clearing itself of extravagance, acquiring art by study and reflection, it would not be easy to limit the admiration and homage he might by this time have won from his countrymen. As it is, he must be content with the praise of amusing the idle hours of the greatest number of readers; not, we may hope, without improvement to their hearts, but certainly without profoundly affecting their intellects or deeply stirring their emotions. (24 September 1853)

Illustrated London News

'WHAT do you think of *Bleak House?*' is a question which everybody has heard propounded within the last few weeks, when this serial was drawing towards its conclusion; and which, when the work was actually closed, formed, for its own season, as regular a portion of miscellaneous chat as 'How are you?' One obvious distinction is, that a great number of people who ask you how you do, make a practice of neither waiting for, nor listening to, your reply; they pay no attention to the meaning of their own interrogatory. But, on the contrary, those who inquire for your ideas about *Bleak House*, think of *Bleak House*; and, if they do not really want to know your opinion, want you at least to know theirs. The same sort of query resounded at the commencement of this latest of Charles Dickens's labours, and for some little time afterwards. Then there was a silence: people read without comment; and now, when they have read to the close, they once more – only with greater noise – make a demand for each other's impressions; volunteering, however, each his own; without much show of heeding anything else. In the meantime, a distinct section have reserved their perusal till they could have the whole production in their hands at once. These last persons will probably have taken the best means of judging of the plot, in its separate and distinctive merits. They will speak, like the rest, when they have mastered the case; and, as they have shown less haste, they may, perhaps, make better speed. They have not felt themselves under the necessity of proving the vividness of their literary intelligence by a hundred contradictory criticisms, and they may say something comprehensible, something 'that will hold water', respecting a work which is likely to last a good while and to provoke praise or animadversion long after most of its present conversational commentators have ceased to comment upon anything. . . .

Bleak House has one grand defect, while exhibiting every quality of its author's undoubted genius. People want some story in a work of fiction; and not only is the desire for a story perfectly natural and perfectly reasonable (as we could prove if we had time, and if, indeed, it were necessary), but it is, in an artistic sense, one of the essential elements of all good prose works of this nature. Now, most unfortunately, Mr Dickens fails in the construction of a plot. This is the very point in which he has generally been weakest. No man, we are confident, could tell a story better, if he had but a story to tell. We suspect that he is not at all unconscious of his own deficiency; for, in *Bleak House* especially – and, we might add, in many of his other novels – he resorts to a thousand artifices to excite curiosity; and lo! there is nothing about which we need have been curious – there is no explanation, by which, when our curiosity has been excited, it will be gratified or satisfied. A lawyer is deeply, and almost pro-vokingly, interesting, because he knows a thousand secrets. What are they? We shall see; but we close the book, and have seen nothing. Here comes a man whom it is even exciting to watch; it is the celebrated detective officer, Buckett [*sic*]. Mark him well. He can find out anything. See him in the streets, in the day time. Follow him at night. Notice how he behaves to various characters. Now, he is in operation – he will infallibly reach what he is seeking. What is it? Again, it is nothing – or nothing which greatly influences what has thereafter to be unfolded. And this marked characteristic of Mr Dickens's story-telling is no slight or trivial blemish. So far as the intrinsic congruities and self-evident laws of fictitious writing demand of the narrator a sort of artistic honesty, from which he may depart without being a bad man, but from which he cannot depart without being (in that at least) a bad author – so far, we say, Mr Dickens violates, to his own injury, one of the obligations which he has undertaken to respect. We are speaking here of an offence which the Germans would call an æsthetic immorality. Of course, it is evident that all the immoralities and all the moralities of the mimic world of fiction are but shadows; that the writer is in that world bound, not under pain of guilt, but under pain of nonsense; that his cul-pabilities affect him not as a member of society, in a personal sense, but as a citizen of the lettered republic, and a citizen whose usefulness, instructiveness, and value are to be estimated; and that, while his materials are permitted to be untrue literally, they are required to be both true and suggestive allegorically – faith-ful in their analogies, strict in their proportions, and scrupulously object-like in their tendency and settlement. Now, a story-teller professing to offer you a representation of real life, yet unable to construct a good plot, is under a disadvantage which we need not enlarge upon. But this describes Mr Dickens's case only in part. The plot is invariably his great difficulty; and, like other gentle-men similarly circumstanced, having failed to overcome his embarrassments, he strives, by every artifice at least, to hide them, for the sake of his credit. He wants the reader to trust him. He has the art of exciting the most lively expectations; he has the

art of sustaining them. Renewal upon renewal he obtains for
these literary bills, during the whole progress of the story's
existence; and, when it dies, there are not assets found to pay
half-a-crown in twenty shillings. Mr Dickens, the noblest, the
most munificent of writers in all other qualities, appealing ever
to the best sympathies of his readers – elevating, instructing, and
charming them throughout; spending the credit which he enjoys
at their hands in the most princely and even royal manner;
honoured, beloved, and admired while his story lasts, is, when it
is wound up, discovered to have been in one point on which he
had required and received unwavering faith, a splendid and
delightful pretender – pretender, however, by whom it is pleasant
to be taken in. It is some comfort to be even deceived in such a
style; and people would sooner be cheated by Mr Dickens than
paid in full by many other writers.

Besides, this is but one small part of the account. Mr Dickens
fulfils his obligations, were they four times told, in the less
mechanical duties of his inspired vocation. *Bleak House*, like so
many of his former works – like all, indeed, of the longer kind –
has beauty enough, and power enough, and is full of passages
which those who read them find reason to be glad they have
read; passages which ever exercise a most decisive influence
where they are designed to exercise it: and which, while they both
warn and delight the unimplicated majority, expose fraud, un-
mask and brand hypocrisy, put selfishness out of conceit with
itself, show the pampered turpitude of cant in all the truth of its
revolting deformity, and confirm, by irresistible impressions,
whatever feelings tend in our day towards the reconciliation of
estranged interests, towards the promotion of healthy sentiment
among the public, and towards the practical amelioration of
society. In these respects the influence of Charles Dickens is,
and has from the beginning been, pure, beneficial, and elevating.
The same could not be said of many writers of equal, or greater,
natural genius, and certainly of greater scholarly attainments. If,
in fact, every author as gifted as Mr Dickens exercised his abilities in a spirit as pure and as excellent as his, the good to the
world would be greater than all that has been conferred by all the

best Kings or Caliphs that ever existed upon the communities
under their sway.

As usual, Mr Dickens has, in this book, given to his readers
many intellectual daguerréotypes to carry away. These are at once
called up by the mere names of the characters; and with those
names they will be identified for evermore. Thus, in society, a
person might be at some loss to convey his impressions
about an individual, whose dispositions, habits, and peculiarities he wanted to describe – but time and power fail. Now,
however, a word bears the significance of half a dozen hours'
delineations – you mean that the fellow is a sort of Harold
Skimpole. Just so – with the exception: and the exceptions are
marked off with ease, leaving one of those vivid ideas of the
original, which could never have been conveyed but for the help
of a great author – in this the most trivial and insignificant of
his collateral uses, and, perhaps, collateral abuses. Very few
modern writers have furnished, with respect to vulgar life, more
of this stenograph – more of this hieroglyphical nomenclature –
more of this algebra of conversational satire, than Dickens.
At present, he has added some new full-lengths to his dreaded
gallery (and may the salutary terror of it increase!) – to his
dreaded gallery of the Denounced. Mr Chadband (though painted
with less than the full possible vigour, because undertaken with
a vehemence of hate unfavourable to the more deadly effects of
art) is a terrific presentment: his false eloquence, and still falser
religion, will avail his class no more. Mrs Jellaby [*sic*], again, is
an admirable effort; and, for the sake of hundreds of families, she
deserves to be at length brought out into the clear light, that
people may see and feel what is the true value of such a wife,
mother, and woman. Mrs Jellaby [*sic*] is not the less, but the
more, original in the hands of Mr Dickens, because she had been
inadequately, and, therefore, unsuccessfully, sketched already a
score of times by less powerful writers. The total omission of a
portrait is not half so good a reason for undertaking the subject
as an omission or defect in the already attempted portrait itself.
No theme can entitle a writer to the praise of being original;
his treatment of any theme may; and Mrs Jellaby [*sic*] is one of

the most genuinely and racily original peculiarities of *Bleak House*.
Mr Turveydrop is more of an abstraction; but that sketch is also
both humorous and moral. As to Mr Guppy and his associates, we
by no means regard them, with a weekly contemporary, as
failures, because they are 'detestable'; nor can we agree that Mr
Dickens has discarded the character of 'low humourist'. Mr
Dickens never was a 'low humourist'; and, therefore, could not
discard the character; and Mr Guppy and his set are meant to
be 'detestable'; and, therefore, cannot be failures on that account.

We cannot afford room for extracts, which, indeed, would be
new to very few. We have not room ourselves to say all that this
work deserves. Besides the humour, the feeling, the originality,
and the freshness which abound in its pages, it is what most of its
author's productions are – a model of honest, powerful, and
beautiful English. In certain passages we have writing so exquisite that, without any merit but that alone, they would be
worth perusing. *Bleak House* is not the best, and not the worst,
of Mr Dickens's fictions; but when we say that we think it
superior to several of them which are in great and just estima-
tion, we give it sufficient praise. (24 September 1853)

Bentley's Monthly Review

'IN *Bleak House* I have purposely dwelt upon the romantic side
of familiar things. I believe I have never had so many readers as
in this book.' So says Charles Dickens in his preface to this, his
lately completed, work of fiction. We do not doubt his statement,
and it is certainly one which proves the great and enduring popularity of this most favorite author. It is now, we believe, more
than seventeen years since 'Boz' first carried away the prize of
popular applause from all competitors in the realms of light
literature, by the publication of the unrivalled *Pickwick Papers*.
From that day to the present he has had no equal in the favor of a
reading public. Perhaps it is not too much to say that every line
he has since written has been read by at least half a million of
people; which is allowing a sale of twenty-five thousand copies

of each of his works and twenty readers to each copy – both of which estimates may be considerably within the mark.

We recollect well the prophecies which were generally uttered as to the fate of the author of the *Pickwick Papers*. 'He will soon write himself out.' 'He cannot keep up that style long.' 'People will soon tire of mere nonsense.' And so on went the croakers, who never can believe in the endurance of brilliancy, and who fancy that dullness and mediocrity are alone perennial.

But those who thus prophesied had taken a very wrong gauge of the intellectual powers of Charles Dickens. *Pickwick*, it is true, had no great purpose beyond that of amusement. To that end it at least succeeded, for it overflowed with the freshest and most genuine humour: young and old, grave and gay laughed over it with the intensest enjoyment, and we will venture to say that the English language has no more perfect specimen of a comic novel than the *Pickwick Papers*.

Something more, however, than mere fun lurked in those sparkling pages. There were touches of pathos which, if sometimes overstrained, shewed evidence of other powers than those of mere comedy. There were glimpses of a poetical feeling scattered here and there; and there was an insight into the human heart displayed in almost every chapter. . . .

Last on the list – and, spite of the very few exceptions, what a proud list it is! – comes *Bleak House*, just completed. Take it for all in all, it is, perhaps, the greatest, the least faulty, the most beautiful of all the works which the pen of Dickens has given to the world.

Intricacy of plot is never one of the characteristics of this author's fictions. The story is generally slight, and not always skilfully arranged. Secret there is none; or if there be, it is like one intrusted to a coterie of old spinsters which every one can somehow *guess*. Occasionally the author assumes an air of mystery, as if he had something wonderful in the back-ground; but we smile at the futile attempt at concealment, and 'see it all' as plainly as if we had been able to dip into the last chapter before the first six had been published. In *Bleak House*, for example, every one knows from the first that Esther Summerson is the daughter of

Lady Dedlock, and that the wretched law-writer is her ladyship's *quondam* lover. We are inclined to suspect that Mr Dickens really meant these two facts to be great secrets, which the seventeenth or eighteenth numbers were to reveal; but we are confident that not one of his readers had the least doubt on the subject after the second or third appearance on the scene of the characters in question.

The only point which is managed with real mystery is the murder of Tulkinghorn, the Attorney. Certainly the first impression of every reader must have been that Lady Dedlock was the criminal. The discarded French waiting-woman proves eventually to be the real murderess; but we cannot admit that all this is well contrived. It is entirely unnatural. The very reason why our suspicions never turn towards Mademoiselle Hortense is because she has no adequate motive for the commission of the act, and therefore she ought not (artistically speaking) to have been guilty of it.

It is not, however, in the conduct of a plot that our author shines – whether he has no ambition to excel in that respect, or whether he is conscious of his deficiency, we know not. Delineation of character is his *forte*, and the power of sketching in life-like colors the scenes of every day existence – especially in London. Places and incidents which would be common place and devoid of interest under ordinary circumstances, are made to afford us the highest amusement from the humorous touches of his pen, or are invested with a quiet charm of pure poetry from the genuine pathos with which they are presented to us by his genius. . . .

As usual in Mr Dickens's works, *Bleak House* has a great number and great variety of characters. The skill with which they are drawn is only equalled by the care, with which their characteristics are preserved throughout. Esther Summerson is decidedly the heroine in the tale, though Esther disclaims anything heroic as belonging to her. And, by the way, one of the peculiarities of this work is, that nearly two thirds of it are related by Esther herself in the first person, and the rest by the author in the third person. We do not know of any similar instance in our literature of the mixture of autobiography and ordinary narrative; but though the idea is novel, the effect is good. It affords the writer a wider range of character and scene than a single autobiography would have done, while its partaking partly of the nature of the latter, gives an additional interest to the character of the heroine.

Esther Summerson is drawn entirely by Esther herself. She scarcely appears on the scene at all, save in her own narrative. Now, among all the amiable and interesting female characters that the pen of Dickens has pourtrayed, we venture to assert that there is not one so perfectly *loveable* in every way as Esther Summerson. Yet we know Esther only from her own account of herself, and anything more simple and modest than that account, cannot be imagined. There is not a grain of self-praise in her autobiography, nor is there on the other hand that mock-depreciation of herself which a person of real vanity, but pretended humility, would assume. All is perfectly natural and easy. She does not once describe her own person – yet, we feel that we know her well, and should recognize her in the street to-morrow. She does not once give us her intellectual or moral portrait, yet we recognize the clever head, and the noble, generous, single-purposed, sympathising heart, which is all that woman's should be, and all that man's so seldom is. Consummate art this in the author! He does not draw his heroine's picture: he does not even make *her* do it: he leaves the reader to do it himself, and yet the latter (be he ever so dull-witted) can draw it only one way, under his unseen guidance, and the result is one of the most exquisite female creations that ever issued from the brain of poet or painter.

The tale has no hero, unless Richard Carstone be meant for him. But we will not notice him yet – *place aux dames*. Ada is a very amiable girl – and that is all. There is no strength of character in her: she would rather afford an example of Pope's meaning.

Most women have no character at all.

Mr Dickens has presented us with many specimens of woman-kind like Ada: we grant that they are natural, but we cannot admire, nor get interested in them – though we suspect the author wishes us to do so.

Lady Dedlock is a grand creation. Every inch a woman – an indomitable spirit, smothering all her griefs and all her remorse. She is not, however, quite original; for Edith Dombey is her prototype. Mr Dickens is as fond of depicting this class of female character as Lord Byron was of drawing Corsairs, and while the latter shewed a 'sneaking affection' for his villains, Mr Dickens gives us the idea of being alarmed at his own 'strong-minded' woman.

Mrs Jellyby is also a strong-minded woman of a different class; but, after all, she is a caricature, though caricatures are occasionally useful. Her daughter Caddy is, on the contrary, true enough to nature.

Mrs Snagsby is a capital bit of Dutch painting – life-like and admirably worked up. And the old housekeeper, Mrs Rouncewell, is a thoroughly genial character.

Of the men who figure in the book, Mr Jarndyce is the best depicted, and Sir Leicester Dedlock, to our taste, the worst. Mr Dickens never displays as much power in dealing with characters in high-life, as in the middle and lower classes. He is too fond of making the former abstractions – impersonifications of one mental or moral quality alone. Thus Sir Leicester Dedlock is simply the incarnation of aristocratic pride. We submit that this is unnatural. Nowhere, out of plays and novels, do we meet with men whose characters are entirely absorbed in one single idea. Pope's 'ruling passion' theory has been questioned by high authorities in the matter of ethics; but Mr Dickens, in the delineation of such men as Sir Leicester Dedlock, pushes Pope's theory *ad absurdum*.

Jarndyce is amiable without much sense or strength of character. Richard Carstone is a weak young man. But Horatio [*sic*] Skimpole is evidently the man on whom Mr Dickens has expended the most pains. He is certainly the most original character in the book; but we fear that we must pronounce him, next to the baronet, the least natural. A little care would have made him otherwise; but when Mr Dickens has hit upon a good thing he is apt to let the notion run away with him; and so the excessive simplicity and innocence assumed by Skimpole to veil his selfishness and want of principle have degenerated into the broadest caricature; till we feel reduced to this assertion – either such a character could not, in the nature of things, exist – or if he did, his imposture would be too gross and palpable to deceive even a Jarndyce.

The rest of the men (with the exception of Tulkinghorn, who is well drawn) are 'minor' characters – some well depicted, and some most admirably finished. We would instance Mr Chadband among the latter.

But we have said that Mr Dickens always writes *with a purpose* now. And what is the task he has set before him in *Bleak House?* No less a one than the exposure of the infamies of Chancery. A great theme and a difficult one. Not difficult in one sense – for it is easy to attack and to abuse any system, and especially one which is confessedly most faulty. But an author who sets out with the intention of running a tilt against any institution, either of our constitution or of society, should first take care to understand his subject. We do not think that Mr Dickens displays this knowledge in *Bleak House*. That Chancery Suits were long and expensive; that people got very weary of them; were occasionally imprisoned in respect of them; and that reform was needed somewhere: all this we knew before, and the whole country knew. But if Mr Dickens wished to effect any good in this matter, why did he not point out the *roots* of the particular evils he complains of, and suggest remedies? The answer will probably be – how can he, a layman (though a 'student for the bar', by the way) understand the subject? Exactly so: then until he *does* understand it, to what practical purpose do his blows, dealt in the dark, serve?

Heartily, most heartily, do we wish for 'Chancery Reform' – some reform there has been, but more is still needed: however, we really do not think that *Bleak House* will aid in obtaining that desideratum. The aim is good and honest, no doubt; but it is futile. And while there are ten thousand social evils which Mr Dickens *does* understand, and against which his pen might be employed with real power and effect, we cannot but regret that his talents should have been wasted, and so much energy spent in a vain attempt to crush the giant of Chancery. Wiser and more experienced heads than his (on *this* subject) are at work to remedy the abuses of this portion of our judicial system: hitherto they have worked well and honestly to that end, and we are sure that Lord St Leonards is as hearty a Chancery Reformer as Mr Dickens, while we humbly opine he will be the more effectual one.

But our space is filled, and we take leave of *Bleak House*. To 'recommend' it would be superfluous. Who will not read it? and who will not be delighted with this last and best of the beautiful fictions of Charles Dickens? (October 1853)

Westminster Review

FROM cathedrals and old palaces, we come to other works of fancy, even novels. There is *Bleak House*, just now more famous than the Duomo of Torcello; it may be even the better work of the two; mind against mind, perhaps there has gone more feeling and more thought to its construction. All the English world is critic of it; we need say but little therefore of its character. There are chapters in it that may be taken as the maturest and best things ever written by their author. All that relates to that type of a class, the poor street outcast, 'Jo', is told with the most exquisite skill and feeling, and will be remembered always as one of the choice things that do honour to our literature. The whole work is full of humour and pathos, yet there are defects in it that are as obvious as its beauties. The tone of the plot is more than usually melodramatic, and it is cumbered in its progress by some people with whom we are not glad to have met. The early decease of Mr Krook, by any calamity, even by spontaneous combustion, was most welcome. The Smallweeds blot the pages of the book wherever they appear. Except in the first well-contrived scene with Lady Dedlock, Mr Guppy appears only as a bad farce character; and even Esther Summerson fatigues us by the pains

she takes to show how wonderfully good she is, and how unconscious of her goodness. Few works written of late by Mr Dickens
have given so much opportunity to make exception against this
point and that, yet in none that he has ever written does there
appear so great a maturity of power; it abounds in pictures
wrought out with the most masterly care and finish, it appeals in
turn to almost every emotion, and, barring the purposeless disgust excited by the Smallweeds, turns every thought suggested
in it towards what is good and pure and noble. They who find
fault with *Bleak House*, and they must be many, can only quarrel
with it as with what they love. (October 1853)

Bentley's Miscellany

ANY record of the current literature of September and October
would be most imperfect without some notice of the completion
of Mr Dickens' last serial fiction. *Bleak House* is finished; Jarn-
dyce-and-Jarndyce is at an end. They who from month to month
have dwelt with eager attention on the narrative of Esther
Summerson, have now placed the volume on their shelves, often,
we will venture to say, to be taken down, and wept over again,
with new interest and new emotion.

A book which, Mr Dickens himself assures us, has had more
readers than any of his former works, is, to a certain extent, independent of criticism. But the critic, nevertheless, must say something about it. That 'something' is very easily said. *Bleak House*
is, in some respects, the worst of Mr Dickens' fictions, but, in
many more, it is the best.

It is the worst, inasmuch as in no other work is the tendency to
disagreeable exaggeration so conspicuous as in this. There are
a great number of *dramatis personæ* moving about in this story,
some of them exercising no perceptible influence upon its action
or in any way contributing to the catastrophe of the piece. They
disappear from the scene, give no sign, and when we come to
look back upon our transient acquaintance with them, we begin

to suspect that the story would have profited more by 'their room than by their company'. Now such characters are only serviceable in fiction, when they represent a class, and something is gained to morality, if nothing to art. When, on the other hand, they are exaggerated exceptions, and represent nothing which we have ever seen, or heard, or dreamt of, we cannot but regard them as mere excrescences which we should like to see pruned away. Of what conceivable use, for example, is such a personage as Mr Harold Skimpole? He does not assist the story, and, apart from the story, he is simply a monstrosity. That there are a great many people in the world who sit lightly under their pecuniary obligations is unhappily a fact, but if Harold Skimpoles are moving about anywhere, we will answer for it that they do not meet, in any known part of this habitable globe, such a number of tolerant and accommodating friends as Mr Dickens' 'child' is represented to have encountered. But, leaving such personages as Mr Skimpole, Mrs Pardiggle, Mr Chadband and others, to advert slightly to those who do exercise some influence upon the development of the plot, we cannot help thinking that Mr Dickens has committed a grave error in bringing together such a number of extraordinary personages, as are to be found huddled *en masse* in this romance, the Smallweeds, the Krooks, the Guppys and others. As for poor Miss Flight [*sic*], we recognize her presence as a legitimacy, for she is the veritable chorus to the great Chancery tragedy, which is here so terribly sustained, even to the dark catastrophe of the death of the young victim. But is it, we ask, within the rightful domain of true art to make the unnatural in character thus predominate over the natural? In *Bleak House*, for every one natural character we could name half a dozen unnatural ones; for every pleasant personage, half a dozen painful ones. Such characters, for example, as the Small-weeds, in which the extreme of physical infirmity, resulting from constitutional decay, is painted with a sickening minuteness, are simply revolting.

There is nothing, indeed, more remarkable in *Bleak House* than the almost entire absence of humour. In this story the grotesque and the contemptible have taken the place of the humorous. There are some passages in the history of Mr Guppy which raise a smile, but beyond these we really do not remember anything provocative of even a transient feeling of hilarity. It would seem, however, that in proportion as Mr Dickens has ceased to be, what he was once believed to be only, a humorous writer, he has been warmed into a pathetic one. The pathos of *Bleak House* is as superior to that of *David Copperfield*, as *David Copperfield* was, in this respect, superior to any of the author's former productions. There are passages, indeed, in it which nothing can excel.

The chief merit of *Bleak House* lies, indeed, in these detached passages. There are *parts* which, without hesitation, may be pronounced more powerful and more tender than anything that Dickens ever wrote – but the whole is disappointing. We feel that the story has not been carefully constructed, and that the undue elaboration of minor and unimportant characters crowding the canvas, and blocking up the space at the author's command, has compelled such a slurring over of required explanations towards the end of the story, that the reader lays down the last number of the series scarcely believing that he is not to hear anything more. The want of art is apparent, if we look only at the entire work. But there is wonderful art in the working out of some of the details. The narrative of the pursuit of Lady Dedlock may be instanced as one of the most powerful pieces of writing in the English language. There is profound pathos, as there is also high teaching, in the description of the death of the poor outcast, Joe [*sic*]; and very touching too is the sketch of the last moments of Richard Carstairs [*sic*]; done to death by his Chancery suit. Of single characters there are some at least which may be cited as new to Mr Dickens' pages. The trooper, George, is a noble fellow, and we are always right glad to meet him. Caddy Jellaby [*sic*] is another who never comes amiss to us. Mr Bucket is a portrait that stands out from the canvas just like a bit of life. And we cannot help thinking that poor Rick, with his *no*-character, is as truthful a bit of painting as there is in the whole book. Of Mr Jarndyce and Esther Summerson we hardly know what to say. We should like to have substantial faith in the existence of such loveable, self-merging natures, whether belonging to elderly gentlemen or young maidens. But we cannot say that we have. Indeed, the final disposal of Esther, after all that had gone before, is something that so far transcends the limits of our credulity, that we are compelled to pronounce it eminently unreal. We do not know whether most to marvel at him who transfers, or her who is transferred from one to another, like a bale of goods. Neither, if we could believe in such an incident, would our belief in any way enhance our admiration of the heroine. A little more strength of character would not be objectionable – even in a wife.

We have instanced these defects – defects which our reason condemns – defects spoken of commonly by hundreds and thousands of readers in nowise professing to be critics, mainly with the intent of illustrating the wonderful genius of the writer, whose greatest triumph it is to take the world captive in spite of these accumulated heresies against nature and against art. Everybody reads – everybody admires – everybody is delighted – everybody loves – and yet almost everybody finds something to censure, something to condemn. The secret of all this, or, rather, for it is no secret, the fact is, that almost every page of the book is instinct with genius, and that Charles Dickens writes to the hearts, not to the heads, of his readers. It is easy to say – as we have said, and not falsely either – that *Bleak House* is untruthful. If there were not wonderful truthfulness in it, it would not have touched so many hearts. But the truthfulness is in the individual details; it is truthfulness in untruthfulness. There are minute traits of character – little scraps of incident – small touches of feeling, strewn everywhere about the book, so truthful and so beautiful, that we are charmed as we read, and grieve when we can read no longer. It is unreasonable to look for perfection anywhere, but if the whole of such a work as *Bleak House* were equal to its parts, what a book it would be! (vol. XXXIV, 1853)

Putnam's Magazine

THE author of *Bleak House* is now about the age of the author of *Waverley* when the appearance of that literary marvel took the reading world by surprise; and he has still the time before him to make new conquests in literature, as the northern magician did when he quitted verse and bent his pliant genius to romances in prose. The thing which Dickens has yet to do, is to write a good story. Hitherto he has attained his brilliant successes by the production of novels, which have lacked one of the essential qualities of that species of literary manufacture. Yet, in spite of this great defect, he has achieved a success in comparison with which even Scott's was almost a failure. Until the appearance of Uncle Tom, Dickens' writings were the only books that could be said to have been really published. Doubtless something of his success must be attributed to the improved machinery of publishing, but much more to the popular character of his productions. We hardly feel warranted in thinking that the author of *Pickwick* lacks the talent of construction, for it may be, that finding he could accomplish his aims by a much easier and cheaper process, he has never thought it worth his while to try to construct a regular epic. He has found the public greedy enough to take his single characters, and has not attempted to add to their value by weaving them together in a plot. As a delineator of persons, and the creator of distinct types of humanity, he stands second only to Shakspeare; while, in fertility of invention, he is fully the equal of the great poet of humanity. If he has given us none of the grander forms of human passion, none of the Othellos, Hamlets and Lady Macbeths, he has created a vastly greater multitude of the baser order than the great dramatist. . . .

We have heard many of the most enthusiastic admirers of *Pickwick* complain that his after stories were failures; but either of his works, we imagine, would have created as great a sensation as that, if it had been his first; and we believe that even *Bleak House* would have been hailed as a greater marvel, if his previous creations had not blunted the keen edge of enjoyment, which that prodigious repertory of character would have gratified. But, such has been the prodigal affluence of his genius in scattering his characters, that we take up a new number of one of his stories, and feel ourselves wronged if we do not find half a dozen or more of new people, whose names and characteristics we can no more forget, than we can those of our own schoolfellows, or the members of our own household. Yet there is nothing so rare in literature as the creation of a new character; from the time of Shakspeare to Fielding, there were not half a dozen added to the realm of fiction, and among these few, Addison's Knight is the only one that has a distinct presence of its own. The forty-nine acted plays of Dryden did not all contain a single character that the world now remembers. Fielding made a very considerable addition to the populousness of the world of fiction, and since his time there have been many more added; but the creations of Dickens are more numerous than those of all the authors that preceded him, from the days of Fielding and Smollet [sic], put together. If any one thinks we make an extravagant statement, let him make a list of the familiar names in fiction, and compare it with a list of those which he can cull from the productions of Dickens. The only contemporary author who can be mentioned in comparison with him, as a creator of character, is Thackeray, who, in the construction of his stories, and the motive of his plots, is infinitely his superior. But, though in quality, the characters of Thackeray are equal to those of Dickens, in fertility of invention he cannot rank with his great rival. As a literary artist, we are inclined to rank the author of *Pendennis* above the author of *Pickwick*, it is in the power of production, and the fertility of invention, that the superiority of Dickens lies – the ease and grace with which he flings his characters from his brilliant pen upon the wondering multitude. . . .

In *Bleak House*, Dickens exhibits his greatest defects, and his greatest excellencies, as a novelist; in none of his works are the characters more strongly marked, or the plot more loosely and inartistically constructed. One-half of the personages might be ruled out without their loss being perceived, for, although they are all introduced with a flourish, as though they had an important part to perform, yet there would be no halt in the story

if they were dropped by the way, as some of them are – Mr Boythorn and his canary, for instance – without our being able to
discover for what purpose they were brought out. Yet, who
would wish not to have known Mr Boythorn? We constantly
meet people in society who in no manner influence our destiny,
whom it is, notwithstanding, a great comfort to have known.
And so it is with Mr Boythorn and his canary, such a great,
honest, healthy, and generous nature, rude and boisterous as his
manners are, makes one more reconciled to the Smallweeds and
Tulkinghorns that cannot be avoided. And Volumnia and her
poor, feeble cousin, all of whose manhood has been refined out
of him by generations of gentlemanly breeding, until the mere
effort of speaking distinctly is too much for his aristocratic
nature, are profitable people to know, although they do not help
on the story an inch, but, on the contrary, retard it by their
inanities. The debilitated cousin, is an enfeebled cousin Feenix,
whose acquaintance we first made in our dealings with the firm
of Dombey & Son; but what of that? is not Master Slender a step
down from Justice Shallow, and Master Silence going a little
below his cousin Slender. Volumnia is always the same, like the
rest of the characters, and every time we encounter her it is like
going into a room and seeing the same portrait simpering to us
out of its gilded frame. The only change in her is that she grows
pinker as to the red of her face, and yellower as to the white. But,
we remember Volumnia and the dilapidated cousin, and doubtless we take a more sober and sensible view of human life from
having made their acquaintance. . . .

Harold Skimpole, when he is first presented to us, is one of the
happiest creations of the author, and yet, so common a character
in real life that every body said at once they knew a dozen Skimpoles. It has been said, too, that Dickens in portraying this
character took Leigh Hunt for his model, and there are many
points in Skimpole to warrant such a supposition; but this is one
of the daguerreotypes that the author has spoiled by putting on
too much color, after the portrait was taken. In making Skimpole
a conscious villain he entirely destroys the consistency and truthfulness of the character, and Skimpole ceases to be the type of a

class. But though Skimpole changes his character, he keeps up his phraseology to the last, and says precisely the same things at the close that he did at the beginning. Quite as worthless a rascal, and very much in the same line, yet wholly different in style, is the incomparable Turveydrop, whose care of himself, and remorseless indifference to the sufferings of others, are by no means contradictory elements of character. He is a splendid satire on society, and it was a most happy idea to make him up after Lawrence's effeminate portrait of George the Fourth. The character of his son, the Prince, the simple-hearted, tender, dutiful and hardworking dancing-master is one of the best characters in the book, and Caddy Jellyby, his wife, is one of the few characters that have grown up under the hands of her master. Caddy is not presented to us as a daguerreotype, but is beautifully and naturally developed by the progress of events. Her precious mother, on the contrary, is always the same, looking off to Borioboola Gha [*sic*], and looking over the immediate objects which are entitled to her attention and sympathy – a perfect type of the philanthropist by trade; her poor neglected husband and children are all happily delineated, even to little Peepy, who is done for by being put into the Custom-House – a remarkable catastrophe for a hero of romance. Many have been the unsuccessful attempts to depict Mrs Jellyby, by inferior artists, but, no sooner does the hand of a genuine master attempt to sketch her than she stands out before the world, the confessed type of the class to which she belongs. Henceforth Mrs Jellyby is to be as real a character as Semiramis or Clytemnestra. When sham philanthropists are mentioned, Mrs Jellyby in her slatternly dress rises instantly in our memory. But Mrs Jellyby was not specially needed in *Bleak House*, she was in no way connected with the Court of Chancery or the suit of Jarndyce and Jarndyce. Neither was Mr Tulkinghorn; and this Mr Tulkinghorn, who comes to his death so needlessly, accomplishing nothing thereby, and filling so large a space in the volume, is one of the non-successes of the author. He is, oddly enough, introduced for the purpose of keeping family secrets, which are not of any importance to any body, and which he never divulges, but seems to be always on the point of doing something tragical, but never does. He is like a gloomy looking dark passage in a building that leads nowhere, and puzzles you to guess what it was intended for. The other lawyers, Carboy and Kenge, and their vulgar clerk, Mr Guppy, and his fast companion, Mr Jobling, and the Lord Chancellor, are all happily and strongly individualized. Conversation Kenge is a good deal of a humbug, but he is a perfectly natural and consistent character, and never forgets himself. Poor Joe [*sic*], down in Tom-all-alone's, has already become a proverb. We read the deaths of a good many eminent men without an emotion – the newspapers accustom us to such events, but we cannot withhold a tear when we read the death of poor Joe [*sic*], and when he is 'moved on' for the last time we too are moved. Yet we know all the time that poor Joe [*sic*] is an unreal phantom – a mere shadowy outline, raised by a few strokes of a steel pen; yet we weep over him and give him the sympathies which we withhold from the real Joes we encounter in our daily walks.

The chief personage of *Bleak House* is Esther Summerson, a gentle, loving, true-hearted and womanly creation; she possesses all the good points of the feminine character; and it was no wonder that Mr Guppy should, at last, entertain so strong an affection for her. It was a redeeming trait in that gentleman's character, and we like him for it. But nothing can be more palpable than the strange contrast between the character of this estimable lady, and the manner in which she narrates it herself, confessing that she never was good for any thing, that she is awkward and so on, and then going deliberately to work to draw her own portrait in the most flattering manner, all the time perfectly conscious, too, that she was doing it. Esther is a perfect character, and naturally developed, with the sole exception that her picture of herself is an unnatural contrivance. Her portraits of Richard and Ada are in the uniform manner of Dickens' young people, but have nothing distinctive about them. Richard is intended as a forcible picture of a chancery victim, but he is, in fact, a victim only to his own weaknesses and want of character. Miss Flite is much more effective, as showing the melancholy effect of long deferred hope, and disappointed expectations. She is a very good companion to Mr Dick in *Copperfield*. Krook is a night-marish character, and his going off by spontaneous combustion, which the author defends so stoutly in the face of science, is quite the unpleasantest thing to read in fiction. Jarndyce is a good old fellow, who can hardly be said to represent any body but himself, for such pure philanthropy, easy good nature, and good sense, are not often found united in the same person. Jarndyce is a prominent figure in the history of Bleak House, and, as the proprietor of that comfortable mansion, he should perform an important part in the drama which takes its name from his property, but he might be spared from the scene without the denouement being changed or interrupted. His proposition to marry Dame Durden is very tenderly and delicately managed; and we would recommend it as an example worthy of being imitated by any soft-hearted old gentleman who may have a desire to marry his housekeeper, or a lady much younger than himself. Mr Vholes must not be omitted in the enumeration of the characters of *Bleak House*, a genuine specimen of the mean nature which the practice of the law, when the practitioner is not eminently successful, engenders, or at least aggravates; the hen-pecked law stationer, who is always afraid of putting too fine a point on things, and his unhappy wife, who will be jealous of him whether he give her cause or not, are bold, distinctly drawn individuals whom we do not readily forget, and their epileptic servant will always be associated with them in our recollection. And Mr Chadband, incomparable Mr Chadband, how superior he is to the Maworms of the stage, and all other attempts to delineate his species. He will for ever stand as the type of that numerous band of evangelists whom he so vividly calls to mind. We can only mention Coavins [*sic*], who makes us respect a sheriff's officer, by the honesty with which he performs his unpleasant task, and whom we cannot but love as the father of Charley, the brave, affectionate and dutiful child.

These are not all the characters; but what a catalogue those form which we have named, to be found in one book. They are not mere names, nor lay figures, but distinct and striking individuals, who are remembered and alluded to as real personages who have impressed themselves upon us by their characteristics of mind and manner. (November 1853)

Eclectic Review

Bleak House is the latest production of Mr Dickens's prolific pen. The public has had to content itself with receiving it in monthly portions – a somewhat tantalizing process to the reader, whose interest is absorbed in the windings of the narrative, and who rises from every number with perplexing surmises as to what will be the end of such a character, or what is the meaning of indistinct allusions to something which has yet to be disclosed. It is needless to repeat the objections that there are to this mode of publication. Perhaps, generally, its chief disadvantage is to the author, rendering it almost impossible to produce that which when completed shall be deemed a good book. But we question whether Mr Dickens loses much by publishing in this way. It is doubtful, whether, in any circumstances, he could work out a good plot. He is not very capable, we should think, of looking right through his story, and marshalling his characters and incidents in their proper order. He sees so much of every part, and takes such delight in dwelling on it, that he is apt to forget the relation it bears to others. He reminds us of some short-sighted persons whom we have met with, who could read the ten commandments if written on a space which a sixpence might cover, but would be at a loss to point from the top of St Paul's to the exact localities of the Post Office, the Mansion House, or the Exchange. . . .

The great centre, around which the events and characters revolve, and a glimpse of which is afforded in the opening chapter, is the Court of Chancery, that tomb into which the fortunes and hopes of so many thousands have slowly descended. A very fruitful theme. Perhaps it would have been well if Mr Dickens had given an earlier exposition of it. Had his present work appeared twenty years ago, it would have been a revelation of strange mysteries to the public, and might now be looked upon as having contributed to promote the beneficial changes effected, or on the way to be effected, by recent legislation. As it is, he is rather late. He only exhibits in a stronger and more romantic light what has been pretty well made known before through the earnest prose of plainer men. In this respect, he reminds us of a fact which has often struck us in regard to the sparkling writers who, in many things, profess to lead the age. They are no prophets. *Punch* deals severe blows at abuses, on which the public eye is fixed, but seldom deserves the credit of discovering them. We have generally noticed that he has followed in the track of the less imaginative *Times*; and even the conductors of the 'leading journal' derive their inspiration, not from their own genius, but from the communications of nameless men of business, who, brought into contact with the evils which still have their roots among us, snatch a few minutes from their ordinary avocations, and relieve their irritated feelings by sending an account of their wrongs to Printing House-square.

But if the theme be not altogether a new one, there is a freshness about our author's manner of setting it forth which is as good as novelty, and again awakens our gratitude that the nuisance is on the road to abatement and removal. . . .

In our opinion, the best portions of Mr Dickens's works are the pictures he draws of characters subordinate to the main personages of the story. He is especially successful in depicting the features of those who dwell amidst the murky gloom of England's lowest life. The gem of *Bleak House* is 'poor Jo', the crossing-sweeper, hapless representative of a class whose very existence from generation to generation cries shame on the land in which they dwell. . . .

It seems ungracious as well as presumptuous – and we feel unwilling to say anything in disparagement of an author to whom the public are indebted for so much pleasant reading – yet we should not do justice to our own feelings nor to the book under notice, if we did not indicate our opinion that as an artist Mr Dickens is not perfect; while as a teacher his lessons are not always to be relied on. One of the faults with which he may be charged is that of *exaggeration*.

No one has a quicker eye to discover, or can better hit off the peculiarities of the odd members of our species with whom we sometimes meet in life. But he fixes his view so intently on the peculiarities that he can see nothing else; and when the portrait is finished, the man is hidden beneath the mask of his eccentricities. It is as if a painter in sketching a countenance in which a large nose is the distinguishing feature, should, for a likeness, draw nothing but a nose, and forget to indicate that there *is* a face behind, though not so much of it to be seen as in other persons.

Mr Skimpole, of *Bleak House*, is an example of the defect of which we are speaking. A well-known popular writer has been pointed out as the original of this picture. We have met with persons of whom Skimpole is evidently designed as a type – persons who are so simple, that they can without misgiving impose themselves as burdens on the world – babies in society – babies, however, who manage to secure easy nursing from the less amiable members of society. We have often wished that some one would take a whip and flog them into the development of a more manly nature. Perhaps the author has intended to do some such service in the character of which we are speaking. But unfortunately it is overdrawn. For a time we half thought that he was describing some crazed being whose madness took this form, and we knew not which to award him, pity or contempt. But when his real character does come out, our speculations are occupied with another subject, and we are at a loss whether to compassionate or despise Mr Jarndyce for keeping his house open for such a creature to prey on his friends. . . .

We regret that before we close we must speak disapprovingly of one part of the design running through this, in many respects, fascinating book. There is an evident attempt to bring odium on the pastors of the *unprivileged* sects, and on the enterprises of world-wide philanthropy which form one of the chief glories of the age in which we live.

Mr Dickens has found it convenient before to introduce the ministers of Bethels, Zions, and Ebenezers, to his readers; and we regret that he has not been charitable enough to give a fairer example of them than is to be found in *Mr Chadband*, a man whose principal characteristics are, speaking abominable English, stuffing himself with hot muffins, drinking we know not how many cups of tea, and rejoicing when he can get a stiff portion of a stronger beverage. The pages of *Bleak House* will be read by many whose knowledge of the clergy is derived from intercourse with nothing lower than the dignified gentlemanly rector or vicar; and we are afraid that the writer may wish to suggest to them, that the personage he has described is a sample of a class which numbers thousands in this land. If so, we can only say, that it is an insinuation which there are hundreds of thousands qualified and prepared to deny. We suppose Mr Dickens has not had opportunities for judging fairly of the men whom he caricatures. We advise him to leave them alone, and to eschew allusions to matters which are beyond his reach. We understand what he means; and we can tell him that the violation of good taste, by what better informed people know to be scandalously false and mischievous insinuations, reflects no credit on his intelligence, and can gratify none but the ignorant and irreligious vulgar in any rank of life.

Mrs Jellyby and Mrs Pardiggle are introduced apparently for no other purpose than to serve as a mark through which arrows may reach missionary and other benevolent institutions, and their agents. The one is a slattern, neglecting her household that she may attend to correspondence in reference to Boriaboola Gha [*sic*]. The other is a forbidding domestic tyrant, making her children hate her, because she forces them to contribute their pocket money to distant objects. Now, if Mr Dickens intended to exhibit these as examples of the friends of missions, and humanity in general, we say again that the truth of the picture is denied by those who are best qualified to form a judgment of the real household character of the parties here represented, and who will think that, in making females the ridiculous butts for his attacks on great institutions, he has shown a lack of chivalry to which gentlemen of his order prefer so loud a claim.

It is evident that, by offensive personifications of the agents of philanthropic societies, the aim is, to hold up to odium the very designs of those societies, as being either culpable or unwise.

If Mr Dickens is right in this, then his censures fall, not so much on present institutions as on Him who gave all nations as a charge to His disciples, and on those who, accepting that charge in its literal signification, sought to carry it out. If this is what the author means, it would be more candid in him to say so, and not to insinuate, as he does sometimes, that he is a truer admirer of the Nazarene Teacher, than those who profess to act up to His broad commands.

The standing argument against Foreign Missions is, that they take away the resources which ought to be employed in meeting the poverty, ignorance, and heathenism which abounds at home. To this assumption we have two replies: *First*, that during the period in which labours among the heathen have engaged the interest of various parties in this country, more, a hundred-fold more, has been done for the health, the education, and the evangelization of the English poor, than was ever done in a like period before; and, *secondly*, this home-work has been done mainly, nearly altogether, by the same classes from which foreign missions derive their support. One of the sayings put into the mouth of Esther is, that she found nobody with a mission cared at all for anybody else's mission – a stroke of wit which falls most directly on the author himself, for, in this work, he is surely decrying every mission but that of befriending 'poor Jo'. We are reminded, however, by the dedication, that he has in a more practical manner enlisted in another mission, viz., the establishment of a 'Guild of Literature and Art', which, we believe, has hitherto been promoted by acting a pleasant drama in aristocratic saloons before the nobility and beauty of the land.

We are not aware that the friends of more vulgar missions have taunted Mr Dickens and his associates for their devotion to this object. It is, perhaps, very benevolent and charitable. Yet we may be allowed to say, that it is a work of charity which can be gone about in full dress without much danger of being soiled. And he who has chosen such a very pleasant 'mission' for himself would, we think, have done more nobly if he had left unmolested those who are engaged in missions of a less attractive kind.

We should have been glad to close our notice of this work as
the eulogists rather than the censurers of a writer who has
afforded us many an hour's delight. But we should have been
wanting in what we felt to be the course of duty had we passed
by the grave matters to which we have referred. We take leave
of Mr Dickens with the encouraging but cautionary counsel –
Go on exhibiting to an increasing number of readers 'the
romantic side of familiar things', pointing out in all their deformity the evils that cluster around our institutions, bringing forth
to daylight the dark haunts and characters which, as plague spots,
are festering beneath the respectabilities of English life; go on as
the graphic exposer of 'poor Jo's' sad wrongs. But be careful
that, in your manner of doing this, you do not lay yourself open
to the charge of being the somewhat rash, heedless slanderer of
that part of the British nation among whom hitherto poor 'Joes'
have found their best *working* friends. Nor vainly expect to
produce the fairest fruits of humanity while you ignore, despise,
or misrepresent the humble sowers of the precious seed of that
divine truth from which alone those fruits have ever sprung.
Trust not too sanguinely the fascination of even your delightful
genius. You have done much to increase our mental pleasures
and to refresh our moral sensibilities, to expose many things that
are hollow among us, and to charm us with ideal pictures on
which it does the heart good to look; but neither your power
now, nor your happiness when you '*begin the world*', will be
increased by attempting to sever the virtues of society from the
principles which have been sent down from heaven on purpose
to implant and ripen them. (December 1853)

Blackwood's Edinburgh Magazine

In Mr Dickens' last great work (an adjective which cannot apply
in any sense to his very last one, *Hard Times*), he makes a beginning as pleasant as in *Copperfield*; but great as are the merits of
Bleak House, we cannot be persuaded into the same thorough
liking for it as we entertain for its predecessor. Here we are again

on the perilous standing-ground of social evil; and the sketch of workhouse tyranny in *Oliver Twist*, and the miserable picture of the miserable school in *Nickleby*, are transcended by this last exposition of a still wider and more extensive desolation. Had the lesson been unlearned, or the truth less universally known, this must have been a very telling revelation of the long-acknow-ledged evils of Chancery litigation; and even admitting that Mr Dickens comes late into the field, it is not to be denied that, for the purposes of his story, he makes very effective use of his suit in Chancery. Not to speak of Miss Flite and Gridley, the earlier victims, who are introduced rather to support the argument than to help the narrative, the manner in which the fatal Jarndyce case engulfs and swallows up poor Richard Carstone is at once extremely well managed, and a quite legitimate use of a public evil. Poor Richard! his flightiness and youthfulness, his enthu-siasm and discontent, and that famous and most characteristic argument of his, by which he proves that, in not making some extravagant purchase he meditated, he has saved so much, and has consequently such a sum additional to spend, are very true – sadly true, and to the life. Poor Ada is a sweet slight sketch, not aiming at very much, but Mr Dickens has been ambitious in Esther. Esther begins very well, but, alas! falls off sadly as she goes on. In her extreme unconsciousness Esther is too conscious by half: we see her going about, rattling her basket of keys, and simpering with a wearisome sweetness. Yes, we are grieved to say it; but it is with a simper that Miss Esther Summerson recalls those loving and applauding speeches which she is so sweetly surprised that everybody should make to her. We are some-times reminded of the diary of Miss Fanny Burney in reading that of Esther; each of these ladies exhibits a degree of delight-ful innocence and confusion in recording the compliments paid to them, which it is edifying to behold. But Esther, though her historian does great things for her, is not so clever as Fanny; and as there is no affectation so disagreeable as the affectation of ingenuous simplicity, we feel considerably tired of Esther before she comes to an end. Nevertheless we must make a protest in behalf of this young lady, little as she interests us: we

cannot be content with this style of unceremonious transfer from
one suitor to another, which so many modern heroines are sub-
jected to. This, which is becoming quite a favourite arrangement
in fiction, especially patronised, to increase the wonder, by lady
novelists, does not seem to us to be particularly flattering even
to the bridegroom, promoted at the eleventh hour to the post of
honour; but how much less flattering to the bride, thus quietly
disposed of, let the first heroine of spirit, threatened with such an
insult, declare indignantly, by casting adrift *both* the wooers, who
barter her between them. Perhaps Esther deserves the indignity,
and she certainly does not seem to resent it; but before she loses
or gives up *all* the honours accorded to her sex, we must make
our stand in behalf of the unfortunate piece of perfection called a
heroine. Take our novels as a criterion, and how much of the
love-making of the present day is done by the ladies? Oh age
of chivalry! oh knightly worshippers of beauty, throned and
unapproachable! What has become of all the reverence and duty
of your magnanimous bestowal, the sacred honours you gave to
woman's weakness, and all the noble fruits it bore?

We are somewhat at a loss to find why so many pseudo-
philanthropists come in to the first stage of this tale, for it does
not seem enough reason for their introduction that they are
simply to play upon the benevolence of Mr Jarndyce, and thence
to disappear into their native gloom. Altogether the author seems
to have intended making more of Jarndyce, and his immediate
surroundings, in his first design – else why the momentary vision
of Mrs Pardiggle, and the elaborate sketch of Boythorne [*sic*], of
whom so very little is made afterwards? Mrs Jellyby, too, disappears placidly, though she leaves a very sufficient representative in her daughter, whose various adventures and simple girlish
character make a pleasant variety in the tale. Then there is Skimpole, a sketch, which *looks* almost too near the life, of the fashionable amiable phase of the most entire and unalloyed selfishness.
The poor boy Joe [*sic*] is a very effective picture, though we fail
to discover a sufficient reason for his introduction; and the household of Snagsby, in spite of the clandestine virtues of its good
little master, is far from an agreeable one. We cannot omit, either,

to remark the horrible catastrophe of the book, a pure outrage upon imagination. It is not of the slightest importance to us if a case of spontaneous combustion occurs somewhere every week or every day, but we know it is quite out of the range of healthful and sound invention, a monstrous and fantastic horror; – worthy of it, and of their relationship to its victim, are the revolting family of Smallweeds. Is this humour? or is it worthy to be offered to a trustful public in any guise? Yet many of these pages, which Mr Dickens can fill so well, are given over to disgust and impatience, that our author may bring before us this miserable family, and prove to us what he can do in the way of exaggerated and uninstructive caricature. We have another quarrel with Mr Dickens – one of long standing, dating back to the period of his first work: the 'shepherd' of Mr Weller's widow, the little Bethel of Mrs Nubbles, have effloresced in *Bleak House* into a detestable Mr Chadband, an oft-repeated libel upon the preachers of the poor. This is a very vulgar and common piece of slander, quite unworthy of a true artist. Are we really to believe, then, that only those who are moderately religious are true in their profession? – that it is good to be in earnest in every occupation but one, the most important of all, as it happens? What a miserable assumption is this! Mr Dickens' tender charity does not disdain to embrace a good many equivocal people – why then so persevering an aim at a class which offends few and harms no man? Not very long since, we ourselves, who are no great admirers of English dissent, happened to go into a very humble little meeting-house – perhaps a Bethel – where the preacher, at his beginning, we are ashamed to say, tempted our unaccustomed faculties almost to laughter. Here was quite an opportunity for finding a Chadband, for the little man was round and ruddy, and had a shining face – his grammar was not perfect, moreover, and having occasion to mention a certain Scripture town, he called it Canar of Galilee; but when we had listened for half an hour, we had no longer the slightest inclination to laugh at the humble preacher. This unpretending man reached to the heart of his subject in less time than we have taken to tell of it; gave a bright, clear, individual view of the doctrine he was considering, and urged it on his hearers with homely arguments which were as little ridiculous as can be supposed. Will Mr Dickens permit us to advise him, when he next would draw a 'shepherd', to study his figure from the life? Let him choose the least little chapel on his way, and take his chance for a successful sitting: we grant him he may find a Chadband, but we promise him he has at least an equal chance of finding an apostle instead.

We are glad to turn from those disagreeable people to the lofty household which adds its state and grandeur to this novel, and we can give nothing but commendation, and that of the highest, to the family of Sir Leicester Dedlock. Lady Dedlock, haughty, imperious, beautiful, elevated to a higher world, above suspicion, like the wife of Cæsar, by the reverential admiration of her husband, is admirably introduced; and the woman's heart weeping behind these disguises – the old secret history so slowly unfolded, the womanish impulses so sudden and stormy, the womanish horror and yet defiance of shame, are nobly developed as the tale goes on. How did her ladyship's daughter chance to have so mild and tame a nature? The fire and passion of Lady Dedlock are things of a very different rank and order from any emotion of Esther Summerson's. The whole house, from the grey-haired pompous ancient gentleman himself – a true gentleman, and tenderly revealed to us, in the end, with the old chivalry alive and noble under these grand pretences of his – down to the debilitated cousin, is worthy of its author. In this sphere he has done nothing so dignified and so perfect. The accessories and dependants of the family are all touched with equal delicacy. What can be better in its way than George, his friends, and his story? – or that stout-hearted trooper's wife, with her far-travelled umbrella and her grey cloak?

In the very highly wrought and tragical pursuit of Lady Dedlock, Mr Dickens makes use of materials long since collected. Strangely different in its superficial garb from the romance of the past is the romance of to-day; yet who ever traced a picturesque fugitive, warned by spectres, and pressed by armed pursuers, with interest more breathless and absorbed than that with which we follow Bucket as *he* follows the faint trace of this unhappy lady? The dash of the horses along the midnight road – the breathless and silent excitement to which the pursuers reach at last, and then the sudden discovery and climax so simply told, form a wonderful picture. And most pathetic is that other scene, where poor Sir Leicester lies in his chamber, listening for their return. These scenes are full of delicacy and power, and are very great efforts, conceived and carried out with unfaltering force. (vol. LXXVII, April 1855)

Fortnightly Review

DICKENS has proved his power by a popularity almost un-exampled, embracing all classes. Surely it is a task for criticism to exhibit the sources of that power? If everything that has ever been alleged against the works be admitted, there still remains an immense success to be accounted for. It was not by their defects that these works were carried over Europe and America. It was not their defects which made them the delight of grey heads on the bench, and the study of youngsters in the counting-house and school-room. Other writers have been exaggerated, untrue, fan-tastic, and melodramatic; but they have gained so little notice that no one thinks of pointing out their defects. It is clear, there-fore, that Dickens had powers which enabled him to triumph in spite of the weaknesses which clogged them; and it is worth inquiring what those powers were, and their relation to his un-deniable defects. (February 1872)

George Gissing

I

TO come to the root of the matter, *Bleak House* is a brilliant, admirable, and most righteous satire upon the monstrous iniquity of 'old Father Antic the Law', with incidental mockery of allied abuses which, now as then, hold too large a place in the life of the English people.

Needless nowadays to revive the controversies which the book excited; we know that the Court of Chancery disgraced a country pretending to civilization; we know that, not long after the publication of *Bleak House*, it submitted to certain reforms; yet it is interesting to remember that legal luminaries scoffed at Dickens's indignation and declared his picture utterly unlike the truth. One of these critics (Lord Denman) published a long and severe arraignment of the author, disputing not only his facts, but his theories of human nature. This novel, asserted Lord Denman, contained all Dickens's old faults and a good many new ones. Especially bitter was his lordship on the subject of Mrs Jellyby, whom he held to be a gross libel on the philanthropic cause of slave emancipation. Many readers, naturally, found subject of offence in Mr Chadband. Indeed, *Bleak House* seems to have aroused emotions in England very much as *Martin Chuzzlewit* did in America, the important point being that in neither case did Dickens's satire ultimately injure him with his public; in the end, the laugh was on his side, and with a laugh he triumphed. Not a little remarkable, when one comes to think of it, this immunity of the great writer. Humour, and humour alone, could have ensured it to him. It is all very well to talk of right prevailing, of the popular instinct for justice, and so on; these phrases mean very little. Dickens held his own because he amused. The noblest orator ever born, raising his voice in divine wrath against Chancery and all its vileness would not have touched the 'great heart of the People' as did these pages which make gloriously ridiculous the whole legal world from His Lordship in his High Court down to Mr Guppy on his high stool.

The satire is of very wide application; it involves that whole system of pompous precedent which in Dickens's day was responsible for so much cruelty and hypocrisy, for such waste of life in filth and gloom and wretchedness. With the glaring injustice of the Law, rotting society down to such places as Tom-all-Alone's, is associated the subtler evils of an aristocracy sunk to harmful impotence. With absurd precedent goes foolish pride, and self-righteousness, and every form of idle egoism; hence we have a group of admirable studies in selfish conceit – Harold Skimpole, Mr Turveydrop, Mr Chadband, Mrs Jellyby. Impossible to vary the central theme more adroitly, more brilliantly. In *Bleak House* London is seen as a mere dependence of the Court of Chancery, a great gloomy city, webbed and meshed, as it were, by the spinnings of a huge poisonous spider sitting in the region of Chancery Lane; its inhabitants are the blighted, stunted and prematurely old offspring of a town which knows not fresh air. Perfect, all this, for the purpose of the satirist. In this sense, at all events, *Bleak House* is an excellently constructed book.

There is no leading character. In Richard Carstone, about whom the story may be said to circle, Dickens tried to carry out a purpose he had once entertained with regard to Walter Gay in *Dombey and Son*. That of showing a good lad at the mercy of temptations and circumstances which little by little wreck his life; but Richard has very little life to lose, and we form only a shadowy conception of his amiably futile personality. Still less convincing is his betrothed, Ada, whose very name one finds it difficult to remember. Nothing harder, to be sure, than to make a living picture of one whose part in the story is passive, and in *Bleak House* passivity is the characteristic of all the foremost figures; their business is to submit to the irresistible. Yet two of these personages seem to me successful studies of a kind in which Dickens was not often successful; I cannot but think that both Sir Leicester Dedlock and John Jarndyce is, each in his way, an excellent piece of work, making exactly the impression at which the author aimed. Compare Jarndyce with Mr Pickwick and with the brothers Cheeryble. It is to their world that he belongs, the world of eccentric benevolence; he is the kind of man Dickens delighted to portray; but Mr Jarndyce is far more recognizably a fellow-mortal than his gay predecessors; in truth, he may claim the style of gentleman, and perhaps may stand for the most soberly agreeable portrait of a gentleman to be found in all Dickens's novels. Sir Leicester, though he shows in the full light of satiric intention, being a figurehead on the crazy old ship of aristocratic privilege, is a human being akin to John Jarndyce; he speaks with undue solemnity, but behaves at all times as *noblesse oblige*, and, when sinking beneath his unmerited calamities, makes no little claim upon our sympathetic admiration. We have travelled far since the days of Sir Mulberry Hawk; the artist, meanwhile, had made friends in the privileged class of his countrymen, and had learnt what the circumstances of his early life did not allow him to perceive, that virtue and good manners are not confined to the middle and lower orders. He would not go so far as to make Sir Leicester intelligent; in spite of personal experience, Dickens never reconciled himself to the thought of 'birth' in association with brains. His instinctive feeling comes out very strongly in that conversation between the Baronet and the Ironmaster which points to Dickens's remedy – the Radical remedy – for all the evils he is depicting.

II

That the Dedlock tragedy is the least impressive portion of the book results partly from Dickens's inability to represent any kind of woman save the eccentric, the imbecile, and the shrew (there are at most one or two small exceptions), and partly from the melodramatic strain in him, which so often misled his genius. Educated readers of to-day see little difference between these chapters of *Bleak House* and the treatment of any like 'mystery' in a penny novelette. There is no need to insist on these weaknesses of the master; we admit them as a matter of critical duty, and at the same time point out the characteristics, moral and intellectual, of Victorian England, which account for so many of Dickens's limitations. Had he not been restrained by an insensate prudishness from dealing honestly with Lady Dedlock's story, Lady Dedlock herself might have been far more human. Where the national conscience refuses to recognize certain phases of life, it is not wonderful that national authors should exhibit timidity and ineptitude whenever they glance in the forbidden direction. Instead of a picture, we get a cloudy veil suggestive of nameless horrors; it is the sort of exaggeration which necessarily results in feebleness.

Dickens was very fond of the effect produced by bringing into close contact representatives of social extremes; the typical instance is Lady Dedlock's relations with crossing-sweeper Jo. Contemporary readers saw in Jo a figure of supreme pathos; they wept over his death-bed, as by those of Paul Dombey and of Little Nell. An ecclesiastical dignitary could not find words of solemn praise adequate to his emotions at the end of chapter 47. 'Uncultured nature is *there* indeed; the intimations of true heart feeling, the glimmerings of higher feeling, all are there; but everything still consistent and in harmony. To my mind nothing in the field of fiction is to be found in English literature surpassing the death of Jo!' That expressed the common judgment; but there were dissentients, especially Lord Denman, who after deploring the introduction of so much squalor – 'the author's love of low life appears to grow on him' – went on to protest against Dickens's habit of discovering 'delicacy of virtuous sentiment in the lowest depths of human degradation'. We know that Lord Denman was here quite right; for, though virtue may exist in the ignorant and the poor and the debased, most assuredly the delicacies of virtue will not be found in them, and it is these delicacies on which Dickens so commonly insists. If one fact can be asserted of the lowest English it is that, supposing them to say or do a good thing, they will say or do it in the worst possible way. Does there, I wonder, exist in all literature a scene less correspondent with any possibility of life than that description of Jo's last moments? Dickens believed in it – there is the odd thing. Not a line, not a word, is insincere. He had a twofold mission in life, and, from our standpoint, in an age which has outgrown so many conditions of fifty years ago, we can only mark with regret how the philanthropist in him so often overcame the artist.

His true pathos comes when he does not particularly try for it and is invariably an aspect of his humour. The two chief instances in this book are the picture of Coavinses's children after their father's death, and the figure of Guster, Mrs Snagsby's slave-of-all-work. Nothing more touching, more natural, more simple, than that scene in chapter 15 where Esther and her companions find the little Coavinses locked up for safety in their cold garret, whilst the elder child, Charley, is away at washing to earn food for them all.

'God help you, Charley!' said my Guardian. 'You're not tall enough to reach the tub!'
'In pattens I am, Sir,' she answered quickly. 'I've got a high pair as belonged to mother.'

That is worth many death-beds of ideal crossing-sweepers. We see it is a possible and intelligible thing that Charley should be a good girl, and her goodness takes precisely the right form. She is healthy in mind and body; her little figure makes one of the points of contrast (others are Mr Boythorn, and Caddy Jellyby, and Trooper George, and the Bagnet household) which emphasize the sordid evil all about her. Anything but healthy, on the other hand, is Mrs Snagsby's Guster, the poor slavey whose fits and starved stupidities supply us with such strange matter for mirth. She belongs to the Marchioness group of characters, wherein Dickens's hand has a peculiar skill.

Guster, really aged three or four and twenty, but looking a round ten years older, goes cheap with this unaccountable drawback of fits, and is so apprehensive of being returned on the hands of her patron saint [the parish] that except when she is found with her head in the pail, or the sink, or the copper, or the dinner, she is always at work. The law-stationer's establishment is, in Guster's eyes, a temple of plenty and splendour. She believes the little drawing-room upstairs, always kept, as one may say, with its hair in papers and its pinafore on, to be the most elegant apartment in Christendom. . . . Guster has some recompense for her many privations.

The wonderful thing about such work as this is Dickens's subdual of his indignation to the humorous note. It is when indignation gets the upper hand, and humour is lost sight of, that he falls into peril of unconsciously false sentiment.

III

Among the characters of this book there is not one belonging to the foremost groups of Dickens's creations, no one standing together with Mr Micawber and Mr Pecksniff; yet what novel by any other writer presents such a multitude of strongly-featured individuals, their names and their persons familiar to everyone who has but once read *Bleak House*? As I have already remarked, most of them illustrate the main theme of the story, exhibiting in various forms the vice of a fixed idea which sacrifices everything and everybody to its own selfish demands. The shrewdly ingenious Skimpole (I do not stop to comment on the old story of his outward resemblance to Leigh Hunt), the lordly Turveydrop, the devoted Mrs Jellyby, the unctuously eloquent Mr Chadband, all are following in their own little way the example of the High Court of Chancery – victimizing all about them on pretence of the most disinterested motives. The legal figures – always so admirable in Dickens – of course strike this key-note with peculiar emphasis; we are in no doubt as to the impulses ruling Mr Kenge or Mr Vholes, and their spirit is potent for evil down to the very dregs of society, in Grandfather Smallweed and in Mr Krook. The victims themselves are a ragged regiment after Dickens's own heart; crazy Chancery suitors, Mr Jellyby and his hapless offspring, fever-stricken dwellers in Chancery's slums, all shown with infinite picturesqueness – which indeed is the prime artistic quality of the book. For mirth extracted from sordid material no example can surpass Mr Guppy, who is chicane incarnate; his withdrawal from the tender suit to Miss Summerson, excellent farce, makes as good comment as ever was written upon the law-office frame of mind. That we have little if any frank gaiety is but natural and right; it would be out of keeping with the tone of a world overshadowed by the Law. To regret that Skimpole is not so engaging as Micawber, with other like contrasts, is merely to find fault with the aim which the novelist sets before him. Yet it is probable enough that the rather long-drawn dreariness of some parts of the book may be attributed to the overstrain from which at this time Dickens was avowedly suffering.

In his Preface he tells us that he had 'purposely dwelt on the romantic side of familiar things'. But the word romantic does not seem to be very accurately applied. In using it, Dickens no doubt was thinking of the Dedlock mystery, the involvement of a crossing-sweeper in aristocratic tragedies, and so on; all which would be better called melodrama than romance. What he did achieve was to make the common and the unclean most forcibly picturesque. From the fog at the opening of the story to Lady Dedlock's miserable death at the end, we are held by a powerful picture of murky, swarming, rotting London, a marvellous rendering of the impression received by any imaginative person who in low spirits has had occasion to wander about London's streets. Nowhere is Dickens stronger in lurid effects; for a fine horror he never went beyond chapter 32 – where it would, of course, be wide of the mark to begin discussing the possibility of spontaneous combustion. Masterly descriptions abound; the Court in chapter 1, the regions of the Law during vacation in Chapter 19, Mr Vholes's office in chapter 39, are among the best. The inquest at the Sol's Arms shows all Dickens's peculiar power of giving typical value to the commonplace; scene and actors are unforgettable; the gruesome, the vile, and the ludicrous combine in unique effects, in the richest suggestiveness. And for the impressive in another kind – still shadowed by the evil genius of the book, but escaped from the city's stifling atmosphere – what could be better than chapter 57, Esther's posting through the night with Inspector Bucket. This is very vigorous narrative. We, of course, forget that an amiable young lady is supposed to be penning it, and are reminded of those chapters of earlier books where Dickens revels in the joy of the road.

As a reminder that even in *Bleak House* the master did not altogether lose his wonted cheeriness by humble firesides, one may recall the Bagnet household, dwelling at a happy distance from Chancery Lane. Compare the dinner presided over by the Old Girl beside her shining hearth with that partaken of by Mr Guppy, Mr Jobling and Mr Smallweed at their familiar chophouse. Each is perfect in its kind, and each a whole world in little.

(from *The Immortal Dickens*, 1925)

PART THREE
Bleak House
in its Period

Humphry House

BLEAK HOUSE: THE TIME SCALE (1941)

Bleak House was published in monthly parts from March 1852 to September 1853, and Dickens seems to have gone out of his way to leave the imaginary time of the story vague. When Esther copies into her narrative the letter in the wonderful legal jargon of Kenge and Carboy, she deliberately says: 'I omit the date.' No year is given anywhere, and there is scarcely even the name of a month. This is more surprising because the sense of the passage of time is so peculiarly vivid, and makes more impression on the memory, perhaps, than the chronology in any of the other novels. This powerful imaginative effect is produced by term succeeding vacation and vacation succeeding term in the Court of Chancery, and by the changes of the seasons down at Chesney Wold. But the tempo of events in the two main strands of the plot is curiously dissimilar. If we isolate the Jarndyce theme from the Dedlock theme, we think of Richard Carstone's failure, entanglement, and decay as slow and long-drawn-out, but of the events which hurried Lady Dedlock to discovery and death as a swiftly moving series of crises. Yet on the whole the two are meant to synchronize: Lady Dedlock does not die many pages before Ada discloses her pregnancy; and the story proper has then less than nine months to run. And at the end, as so often with Dickens, even what should be slow is hurried.

By watching the seasons and the terms it might appear that from Esther's first going to Bleak House to the death of Richard was something just less than three years. But at several points the time-table is congested and obscure, and John Jarndyce himself suggests that it is probably wrong. The main story cannot have happened later than 1843–6, and is also assumed to be much earlier.

The personal experience on which Dickens was drawing when he described Guppy and Jobling clearly belonged to the same years which produced Lowten and the 'Magpie and Stump'; that is, to 1827–31, the period between leaving school and becoming a reporter in the Gallery of the House of Commons. During this time he was seen to be reporting cases in the Lord Chancellor's Court, and the Lord Chancellor from 1827 to 1830 was Lord Lyndhurst.* But Lyndhurst was Chancellor again, in 1834 and for a third time from 1841 to 1846. So, even if we boldly say that he was the Chancellor of *Bleak House*, it proves very little about the date of Caddy's marriage or the dispute between Coodle and Doodle.

But, dotted about in the book, there are other quite clear indications of time – all rather contradictory, though they seem to be so definite. One of the most unexpected is the sudden statement in chapter 43 that Harold Skimpole 'lived in a place called the Polygon, in Somers Town, where there were at that time a number of poor Spanish refugees walking about in cloaks, smoking little paper cigars'. Their identity is plain enough: they were the 'group of fifty or a hundred stately tragic figures, in proud threadbare cloaks' described by Carlyle in his *Life of John Sterling*, the exiles of the Torrijos party, well known round St Pancras between 1823 and 1830, whom Dickens must often have seen as a boy. But their picturesque irruption into *Bleak House* hardly tallies with the landscape measured and broken for the coming railway out of Lincolnshire (ch. 55). The scorn with which the shining hatted and belted policeman looks down on the beadle (ch. 11) as 'a remnant of the barbarous watchmen-times' suggests a superiority in the 'Peelers' not acquired too soon after 1829. Mr Bucket, too, belongs very much to the

---

* W. S. Holdsworth in *Charles Dickens as a Legal Historian* (New Haven, Conn., 1928) accepts the Lyndhurst identification from J. B. Atlay's *Lives of the Victorian Chancellors*, 2 vols (1906–8), I 143, but goes on (p. 79): 'If it be true that the Lord Chancellor described in the third chapter of *Bleak House* is Lord Lyndhurst, the time at which the action of the story takes place must be taken to be in or about 1827, when he was made Chancellor in succession to Lord Eldon.'

reformed world.* Mrs Pardiggle's Puseyism, and the Carlyle-like attack on the latest dandyism (ch. 12), which seems to mean partly the Oxford Movement and partly Young England, would, taken by themselves, commit the story at least to the later 'thirties. Mr Turveydrop seems to have maintained his lonely deportment for some years since the death of George IV. Mrs Jellyby and all her works belong in spirit and in detail to the 'forties. And one of the originals for Jo was almost certainly a boy called George Ruby, 'who appeared about fourteen years of age' when he was called at the Guildhall on 8 January 1850 to give evidence in a case of assault.

> *Alderman Humphery.* Well, do you know what you are about? Do you know what an oath is?
> *Boy.* No.
> *Alderman.* Can you read?
> *Boy.* No.
> *Alderman.* Do you ever say your prayers?
> *Boy.* No, never.
> *Alderman.* Do you know what prayers are?
> *Boy.* No.
> *Alderman.* Do you know what God is?
> *Boy.* No.
> *Alderman.* Do you know what the devil is?
> *Boy.* I've heard of the devil, but I don't know him.
> *Alderman.* What do you know?
> *Boy.* I knows how to sweep the crossings.
> *Alderman.* And that's all?
> *Boy.* That's all. I sweeps a crossing.†

These things are of varying importance; but if we try to fix a precise date to the story, some at least of them must be misplaced. It seems unlikely that even Dickens, careless as he was, would have brought to life such marked and dated people as Mrs Pardiggle, Mrs Jellyby, and Inspector Bucket, in a world

* The C.I.D. had its origin in the plain-clothes detectives first appointed by Sir James Graham, Home Secretary, in 1844.

† Dickens almost certainly read these exact words, as they are taken from *The Household Narrative*, Jan 1850, the monthly supplement to *Household Words*.

that could not possibly have known them. It is quite possible that when Esther wrote the last section of her narrative 'full seven years' after the story proper was ended, she wrote at the same time as Dickens, in 1853; which would mean that Richard died in about 1846, and that the story probably began in the early 'forties. But the whole atmosphere of the legal parts of the book and numbers of the small details – the Spanish exiles among them – are drawn out of the inexhaustible store of memories from Dickens's early days.

Overlaid on this confusion of the past was a reformist's anger with the immediate present. Both the Court of Chancery and the slums were topical subjects in 1852, for other reasons than because Dickens made them so. People were then in fact dying of litigation and of cholera. It is on the relation between this topicality and the material from other dates that we must focus, if we want to find its historical interest.

SOURCE: *The Dickens World* (1941).

John Butt and Kathleen Tillotson

THE TOPICALITY OF
BLEAK HOUSE (1957)

I

NONE of Dickens's novels is innocent of topical appeal. His naturally keen eyes were sharpened by a journalist's training to render his account of contemporary men and manners, and his sympathies were trained in the same school to detect social abuses. In the early novels he followed the practice of his master Smollett and kept shifting his scene to permit the light to play on a wide diversity of experiences. Thus in the first number of *Nicholas Nickleby* we are prepared, by meeting Squeers, for a visit to Dotheboys Hall; but we have already attended a public meeting held 'to take into consideration the propriety of petitioning Parliament in favour of the United Metropolitan Improved Hot Muffin and Crumpet Baking and Punctual Delivery Company'; and later in the novel we are to learn what life is like in a strolling players' troupe. There is no connexion between Squeers's slum and Crummles's more genial slum except that Nicholas Nickleby lives for a time in each – the Company Meeting he did not even attend – and there might have been even greater diversity of scene, if Dickens had acted upon an impulse, after a visit to Manchester, of striking a blow for the cotton-mill operatives.*

* Dickens wrote to Edward FitzGerald on 29 Dec 1838: 'I went, some weeks ago, to Manchester, and saw the *worst* cotton mill. And then I saw the *best. Ex uno disce omnes.* . . . So far as seeing goes, I have seen enough for my purpose, and what I have seen has disgusted and astonished me beyond all measure. I mean to strike the heaviest blow in my power for these unfortunate creatures, but whether I shall do so in the *Nickleby* or wait some other opportunity I have not yet determined' (E. Hodder, *Life and Work of the Seventh Earl of Shaftesbury* (1888 edn, p. 120). At the time of writing this letter, he had just

This discursiveness of incident is gradually controlled in later novels, but it is not until the eighteen-fifties that a unifying principle can be detected in these heterogeneous topicalities. As late as *David Copperfield* such unrelated topics of contemporary discussion as model prisons, the redemption of prostitutes, and the treatment of lunatics, can be discovered cheek by jowl. But in the next novel, *Bleak House*, a great and largely successful effort was made to integrate the diversity of detail into a single view of society. The 'Condition-of-England question' was perfectly familiar. It was Carlyle who had raised it as long ago as 1839 in his *Chartism*, and he had recently presented another formulation of it in *Latter-Day Pamphlets*:

The deranged condition of our affairs is a universal topic among men at present; and the heavy miseries pressing, in their rudest shape, on the great dumb inarticulate class, and from this, by a sure law, spreading upwards, in a less palpable but not less certain and perhaps still more fatal shape on all classes to the very highest, are admitted everywhere to be great, increasing and now almost unendurable.[1]

Carlyle goes on to define two attitudes currently adopted, one being to admit the miseries and pronounce them to be incurable except by Heaven, the other being to alleviate the evil by charities, 'to cure a world's woes by rose-water':

A blind loquacious pruriency of indiscriminate Philanthropism substituting itself, with much self-laudation, for the silent divinely awful sense of Right and Wrong; – testifying too clearly

---

completed no. x (chs 30–3), in which Nicholas returns to London, after leaving Crummles's troupe of players, removes his sister from Mrs Wititterly's, and establishes her once more with his mother in Miss La Creevy's apartments. In the following number (chs 34–6) he begins life afresh as a clerk in the Cheeryble Brothers' counting-house. The originals of the two Cheerybles are well known to have been Daniel and William Grant of Ramsbottom and Manchester (F. G. Kitton, *Charles Dickens: His Life, Writings, and Personality* (1902) p. 65). By placing the Cheerybles' business in Lancashire and sending Nicholas to work there, Dickens would have taken a satisfactory stance for striking his 'blow' in *Nickleby*.

that here is no longer a divine sense of Right and Wrong; that, in the smoke of this universal, and alas inevitable and indispensable revolutionary fire, and burning up of worn-out rags of which the world is full, our life-atmosphere has (for the time) become one vile London fog, and the eternal loadstars are gone out for us!

There is no need to ask whether Dickens recalled these particular passages. This in general terms was the diagnosis he accepted of the troubles of mid-Victorian England; and in *Bleak House* he set himself to translate this diagnosis into the terms of his own art, choosing individual characters and groups of characters to represent 'the great dumb inarticulate class', those who regarded social iniquities as inevitable, and the rose-water philanthropists; finding symbols in the images of fog and fire; and representing by a plot the way the evil spreads upwards till it impinges 'on all classes to the very highest'.

'The great dumb inarticulate class' is represented by Jo the crossing-sweeper, and to a lesser extent by the brickmaker's family. These are the typical inhabitants of Tom-all-Alone's, a typical slum. They are the victims of our social iniquities, and in a different way they are victims of such ineffectual philanthropists as Mr Chadband and Mrs Pardiggle. The class who admit that the country is in a parlous state are represented by Sir Leicester Dedlock and those attending his house parties at Chesney Wold. These Regency survivals are content with their old-established ways – just as the lawyers are content with their antiquated routine – and are scornful of such men as Mr Rouncewell who tackle the problem by providing productive work. Fire will sweep away the confusion of the Law, as Spontaneous Combustion disposed of Lord Chancellor Krook; and Chesney Wold will slowly decay in the persistent rain. But before that happens, its secrets will have been found buried in Tom-all-Alone's, for that is where Lady Dedlock's lover lay and that is where she herself comes to die. Tom-all-Alone's must have its inescapable effect upon society; this is as unavoidable, in the present state of affairs, as the smallpox which Esther catches from Jo. It is not surprising to find that 'Tom-all-Alone's: The

Ruined House' was the first title drafted for the novel in the manuscript.

The fable has indeed been frequently interpreted, but what has hitherto been overlooked is the topicality of Dickens's particularization. This was a fable for 1852, related to a large extent in terms of the events, the types, and the social groups which the previous year had thrown into prominence.

II

1851 was the year of the Great Exhibition in Hyde Park. It was also a time of public anxiety caused by the establishment of the Roman Catholic hierarchy in England during the previous twelve months. Dickens was aware of both. As to what Lord John Russell called 'papal aggression', he seems to have followed the Prime Minister's lead in blaming it upon the Puseyites: 'if the Universities', he wrote to Miss Coutts on 22 August 1851, 'had been forced to adjust themselves to the character of the times, we never should have had to bless Oxford for the intolerable enormity it has dug out of the mire'.[2]

The principal representative of the Puseyites in *Bleak House* is Mrs Pardiggle. Her allegiance is not asserted, but it is clearly enough implied, in the names she has given to her sons – Egbert, Oswald, Francis, Felix, and Alfred, the names of saints or heroes of the primitive Church – and in her custom of pressing her young family to attend Matins with her '(very prettily done), at half past six o'clock in the morning all the year round, including of course the depth of winter'. But she is not the only Puseyite in the novel. Other suspects are the ladies who pestered Mr Jarndyce for a subscription 'to establish in a picturesque building (engraving of proposed West Elevation attached) the Sisterhood of Mediæval Marys',* and the ladies and gentlemen of the newest

---

* *Bleak House*, ch. 8. The first Anglican sisterhoods had been founded in the eighteen-forties. Miss Sellon's Sisterhood of Mercy at Devonport had been in the news in 1849 owing to an inquiry conducted by the Bishop of Exeter. See H. P. Liddon, *Life of E. B. Pusey*, 4 vols (1893–4) vol. III, ch. viii.

fashion assembled at one of Sir Leicester Dedlock's country house parties. Theirs was a 'dandyism' in religion:

in mere lackadaisical want of an emotion, [they] have agreed upon a little dandy talk about the Vulgar wanting faith in things in general; meaning, in the things that have been tried and found wanting, as though a low fellow should unaccountably lose faith in a bad shilling, after finding it out! Who would make the Vulgar very picturesque and faithful, by putting back the hands upon the Clock of Time, and cancelling a few hundred years of history. (ch. 12)

Bearing in mind the terms of his letter to Miss Coutts, we must attribute this attack upon the Oxford Movement in 1852 to Dickens's disgust at the establishment of the Roman Catholic hierarchy in England in 1850. The Puseyites were to blame for this 'intolerable enormity'.

No one in 1851 could escape being aware of the Great Exhibition, least of all the editor of a weekly journal. But readers of *Household Words* could not complain of being satiated with description and comment. The third in a series of articles by Charles Knight on 'Three May Days in London' was devoted to the Great Exhibition, and William Howitt was allowed to describe a 'pilgrimage' to Hyde Park; but when his wife offered an article on the May Festival at Starnberg, Dickens wrote impatiently to Wills (10 August 1851):

In the May Festival of Miss [*sic*] Howitt (very good) for the Lord's love don't let us have any allusion to the Great Exhibition.[3]

This is what earlier letters might have led us to expect. He is 'used up' by the Exhibition, he tells Mrs Watson on 11 July:

I don't say 'there is nothing in it' – there's too much. I have only been twice; so many things bewildered me. I have a natural horror of sights, and the fusion of so many sights in one has not decreased it;[4]

and he left Miss Coutts to take the children. In fact, he had always had 'an instinctive feeling against the Exhibition', so Wills was told on 27 July, 'of a faint, inexplicable sort'.[5] Some explanation of this feeling, however, may be found in an article, which he wrote for *Household Words* (published 4 January 1851), entitled 'The Last Words of the Old Year'. The Old Year lies dying; on his death bed he surveys his life, and makes his bequests to his successor. It is a melancholy retrospect. ' "I have been," said the good old gentleman, penitently, "a Year of Ruin".' Farmers have been blighted, and the land destroyed; many valuable and dear lives have been sacrificed, in steamboats, 'because of the want of commonest and easiest precautions for the prevention of those legal murders'; forty-five persons in every hundred are found to be incapable of reading or writing; starving children who stole a loaf out of a baker's shop have been sentenced to be whipped in the House of Correction. ' "I have seen," he presently said:

a project carried into execution for a great assemblage of the peaceful glories of the world. I have seen a wonderful structure, reared in glass, by the energy and skill of a great natural genius, self-improved: worthy descendant of my Saxon ancestors: worthy type of ingenuity triumphant! Which of my children shall behold the Princes, Prelates, Nobles, Merchants, of England equally united, for another Exhibition – for a great display of England's sins and negligences, to be, by steady contemplation of all eyes, and steady union of all hearts and hands, set right?

The Great Exhibition, he seems to infer, may encourage, rather than temper, the mood of self-satisfaction, which the mechanical achievements of the age have aroused. In a novel where the life of England in 1851 is otherwise fully represented, the Great Exhibition is deliberately, even conspicuously, excluded.

III

At the end of his survey the Old Year makes some bequests. Not all of them are relevant to this discussion, but a note of prophecy may be easily detected in the following:

I bequeath to my successor ... a vast inheritance of degradation and neglect in England; and I charge him, if he be wise, to get

speedily through it ... I do give and bequeath to him, likewise,
... the Court of Chancery. The less he leaves of it to his successor, the better for mankind.

The centre of *Bleak House* is the great chancery case of Jarndyce and Jarndyce. Dickens himself had suffered from chancery
proceedings in 1844, when he had attempted to stop publication
of a plagiarism of *A Christmas Carol*, and had ultimately dropped
a chancery suit against the bankrupt pirates. More recently he
had published two papers, entitled 'The Martyrs in Chancery', in
Household Words.* Those papers show that he was aware of the
injustices of chancery as early as 7 December 1850, when the first
of them was published; but they do not foreshadow the treatment of chancery in *Bleak House*. There he complains of intolerable delays and legal obfuscation: the articles revert to a theme
which he himself had already touched in *Pickwick Papers*, chapters 41 and 43, and deal with the cases of men who have lan-
guished in prison over long periods of years, because as executors
they had failed to defend a suit in which another party was
interested, or to hand over property of which they were never in
possession. His theme in the *Pickwick* chapters, and his contributor's theme in the *Household Words* articles, is long-term imprisonment.† It is possible to see how that might have turned his
mind to the theme of *Little Dorrit* or of *A Tale of Two Cities*, but
scarcely to the theme of *Bleak House*.

* The *Household Words* contributors' book shows that the author,
A. Cole, was assisted in the second article by Dickens's assistant
editor, W. H. Wills.

† In Sept 1852, Lord Denman, a former Lord Chief Justice, attacked
Dickens in a series of articles in the *Standard*, which were reprinted as
a pamphlet with the title, *Uncle Tom's Cabin, Bleak House, Slavery
and Slave Trade* (1853). Commenting on it in a letter to Lord Denman's daughter, Mrs Cropper, 20 Dec 1852, Dickens wrote: 'The
pamphlet ... objects that I come in at the Death of Chancery and
might have attacked it before. – The most serious and pathetic point
I tried with all indignation and intensity to make, *in my first book*,
(Pickwick) was the slow torture and death of a Chancery prisoner.
From that hour to this, if I have been set on anything, it has been on
exhibiting the abuses of the Law.' For the reasons for Lord Denman's
attack see *Letters*, II 445 and note.

What had directed Dickens's attention to the Court of Chancery in 1851 was the interest which everyone was taking in chancery that year. The reader of *The Times* who opened his newspaper on 1 January would have noticed a leading article on the subject, in the course of which the writer remarked:

We believe that the time is rapidly approaching when the public necessities and the public will must triumph over the *inertia* of an antiquated jurisprudence and the obstacles raised by personal or professional interest . . . the community suffers . . . from a confused mass of laws, from costly and dilatory procedure, and from an inadequate number of Judges. . . . This opinion has now become so strong and universal in the country that active measures for the reform of the law . . . are becoming the test by which a large proportion of the Liberal party are disposed to try the sincerity and the capacity of their present leaders. We could crowd our columns day after day with the remonstrances which are addressed to ourselves, especially with reference to the present state of the Court of Chancery.

The words are not such as Dickens would have used, but the indictment is Dickens's indictment. The writer points, as Dickens was a few months later to point, to the inertia, the confusion, the costly and dilatory procedure, and (most significantly) to the vested interests impeding reform, 'the obstacles raised by personal or professional interest'.

In *The Times* of 24 December 1850, there had been an even stronger protest, and once again the complaint has a familiar ring:

If a house be seen in a peculiarly dilapidated condition, the beholder at once exclaims, 'Surely that property must be in Chancery': and the exclamation very correctly expresses the popular opinion as to the effect of legal proceedings generally upon all property which unluckily becomes the subject of litigation in any shape. . . . Success and defeat are alike fatal to litigants;

and again, later in the same article,

the lingering and expectant suitors waste their lives as well as their substance in vain hopes, and death robs them of their wished-for triumph, if ruin have not already rendered it impossible.

Richard Carstone, Miss Flite, and Gridley, as well as Tom-all-Alone's can there be seen casting their shadows before. Gridley's case is known to have been based upon an actual case in Staffordshire. Forster mentions that a certain Mr Challinor of Leek had sent Dickens a pamphlet setting out its details after the publication of the first monthly number of *Bleak House*, and that Dickens had embodied the facts in a later chapter.* Challinor had already drawn attention to the case at a meeting of the Chancery Reform Association on 30 January, and *The Times* carried a long report of it the following day. At that meeting a barrister told an anecdote which might have appealed to Conversation Kenge:

A man young in his profession . . . came to tell his father-in-law that he had at last succeeded in bringing a suit long in dependence to a termination. 'You simpleton,' said the grave senior; 'it was by means of that Chancery suit that I accumulated the money by which I was able to give a portion to my daughter, your wife. If you had known which side your bread was buttered on, you might have made that lawsuit a patrimony for your children's children';

and another barrister reported that in a case where the parties desired to get out at any sacrifice, 20,000 sheets of brief paper would have to be looked over before the estate could be sold.

Thus in December and January alone the columns of *The Times* contain most of the charges in Dickens's indictment of chancery. There was more to come. A new session of Parliament was opened early in February, and in the course of the Queen's speech it was predicted that the administration of justice in the several departments of law and equity would 'doubtless receive

* John Forster, *The Life of Charles Dickens*, Library edn, 2 vols (revised 1876) bk VII sect. i. The pamphlet was *The Court of Chancery: Its Inherent Defects as Exhibited in Its System of Written Proceedings* . . . By a Solicitor. London. Stevens and Norton, 26, Bell Yard. 1849. Dickens wrote to Challinor on 11 Mar 1852 sending him a formal 'receipt of his pamphlet and obliging note'. In a letter to Wills of 7 Aug 1853 Dickens asked for details of the Day case, which had been instituted in Chancery in 1834 and was still incomplete (*Letters* II 481).

serious attention'. The announcement was welcomed; but a week later *The Times* had already heard rumours that legislation might be delayed till the end of the session, although 'the state of the Court of Chancery is an evil . . . of extreme magnitude'. The rumour proved to be correct. Several weeks were consumed in the search for a Prime Minister who would form a government, and when at last Russell was persuaded to resume office he had first to complete the discussion of the Ecclesiastical Titles Bill which the establishment of the Roman Catholic hierarchy had prompted. It was not until the Act had been placed on the statutes at the end of March that Russell was able to propose a measure of chancery reform. At first *The Times* was inclined to welcome any bill which promised to improve existing conditions:

To the common apprehension of Englishmen the Court of Chancery is a name of terror, a devouring gulf, a den whence no footsteps return. Ask why such a family was ruined, why the representatives of a wealthy man are wanderers over the face of the earth, why the butlers, and housekeepers, and gardeners of the kindest master in the world, in spite of ample legacies in his will, are rotting on parish pay, why the best house in the street is falling to decay, its windows all broken, and its very doors disappearing, why such a one drowned himself, and another is disgraced – you are just as likely as not to hear that a Chancery suit is at the bottom of it. There is no word so terrible to an Englishman as this. An honest, industrious man . . . will turn pale and sick at heart at the bare mention of Chancery. A suit in that court is endless, bottomless, and insatiable. (28 March)

But second thoughts were not so favourable. Russell's proposals were discovered to be quite insufficient, and less than a week after its first article *The Times* was remarking that the bill was nothing and would come to nothing. *The Times* was right again, for within a month of introducing his bill, Russell withdrew it in deference to legal criticism in the House of Lords.

A revised bill was not ready until the middle of June at almost the last possible moment before the end of the Parliamentary session. Though the bill was welcomed by Lord Brougham as 'a step – not a great or a long step, but still a step – in the right direction',[6] and though it passed all its readings before Parliament was prorogued in August, criticism was by no means silenced. *The Times*, which was describing the feeling of the public as 'one of angry and restless impatience',[7] permitted itself to adopt a more sardonic approach to the question. A clever young leader-writer, Robert Lowe,[8] later to become Chancellor of the Exchequer, discovered a chancery suit which had been introduced as long ago as 1815:

Thirty-six years [he commented] are something in the life of a man, of a nation, of a dynasty, or even of a planet, but in the history of a Chancery suit they are a brief interval . . . a mere decent pause in the slow and stately march by which parties proceed to what, by a fine irony, we are in the habit of calling 'equitable relief'. When this old suit was new, the counsel who have succeeded to its management were probably babes in arms, and the judge before whom it is heard a truant schoolboy. Since the parties first applied to this dilatory tribunal for the determination of their rights three Monarchs have succeeded to the aged Prince in whose reign it was commenced. . . . The occupant of every throne in Europe, and every prominent office in the English church and State, has been changed, but still the inexorable Chancery suit holds on its way, permanent in the midst of never-ending change, the only immutable thing in an era of restless transition. . . .

And he continues, in words which bring Richard Carstone to mind:

It is usual to speak of lawsuits as embittering the lives of those who embark in them; but such an expression does but little justice to the hereditary curse which a suit in equity on the present system hands down to the children who are to inherit it. We leave our suits to our children just as we bequeath to them too often our mental peculiarities and bodily infirmities. The little plaintiffs and defendants grow up for the benefit of Chancery; and she adopts them as naturally as they succeed to us. (14 June)

Bleak House was not begun until the end of November, though Dickens's letters show that as early as 7 September his

'new book [was] waiting to be born'.[9] By that date Russell's
Chancery Reform Act was a month old; but the public was still
critical. Throughout those weeks when the new story was 'whirl-
ing through' Dickens's mind,[10] *The Times* kept hammering at
the inadequacies of legal education, and at the eminent members
of the legal profession who were thwarting legal reform. The
opening of the law courts on 3 November had provided one
more occasion for insisting that 'not one whiff of wholesome
fresh air has been let into the Court of Chancery and its pur-
lieus'.

Thus Dickens's indictment of chancery was more than merely
topical. It followed in almost every respect the charges already
levelled in the columns of *The Times*. In both we read of houses
in chancery and wards in chancery, of dilatory and costly procedure, of wasted lives, and of legal obstructionists. *The Times*, as
befitted a national newspaper, was concerned to report the efforts
made in Parliament to procure reform, even while it deplored the
delays in Parliament itself. Dickens had no faith in the powers of
Parliament to bring any good thing about. He makes no reference to Russell's bills. But the behaviour of Parliament during
these months had not escaped him. Some of the most brilliant
scenes in the novel display, with evident mockery of Disraeli's
manner, a country house party of the governing classes at
Chesney Wold. Like their fellow guests the Puseyites, these are
Dandies too – 'of another fashion, not so new, but very elegant,
who have agreed to put a smooth glaze on the world, and to
keep down all its realities'. Among them is my Lord Boodle,
who 'really does not see to what the present age is tending', who
finds that 'the House is not what the House used to be; even a
Cabinet is not what it formerly was', and who 'perceives with
astonishment, that supposing the present Government to be
overthrown, the limited choice of the Crown, in the formation
of a new Ministry, would lie between Lord Coodle and Sir
Thomas Doodle – supposing it to be impossible for the Duke
of Foodle to act with Goodle'. (ch. 12)

Lord Boodle was not the only politician to be voicing his discontent with Parliament and Government in 1851. Scarcely had the session opened in February before Russell was defeated and the country was without a government for a fortnight, while first one statesman and then another tried to form an administration. And when a government was formed, it was clearly too weak to last. It is not surprising that Greville should record in his diary that 'there is no respect for, or confidence in, any public men or man' and that 'there is a lack of statesmen who have either capacity to deal with political exigencies, or who possess the confidence and regard of the country'.[11] Throughout this period *The Times* was unsparing in its attacks upon Parliament and Government alike for failing to perform their duties. One leading article in particular has a familiar ring. Lansdowne, Stanley, and Russell, however much they differed in policy, were all 'wonderfully agreed about the very small number of men at all fit, or likely, for power'. Lansdowne in particular 'is so honestly persuaded that orthodox statecraft is vested in a very small clique, that he is convinced it would be a national calamity to let in new hands. His is a wholesome jealousy and depreciation of outsiders. It is the old quarrel between "the trade" and interlopers, between fully qualified artisans and independent workmen.'

The moral may be taken in the words of Dickens or in the words of *The Times*, for it amounts to the same thing.

It is an insult [said *The Times*] to a free people and a constitutional State to allege that the faculty of government is confined among us just to a score or two hands. What becomes of all our numerous institutions for self-government . . . if, with all this apparatus of political training, the sacred gift of government, is after all, an heirloom in two or three families? (5 March)

and Dickens:

as to some minor topics, there are differences of opinion; but it is perfectly clear to the brilliant and distinguished circle, all round, that nobody is in question but Boodle and his retinue, and Buffy

and *his* retinue. These are the great actors for whom the stage is
reserved. A People there are, no doubt – a certain large number
of supernumeraries, who are to be occasionally addressed, and
relied upon for shouts and choruses, as on the theatrical stage;
but Boodle and Buffy, their followers and families, their heirs,
executors, administrators, and assigns, are the born first-actors,
managers, and leaders, and no others can ever appear upon the
scene for ever and ever. (ch. 12)

Contemporary readers could be trusted with so obvious a reference; and when they reached chapter 40, published in March
1853, where Sir Leicester and his circle comment on the election
campaign then in progress, they would readily recall the general
election of July 1852, of which Greville considered that the most
deplorable feature was 'the exclusion of so many able and
respectable men'.[12]

v

Dickens's indictment of Boodle and Buffy is that they are content to fiddle while Rome is burning: and *The Times* would have
agreed. On 5 March it declared that the most serious evil of the
political *deadlock* was 'the indefinite postponement or defeat of
various measures of great public utility, but yet unconnected
with the passions, the prejudices, or the interest of political
parties'. A modern reader, recalling the conditions in which the
brickmaker and his family lived and the filth of Tom-all-Alone's,
might ask whether there could have been any more important
'measure of great public utility' than a bill for cleansing the
slums. Thinking people in 1851 were fully aware of these horrors.
Dr Simon's report on the Sanitary Condition of the City, presented to the Commissioners of Sewers, was reviewed in *The
Times* at great length on 31 December 1850, and 2 January 1851.
In that review the reader would have learned

that the main conditions which constitute the unhealthiness of
towns are definite, palpable, removable evils; that dense overcrowding of a population; that intricate ramification of courts
and alleys, excluding light and air; that defective drainage; that

the products of organic decomposition; that contaminated water and a stinking atmosphere – are distinct causes of disease and death . . . that each is susceptible of abatement or removal, which will at once be followed by diminution of its alleged effects upon the health of the population.

Sanitary reform was not so actively canvassed in the columns of *The Times* as chancery reform; but no careful reader could have overlooked it. He would have been impressed by the resolution with which Lord Shaftesbury was campaigning for better housing conditions; he would have noticed Shaftesbury's description, in *The Times* of 9 April 1851, of the squalor in the cheap lodging houses of London, and very probably he would have approved of the Lodging Houses Bill sponsored on 8 July by Shaftesbury, who pointed out the consequences of overcrowding in the spread of disease and the undermining of morality. He would probably have approved of Shaftesbury's bill, for *The Times* on 6 August declared that on sanitary questions there is happily a general measure of agreement. Perhaps it was because of this general agreement that *The Times* was less active in pressing sanitary reform than in pressing chancery reform where there were vested interests to be overcome; but even so, there was no attempt to minimize the ghastly truth. In a leading article written on 4 September, when Dickens was meditating his new book, *The Times* reported as established fact that

In English towns generally half the attainable period of life is lost to all who are born. . . . This loss of life is in no degree attributable either to the situation, soil, or climate of a locality, or to the density of a population, or to the employments generally prevailing. . . . The destroying agent is typhus fever, generated by localized filth and excessive moisture. . . . Bad drainage and immoderate dampness – that is to say, too little water where it is needed, and too much where it is out of place, are the generating elements.

In illustration of those generating elements of typhus, 'localized filth and excessive moisture', no more is needed than two details in the description of Tom-all-Alone's and the brickmaker's house and garden: 'the stagnant channel of mud which is the

main street of Tom-all-Alone's'; and in the earlier chapter of
Mrs Pardiggle's visit: 'miserable little gardens . . . growing
nothing but stagnant pools. Here and there, an old tub was put
to catch the droppings of rain-water from a roof, or they were
banked up with mud into a little pond like a large dirt-pie.'

Dickens did not need *The Times* to draw his attention to sanitary reform. The author of *Oliver Twist* knew something of 'the
foul and frowsy dens, where vice is closely packed and lacks the
room to turn'. This was an old campaign of his to which he
proudly alludes in the Preface to a new edition of *Martin Chuzzlewit* in November 1849: 'In all my writings, I hope I have taken
every available opportunity of showing the want of sanitary
improvements in the neglected dwellings of the poor.' The recognition of his claim may have led to his choice as speaker at the
dinners of the Metropolitan Sanitary Association in February
1850 and again in May 1851. At the first of these dinners the
Bishop of London, who presided, referred to plans for the clearance of Jacob's Island, the very slum described in *Oliver Twist*,
and paid a tribute to Dickens who had first drawn attention to
this scandal. But in spite of the general measure of agreement on
sanitary matters discerned by *The Times*, it was not everyone
who recognized the need. A few days later Alderman Sir Peter
Laurie, the Mr Filer of *The Chimes*, told a vestry meeting of the
parish of St Marylebone that Jacob's Island existed only in
Dickens's imagination. The opportunity was too good to miss;
and having occasion to reissue *Oliver Twist* in a cheap edition the
following month, Dickens made a sarcastic retort:

Remembering that when Fielding described Newgate, the prison
immediately ceased to exist; that when Smollett took Roderick
Random to Bath, that city instantly sank into the earth. . . . I was
inclined to make this preface the vehicle of my humble tribute of
admiration to Sir Peter Laurie. But, I am restrained by a very
painful consideration – by no less a consideration than the im-
possibility of *his* existence. For Sir Peter Laurie having been
himself described in a book (as I understand he was, one Christmas time, for his conduct on the seat of Justice), it is but too
clear that there CAN be no such man!

The same Preface also bears witness to Dickens's abiding concern for slum clearance:

I have always been convinced that this Reform must precede all other Social Reforms; that it must prepare the way for Education, even for Religion; and that, without it, those classes of the people which increase the fastest, must become so desperate and be made so miserable, as to bear within themselves the certain seeds of ruin to the whole community.

This shows that his mind was already alive to the wider issues involved. In his speech at the second Metropolitan Sanitary Association dinner he explored the subject further, and in his remarks can be detected some of the interrelated themes of *Bleak House*. The smallpox infection which Charley and Esther catch from Jo is the novelist's way of expressing a truth already perceived by the orator:

That no man can estimate the amount of mischief grown in dirt, – that no man can say the evil stops here or stops there, either in its moral or physical effects, or can deny that it begins in the cradle and is not at rest in the miserable grave, is as certain as it is that the air from Gin Lane will be carried by an easterly wind into Mayfair, or that the furious pestilence raging in St Giles's no mortal list of lady patronesses can keep out of Almack's.*

Mrs Pardiggle visiting the brickmaker and Allan Woodcourt succouring the dying Jo are foreshadowed in the following questions:

* *The Speeches of Charles Dickens*, ed. R. H. Shepherd (1884) p. 127: the point had been forcibly made by Carlyle (*Past and Present* (1843) ch. III sect. 2) when telling the story of a widow refused charity by the Charitable Establishments of Edinburgh:

The forlorn Irish Widow applies to her fellow-creatures, as if saying, 'Behold I am sinking, bare of help: ye must help me! I am your sister, bone of your bone; one God made us: ye must help me!' They answer, 'No; impossible; thou art no sister of ours.' But she proves her sisterhood; her typhus-fever kills *them*: they actually were her brothers, though denying it! Had human creature ever to go lower for a proof?

Of what avail is it to send missionaries to the miserable man condemned to work in a foetid court, with every sense bestowed upon him for his health and happiness turned into a torment, with every month of his life adding to the heap of evils under which he is condemned to exist? What human sympathy within him is that instructor to address? what natural old chord within him is he to touch? Is it the remembrance of his children? – a memory of destitution, of sickness, of fever, and of scrofula? Is it his hopes, his latent hopes of immortality? He is so surrounded by and embedded in material filth, that his soul cannot rise to the contemplation of the great truths of religion. Or if the case is that of a miserable child bred and nurtured in some noisome, loathsome place, and tempted, in these better days, into the ragged school, what can a few hours' teaching effect against the ever-renewed lesson of a whole existence? But give them a glimpse of heaven through a little of its light and air; give them water; help them to be clean; lighten that heavy atmosphere in which their spirits flag and in which they become the callous things they are; take the body of the dead relative from the close room in which the living live with it, and where death, being familiar, loses its awe; and then they will be brought willingly to hear of Him whose thoughts were so much with the poor, and who had compassion for all human suffering.[13]

It is interesting to note that during the next two years, while *Bleak House* was in the course of publication, Dickens was himself engaged in the preliminaries of slum clearance by advising Miss Coutts on acquiring ground in a suitable locality for building blocks of flats.[14] On 7 January 1853, he paid a visit to Bermondsey to inspect a possible site adjoining Jacob's Island, and sent Miss Coutts a description.[15] It is not unlikely that this visit served to supply his mind with some details in the description of Tom-all-Alone's in *Bleak House*, chapter 46, published in Number xiv the following April.

Even without any external evidence showing that Dickens habitually read *The Times*, the internal evidence would be strong enough. Of the five subjects to which *The Times* kept recurring during the months immediately preceding the inception of *Bleak House*, three take a prominent place in the novel, and one of the remaining two is memorably represented. What is of greater significance is that both the policy of the newspaper and its interpretation of facts are represented without much distortion in the novel. Dickens followed *The Times* in deploring the ineffectuality of Parliament, its incapacity for dealing with the important issues of the day; he shared *The Times*'s view that the unhealthiness of the towns was a removable evil, and an evil which must be removed unless the whole community was to suffer; and he agreed with *The Times* in thinking that chancery reform was a crying need, and was being obstructed by certain lawyers who profited from the existing system.

VI

The characters are no less of their time than the action which they support. Mention has already been made of Mrs Pardiggle, the representative of Puseyism. She and her fellow-worker, Mrs Jellyby, are not the only managing females in the novel. There were also Mr Jarndyce's numerous correspondents amongst 'the Women of England, the Daughters of Britain, the Sisters of all the Cardinal Virtues separately, the Females of America, the Ladies of a hundred denominations', all of them consumed with 'rapacious benevolence': 'excellent people, you know', confessed Mr Jarndyce, in a passage removed in proof from chapter 8,

excellent people, you know, . . . Mrs Pardiggle and all the rest of 'em. Excellent people! Do a deal of good, and mean to do a good deal more. But they want one pattern out of all varieties of Looms, they *must* be in extremes, they *will* knock in tin tacks with a sledge hammer, they make such a bustle and noise, and they are so confoundedly indefatigable!

One or two of these women make a more extended appearance at Caddy Jellyby's wedding in chapter 30, notably Miss Wisk, whose mission 'was to show the world that woman's mission was man's mission; and that the only genuine mission, of both man and woman, was to be always moving declaratory resolutions about things in general at 'public meetings'.

In no other novel does Dickens make so much play with

female emancipation and female management, and perhaps in no
other novel could he have used these themes so satisfactorily.
Every reader of *Bleak House* can see in what directions the energy
of these women might more properly have been turned; but the
contemporary reader would have recognized their living proto-
types. A few might have seen in Mrs Jellyby a representation of
Mrs Caroline Chisholm, whose Family Colonization Loan
Society, established in May 1850, won Dickens's support, but
whose housekeeping and dirty-faced children haunted his
dreams, but[16] more readers would have recalled the failure of an
expedition in 1841 to abolish the slave trade on the River Niger
and to introduce there an improved system of agriculture.
Dickens reviewed the published narrative of the expedition in the
Examiner on 19 August 1848. The expedition appeared to him an
exemplary instance of the type of misguided philanthropy
associated at that time with Exeter Hall in the Strand:

It might be laid down as a very good general rule of social and
political guidance, that whatever Exeter Hall champions, is the
thing by no means to be done. If it were harmless on a cursory
view, if it even appeared to have some latent grain of common
sense at the bottom of it – which is a very rare ingredient in any
of the varieties of gruel that are made thick and slab by the weird
old women who go about, and exceedingly roundabout, on the
Exeter Hall platform – such advocacy might be held to be a final
and fatal objection to it, and to any project capable of origina-
tion in the wisdom or folly of man.

The African Expedition . . . is in no respect an exception to
the rule. Exeter Hall was hot in its behalf, and it failed. Exeter
Hall was hottest on its weakest and most hopeless objects, and in
those it failed (of course) most signally.

The Niger expedition succumbed to fever, the few surviving
colonists of the model farm were murdered by 'King Boy', and
'King Obi' returned to his profitable trade in slave selling: Borrioboola Gha failed 'in consequence of the King of Borrioboola
wanting to sell everybody – who survived the climate – for Rum'.
The connexion between the actual and the imagined episodes
would have been clear enough, even if Hablôt Browne had not

inserted on his cover-design the figure of a woman embracing
two black children, and by her side a man who wears a foolscap
and carries a sandwich board bearing the legend 'Exeter Hall'.

The moral, as Dickens expressed it in his review, was that 'the
work at home must be completed thoroughly, or there is no hope
abroad. To your tents, O Israel! but see they are your own tents!
Set *them* in order; leave nothing to be done *there*; and outpost will
convey your lesson on to outpost, until the naked armies of King
Obi and King Boy are reached, and taught.'* But Mrs Jellyby did
not see her disappointment in that light; we learn that 'she has
taken up with the rights of women to sit in Parliament . . . a
mission involving more correspondence than the old one'.

The only occasion for surprise is that Mrs Jellyby did not reject
the petticoat in favour of the trousers. In the early summer of
1851 *Punch* received the intelligence that an American lady, 'a

---

* Lord Denman, in a pamphlet already quoted (p. 111 n), fell foul of
Mrs Jellyby, through whom 'the attempt at commerce and cultivation
is to be ridiculed as a wilder absurdity than even the preaching of
religion'. In defending himself Dickens restates his moral, but surprisingly and untenably claims that he was 'inventing' the notion of an
African expedition: 'Mrs Jellyby gives offence merely because the
word "Africa", is unfortunately associated with her wild Hobby. No
kind of reference to Slavery is made or intended, in that connexion. It
must be obvious to anyone who reads about her. I have such strong
reason to consider, as the best exercise of my faculties of observation
can give me, that it is one of the main vices of this time to ride objects
to Death through mud and mire, and to have a great deal of talking
about them and *not* a great deal of doing – to neglect private duties
associated with no particular excitement, for lifeless and soulless public
hullabaloo with a great deal of excitement, and thus seriously to
damage the objects taken up (often very good in themselves) and not
least by associating them with Cant and Humbug in the minds of
those reflecting people whose sympathies it is most essential to enlist,
before any good thing can be advanced. I *know* this to be doing great
harm. But, lest I should unintentionally damage any existing cause, I
invent the cause of emigration to Africa. Which no one in reality is
advocating. Which no one ever did, that ever I heard of. Which has
as much to do, in any conceivable way, with the unhappy Negro
Slave as with the Stars.' (Letter to Mrs Cropper, 20 Dec 1852, in the
Free Library, Philadelphia.)

Mrs Bloomer', had adopted male attire: 'so far so good', was the comment; 'when does the lady begin to shave?' Whether Mrs Bloomer's initiative was followed to any great extent in England is uncertain; but interest was excited, and the pages of *Punch* in the late summer and autumn were stuffed with fantastic prophecy of the 'tremendous accession of physical energy to the ladies if they once get into trousers'. *Punch* foresaw the new garb becoming generally adopted; but in the van of the movement was the 'most superior and very strong-minded woman, settling into the forties, and owning to thirty-six . . . full of enthusiasm for "isms", and of scorn for conventionalities', the type of managing female who asserts her equality with the male.*

It was not long before Dickens offered his comments. In an article entitled 'Sucking Pigs', published in *Household Words* on 8 November 1851, he showed his strong distaste, not so much for the change of fashion, as for the state of mind implied in the change and for the proselytizing fervour accompanying it. Even if a woman

chooses to become, of her own free will and liking, a Bloomer, that won't do. She must agitate, agitate. She must take to the little table and water-bottle. She must go in to be a public character. She must work away at a Mission. It is not enough to do right for right's sake. There can be no satisfaction . . . in satisfying her mind after due reflection that the thing she contemplates is right, and therefore ought to be done, and so in calmly and quietly doing it, conscious that therein she sets a righteous example which never can in the nature of things be lost and thrown away.

This article was published a few weeks before the first pages of *Bleak House* were written, and assuredly it expresses the mood in which Mrs Pardiggle, Mrs Jellyby, and their associates were conceived. They did not adopt the bloomer costume, but in all other respects they were enlisted under the banners of Bloomerism. When it came to defining the missions at which they should

* *Punch*, xx 220, xxi 168, 192. Mrs Chisholm herself was described by Lord Shaftesbury as having attained 'the highest order of Bloomerism' in that she had 'the heart of a woman, and the understanding of a man' (xxi 156).

work, Puseyism lay ready to hand in the year of 'papal aggression' (as the pages of *Punch* bear witness), and though it was three years since he had touched upon the Niger expedition, 'the Nigger question', as Carlyle called it, was still a lively issue, and Exeter Hall with all it stood for was still a powerful force.

VII

Another dateable character is Inspector Bucket, whose identity was soon guessed. The detectives were a recently-formed[17] branch of the Metropolitan Police Force, and Dickens himself had given them ample publicity in *Household Words*. An article of 13 July 1850, on 'The Modern Science of Thief-taking', explained the organization of the branch and described instances of the detective at work; his duty, it may be noted, was 'not only to counteract the machinations of every sort of rascal . . . but to clear up family mysteries, the investigation of which demands the utmost delicacy and tact'. A fortnight later (27 July), an article entitled 'A Detective Police Party' recounted an interview in Dickens's Wellington Street office with Inspectors Wield and Stalker, and was designed to convey 'some faint idea of the extraordinary dexterity, patience, and ingenuity, exercised by the Detective Police'.

Inspector 'Wield' was to become familiar to readers of *Household Words*. In Number 18 (27 July) he is described as 'a middle-aged man of portly presence with a large, moist, knowing eye, a husky voice, and a habit of emphasizing his conversation by the aid of a corpulent forefinger, which is constantly in juxtaposition with his eyes or nose'. (Mr Bucket also was 'a stoutly-built, steady-looking, sharp-eyed man . . . of about the middle age' (ch. 12), and as to his forefinger, 'when Mr Bucket has a matter of this pressing interest under his consideration, the fat forefinger seems to rise to the dignity of a familiar demon. He puts it to his ears, and it whispers information; he puts it to his lips, and it enjoins him to secrecy; he rubs it over his nose, and it sharpens his scent; he shakes it before a guilty man, and it charms him to destruction' (ch. 53).) In Number 25 (14 September 1850) his experience was called upon to supply three 'detective' anecdotes, and in Numbers 63 and 64 (7 and 14 June 1851) he appears again, the last time under his proper name of Field, and shows his familiarity with the criminal underworld and his easy jocular intercourse with its inhabitants. It was therefore not an unwarrantable assumption that Bucket, so similar in build and manner and so well acquainted with the warrens of Tom-all-Alone's, was a representation of Field. But when *The Times* on 17 September 1853 reprinted an article from the *Bath Chronicle* ('A Detective in his Vocation'), which credited Dickens with making 'much use of Mr Field's experiences in Inspector Bucket, of the *Bleak House*', and with being 'engaged in writing his life', Dickens issued a denial (20 September): 'Allow me to assure you that, amid all the news in *The Times*, I found nothing more entirely and completely new to me than these two pieces of intelligence.' Had Pope written this letter, he might have boasted of having equivocated pretty genteelly. Dickens may have had no intention of writing Field's life, and may not have 'availed' himself of Field's 'experiences', even though they extended to clearing up 'family mysteries'; but it seems clear that he saw Bucket as Field, and endowed him with Field's peculiar yet limited sagacity, his energy, his good nature, his mannerisms, and above all with his intimate knowledge of the haunts of vice. Tom-all-Alone's, which Bucket knows so well, is a slum overripe for clearance. A similar association of mind led Dickens to think of Field when Miss Coutts was looking for an appropriate slum to clear; but just as Allan Woodcourt, a doctor, sees the human problem of Tom-all-Alone's more clearly than Bucket, so Southwood Smith's advice was considered more dependable than Field's:

I am disposed to doubt the efficacy of [Field's] peculiar sort of knowledge and sagacity in this stage of the matter. A locality chosen, I have no doubt that, at a small expence, his assistance in the beginning would be of immense service; or, a locality suggested, that his observations upon it would also be very important – for, if there were a serious objection, he would be

certain to know it. But the habits of his mind hardly lead him
. . . to the present point before us.

. . . Dr Southwood Smith is the man, of all others, to consult
first. His fever-practice has made him, for many years, well
acquainted with all the poor parts of London . . . and he knows
what work there is in this or that place; and how the people live;
and how their tenements are held; and all about them.[18]

<h2 style="text-align:center">VIII</h2>

At least two more characters, Mrs Bagnet and Mr Rouncewell,
can be shown to have been in the public mind as well as in
Dickens's mind in the early eighteen-fifties. A brief note in
Household Words on 6 September 1851 had drawn attention to
the difficult conditions in which soldiers' wives were living. Only
five per cent of private soldiers could marry; and if they did, they
received no more than 7*s* 7*d* a week with no married quarters,
though a sergeant would be permitted to curtain off a narrow
space from the public dormitory for himself and his wife. The
contributor of this note was herself the wife of an officer. In
twenty years' experience of her husband's regiment, she could
not single out three respectable women, for in such conditions
only 'a will strong in virtue can set temptation at naught'. These
then were the conditions in which Mrs Bagnet had learned to
practise her virtues, conditions which had recently been brought
to light in Dickens's own journal.

Mrs Rouncewell's eldest son was a manufacturer whose sturdy
independence we are asked to admire. Some trade he needs must
practise, but Dickens seems not to have chosen haphazardly in
making him an ironmaster. It is possible that he had been reading
The Times reports of the ironmasters' quarterly meetings at
Dudley. Those were difficult days in the iron trade, for the
demand for iron was much reduced; but the action of the ironmasters was exemplary, as *The Times* showed in its report on
29 March 1851:

A reduction of make, or a reduction of wages, [was] suggested,
but [either way] the work people must be the sufferers. The

ironmasters of South Staffordshire are, and ever have been, particularly anxious not to curtail the employment or reduce the remuneration of their men; to such an extent has this considerate feeling been exhibited that many works have been carried on which, if profit only had entered into the master's minds would have been closed, for the purpose of giving employment and support to the neighbouring population.

Whether or not this report had caught his eye, Dickens knew the ironmasters and respected them. Having occasion, a year later, to advise Miss Coutts where to send her 'suggestion-paper' on slum clearance and the principles of building a model community, he recommended the 'large ironmasters – of whom there are some notable cases – who have proceeded on the self-supporting principle, and have done wonders with their workpeople'.[19] It seems probable, therefore, that when Dickens was deciding what trade Mr Rouncewell should practise, he recollected the behaviour of a large group of manufacturers which he could wholeheartedly admire.

IX

As in *Martin Chuzzlewit, Little Dorrit*, and other novels, so in *Bleak House* there are certain indications that Dickens intended to place the action at a greater distance in time. Thus it has been observed that for the details of chancery procedure he was drawing upon his memories of his career as a reporter in the Lord Chancellor's court in the late 'twenties, that the Spanish refugees who were neighbours of Harold Skimpole in Somers Town (ch. 43) were known to be living there at much the same period,* and that Esther wrote the last section of her narrative 'full seven years' after the story was ended.[20] Contemporary readers who were well acquainted with chancery procedure might be trusted to note the discrepancies between chancery as it had been and chancery as it then was; but it is safe to say that the majority

* The Dickens family also was living in Somers Town (No. 13 Johnson Street) from July 1824 till Jan 1829 (Kitton, *Charles Dickens*, p. 19 n).

would fail to notice them and that Dickens himself can never have intended them to be used in evidence of the date of the action. He was content to draw upon his memory of chancery procedure without reflecting, or perhaps even caring, whether in every respect his knowledge was up to date. Nor are those 'full seven years' to be taken at their face value, for he is repeating once more the device, already used at the end of *Dombey and Son* and *David Copperfield*, of distancing the action of the story in time so as to emphasize the calm of mind which rewards the surviving actors.

More difficult to reconcile is the appearance of the Spanish refugees,* and the description (ch. 55) of preparations for the coming of the railways to Lincolnshire, where at the time of the action no railways evidently existed. But neither of these isolated references is enough to counteract the strong flavour of contemporaneity in the action and in the characters. *Bleak House* began as a tract for the times, and the more fully this is recognized, the more fully we shall appreciate the 'esemplastic power' which imposed upon a mass of seemingly heterogeneous material a significant and acceptable form.

SOURCE: *Dickens at Work* (1957).

NOTES

1. 'Model Prisons', Mar 1850.
2. *Letters from Charles Dickens to Angela Burdett-Coutts, 1841–1865*, selected and edited by Edgar Johnson (1953) p. 186.
3. *The Letters of Charles Dickens*, ed. Walter Dexter, 3 vols (1938, the Nonesuch Dickens) II 336. To complete the tally, mention must be made of two articles by Henry Morley, one on the future of the Crystal Palace (19 July) and one on the Catalogue of the Exhibition

* Though Dickens could have recalled them from his boyhood recollections of that district of London, it seems possible that his memory was stimulated by reading Carlyle's *Life of Sterling* (1851), where they are described in pt I, ch. ix.

(23 Aug) which was reviewed by Dickens, and one by Horne contrasting the Great Exhibition with the Little (Chinese) Exhibition beside it.

4. *The Letters of Charles Dickens*, II 327.

5. Ibid. II 333.

6. *The Times*, 15 July.

7. Ibid. 4 July.

8. *The History of The Times 1841–1884* (1939) II 130.

9. *Letters*, II 341. The first reference to the new novel is even earlier: on 17 Aug he had written to Miss Coutts, 'I begin to be pondering afar off, a new book' (*Coutts Letters*, p. 184).

10. *Letters*, II 349.

11. *Journal of the Reign of Queen Victoria from 1837 to 1852* (1885) III 391, 406

12. *Journal*, III 459.

13. Shepherd, *Speeches of Dickens*, pp. 128–9.

14. Letters of 13 Jan, 16 Mar, 18 Apr 1852; *Coutts Letters*, pp. 191–200.

15. Ibid. pp. 219–20.

16. See 'A Bundle of Emigrants' Letters' in the first issue of *Household Words*, and a letter of 4 Mar 1850 (*Coutts Letters*, p. 166).

17. In 1842; see G. Dilnot, *The Story of Scotland Yard* (London, n.d.) p. 207.

18. *Coutts Letters*, pp. 191–2. Letter of 13 Jan 1852, written during the composition of *Bleak House*, no. 1.

19. 18 Apr 1852; *Coutts Letters*, p. 199.

20. The case is argued by Humphry House in *The Dickens World* (1941), reprinted here on pp. 101–4.

PART FOUR
Recent Studies

Edgar Johnson

THE ANATOMY OF SOCIETY (1952)

THE key institution of *Bleak House* is the Court of Chancery, its key image the fog choking the opening scenes in its dense brown obscurity and pervading the atmosphere of the entire story with an oppressive heaviness. But both law and fog are fundamentally symbols of all the ponderous and murky forces that suffocate the creative energies of mankind. They prefigure in darkness visible the entanglements of vested interests and institutions and archaic traditions protecting greed, fettering generous action, obstructing men's movements, and beclouding their vision. Surviving out of the miasmal swamps and ferocities of the past, these evils, like prehistoric monsters, unwieldly, voracious, and dreadfully destructive to human welfare, move stumbling and wallowing through layer upon layer of precedent as if through quagmires of encrusted mud. *Bleak House* is thus an indictment not merely of the law but of the whole dark muddle of organized society. It regards legal injustice not as accidental but as organically related to the very structure of that society.

Though the fog-enshrouded Court is only a symbol for this more sweeping arraignment, it is nevertheless the central symbol of the book. 'The raw afternoon is rawest,' the opening chapter tells us, 'the dense fog is densest, and the muddy streets are muddiest, near that leaden-headed old obstruction, appropriate ornament for the threshold of a leaden-headed old corporation: Temple Bar. And hard by Temple Bar, in Lincoln's Inn Hall, in the very heart of the fog, sits the Lord High Chancellor in his High Court of Chancery.' Here, surrounded by innumerable barristers mistily engaged upon an endless case, 'tripping one another up on slippery precedents, groping knee-deep in technicalities', running their heads against walls of words, in a courtroom like a well where 'you might look in vain for Truth at the bottom', all dim with wasting candles and wasting lives, the Chancellor gazes up from his dais 'into a lantern that has no light in it, and . . . the attendant wigs are all stuck in a fog-bank!' (ch. 1)

'This', Dickens continues, 'is the Court of Chancery; which has its decaying houses and its blighted lands in every shire; which has its worn-out lunatic in every madhouse, and its dead in every churchyard; which has its ruined suitor, with his slipshod heels and threadbare dress, borrowing and begging through the round of every man's acquaintance; which gives to monied might, the means abundantly of wearying out the right; which so exhausts finances, patience, courage, hope; so overthrows the brain and breaks the heart; that there is not an honourable man among its practitioners who would not give – who does not often give – the warning: 'Suffer any wrong that can be done you, rather than come here!' (ch. 1)

From this point the story sweeps relentlessly on, showing how the glacial processes of the court wreck the lives of countless victims. The protracted struggle destroys Gridley, the angry man from Shropshire, 'who can by no means be made to understand that the Chancellor is legally ignorant of his existence, having made it desolate for half a century' (ch. 1). Prolonged waiting overthrows the sanity of poor little Miss Flite, the tiny spinster dwelling with her birds in her starved tenement, and saying, 'I was a ward myself, I was not mad at that time. I had youth and hope. I believe, beauty. It matters very little now. Neither of the three served, or saved me . . . I have discovered', she goes on, 'that the sixth seal mentioned in the Revelations is the Great Seal'; she expects a judgment 'on the Day of Judgment'. How heart-rending is this crazed and helpless small creature, curtsying and smiling, and repeating, 'Youth. And hope. And beauty. And Chancery' (ch. 3). She and Gridley bathe the long perspective of waste in flames of molten indignation and pathos.

The great lawsuit of the book is the classic case of Jarndyce and Jarndyce, 'a monument', as the lawyer Conversation Kenge remarks, 'of Chancery practice'. In it, 'every difficulty, every contingency, every masterly fiction, every form of procedure known in that court, is represented over and over again', and in it the court costs have already amounted to between sixty and seventy thousand pounds. 'It is a cause', he adds with unconscious irony, 'that could not exist, out of this free and great country' (ch. 3). And in it, in one way or another, almost every character of the story is involved.

There are the parties to the case, John Jarndyce, his wards Ada Clare and Richard Carstone, Esther Summerson through her aunt Miss Barbary, Sir Leicester Dedlock through his wife Honoria Dedlock. There are those who have only some vague connection with it, like Miss Flite and Gridley. There are the lawyers, Kenge and Carboy, Sir Leicester's solicitor Mr Tulkinghorn, and Richard Carstone's representative Mr Vholes. There are the lawyers' clerks and law writers, Mr Guppy, his friend Tony Jobling, and 'Nemo', the mysterious lodger above Krook's legal junkshop. There are the bailiff Neckett and his children. There is Snagsby, the law stationer. There are the rapacious Smallweeds, moneylenders, and through them Trooper George, who is in their clutches and who possesses letters that Tulkinghorn wants to secure as evidence. There is the illiterate and half-mad Krook, who calls himself 'the Lord Chancellor', with his crazy collection of tattered lawbooks, ink bottles, old bones, skinned cats, rags, crackled parchment, and dog's-eared law papers. There is the police detective, Inspector Bucket. There is the foul and decaying slum tenement, Tom-all-Alone's, which is going to ruin while the case remains unsettled, in the noisome corners of which sleeps the waif and crossing-sweeper Jo. All these and many more are caught up in the convolutions of Jarndyce and Jarndyce.

What Dickens has done here, in fact, has been to create the novel of the social group, used as an instrument of social criticism. Though to a certain extent, in *Vanity Fair*, Thackeray had anticipated him, Thackeray used his story more in the spirit of *Everyman* or *Pilgrim's Progress*, as a moral commentary upon human nature, hardly more than suggesting that people's lives were shaped and twisted by social institutions. But Dickens had from the beginning of his career been deeply concerned with institutions, although at first he was able to do no more than sandwich his attacks on them between episodes of melodrama and comedy or relate them to his story only by implication. With *Dombey and Son* he had attempted a more integral suffusion of social criticism and narrative, but for all its successes *Dombey* achieves neither the scope nor the depth of *Bleak House*. Modern writers who have followed Dickens in employing the novel to criticize society and its institutions – like Wells and Galsworthy, and even Shaw, in *An Unsocial Socialist* – have striven for no such close-knit cohesion of dramatic plot; Aldous Huxley, in *Point Counter Point*, drops out the plot almost entirely, and leaves many of his characters either quite unconnected with each other or associated only by the most fortuitous of links.

From one point of view this is a gain in 'realism', but from another it is an artistic loss. For if there is a danger of Dickens's intricate structures seeming contrived and overmelodramatic, with their missing documents and hidden sins rising up out of the past, there is also a strength in tightness and intensity of development. This advantage Dickens potently exploits by creating a sense of taut inevitability that deepens immeasurably the emotional impact. The movement of *Bleak House* becomes a centripetal one like a whirlpool, at first slow and almost imperceptible, but fatefully drawing in successive groups of characters, circling faster and faster, and ultimately sucking them into the dark funnel whence none will escape uninjured and where many will be crushed and destroyed. In pure emotional power *Bleak House* ranks among Dickens's greatest books.

This is not to say that it has no weaknesses. Among them is the almost purposeless malignance with which Mr Tulkinghorn pursues Lady Dedlock, a deep animosity that patiently unearths her secret and strives only to reduce her pride to subservience. But he has no practical goal, and it is not merely her proud indifference that challenges him; Sir Leicester is no less proud, and Mr Tulkinghorn has no desire to humiliate him. When this sinister and implacable old man has gathered all the threads in his hands, knows about Lady Dedlock's soldier lover and her bastard child, he himself is uncertain what to do with his knowledge – whether or not to tell Sir Leicester, how to tell him, what the consequences may be. He knows merely that he could not rest until he had dragged up all the facts out of the past and forced this haughty woman to cringe before him.

If Mr Tulkinghorn has no clearly defined motives, Lady Dedlock's motives and her situation fall too much into the domain of melodrama, although Dickens has tried to give them deeper significance. Like Edith Dombey, she is one of those defiant spirits who have got into a false position and who therefore despise themselves and revenge their own self-contempt by treating the world with arrogant scorn. Ambitious for aristocratic rank, she had not married Captain Hawdon and had been deceived into believing that their baby daughter had died at birth. Later, as Sir Leicester's wife and a leader of fashionable society, she has found her triumph dead-sea fruit. Having denied the forces of love and life, she can find no sound basis for rebellion. Mingled with the false guilt imposed by a conventional code of ethics is the real guilt of her submission to its standards, her hidden cowardice, her failure to be faithful to her lover and child. The fictitious conception of honor dictated by the morality of society has involved her in a tragic emotional dilemma, of which her very name, Honoria Dedlock, is symbolic.

Esther Summerson, the daughter of whose survival she has been kept in ignorance, is completely successful neither as a character nor as an instrument of the story's literary technique. Suggested probably, like Agnes Wickfield in *David Copperfield*, by what Dickens saw as Georgina Hogarth's sacrificial dedication to the welfare of others and her immersion in household duties, Esther is almost cloyingly unselfish, noble, and devoted, and rather tiresome in her domestic efficiency. The reader wearies of her jingling her keys as the little housekeeper of Mr Jarndyce's home, and of her being called Dame Durden, Dame Trot, and Little Old Woman, and other nicknames, of everyone's affectionately confiding in her and seeking her advice, and of her so invariably resigning her own desires, repressing her griefs, and telling herself that she is very fortunate.

The fact that she sometimes exasperates us, however, reveals that she has genuinely been endowed with life, even if we do not share the estimate of her that we are intended to accept. But technically she exemplifies another defect in the handling of the narrative. All the scenes in which she appears are represented as seen through her eyes and are told in the first person as her story. This fact involves her in the difficulty of constantly reporting the tributes others pay to her virtues, which none of her own modest disclaimers can make sound quite ingenuous. In addition, although Dickens begins by trying to portray the things she tells through her eyes and to tell them in her words, he often loses sight of that objective and has her say things much more natural to him than to her. Her first visit to Krook's junkshop, when she sees the rags as looking like counsellors' gowns torn up and the bones as those of legal clients picked clean (ch. 5), is brilliant satire, but it is not the observation of a young girl who has had no experience of the law. And only a little later there is the same mordancy in her description of the domineering Mrs Pardiggle and the hordes of clamoring philanthropists as distinguished by a 'rapacious benevolence' (ch. 8). Throughout many other passages one has to concede and overlook the fact that Dickens himself wrests from Esther Summerson the pen he placed in her hands.

Few of the other main characters are so richly or deeply realized as those in either *Dombey and Son* or *David Copperfield*. Ada Clare, one of the wards in Chancery under Mr Jarndyce's protection, is a reversion to the colorlessness of Madeline Bray and Mary Graham. Richard Carstone, the other ward, is a spirited sketch – but only a sketch – of psychological and moral deterioration. (It was a theme Dickens had conceived in his original plans for Walter Gay, before deciding to have him marry Florence Dombey, but only much later, in the hero of *Great Expectations*, was he to be entirely successful in painting a gradually changing character.) Mr Jarndyce probably makes amends to the nobler aspects of Dickens's father for the good-humoredly derisive caricature of Micawber; even the name John Jarndyce is a softened echo of John Dickens. Like Mr Pickwick, a lovable old fool who rescues all the victims of oppression (just as John Dickens had brought his son out of the despair of the blacking warehouse), John Jarndyce is a noble-hearted eccentric who protects every sufferer from misfortune and saves those who will let themselves be saved. Unlike Mr Pickwick, however, he is gently purged of all trace of absurdity. But though his harmless oddities help to humanize his goodness, he does not escape a certain sentimentality of delineation.

Surrounding these central characters crowd a host of others who stand for all the forces or classes of society – philanthropy, art, manners, religion, trade, industry, the poor, the aristocracy, law, government, politics. And, aside from those altogether broken or brutalized by misery, like the crossing-sweeper Jo and the colony of brickmakers near St Albans, almost all these figures are revealed as corrupted by a predatory and selfish pursuit of their own interests. Those who come off best are the small trades-man and the industrialist – Mr Snagsby the law stationer and Mr Rouncewell the ironmaster. But even Mr Snagsby is portrayed as afraid of and subservient to Mr Tulkinghorn and unable to pre-vent his wife from exploiting the poor workhouse slavey Guster, who comes cheap because she is subject to fits; he can express his gentle heart only by silent donations of half-crown pieces to those who have touched his sympathies. And Mr Rouncewell is one of those craftsman entrepreneurs who have made their way by invention and hard work; he has contributed to the welfare of society and is not a financial spider preying on its prosperity like Mr Bounderby, the banker industrialist of *Hard Times*. In *Bleak House* the nearest analogues to Mr Bounderby are the Small-weeds, that horrible family of little goblin usurers.

What a gallery are all the rest! There is Mrs Jellyby, dreaming moonily of helping the African natives on the banks of Borio-boola-Gha while she ignores the horrors of the London slums and neglects her own family. (In her unconcern for her children, Mrs Jellyby was suggested by Mrs Caroline Chisholm, whose Australian emigration schemes Dickens had aided.[1]) There is Mrs Pardiggle, who browbeats the poor and bullies her children to enhance her own sense of power. There is Harold Skimpole,

with his iridescent chatter about art and music and his whimsical
paradoxes disguising his parasitic idleness. There is Mr Turveydrop, that bloated parody of the Prince Regent, in his stays and
rouge and padding, using his elegant deportment to batten on
his devoted son and deluded daughter-in-law. There are the oily
Chadband and the bitter Mrs Chadband, he with his flatulent
pseudo-religious magniloquence and she with her gloomy iron-
bound harshness satirizing the emptiness and the cruelty of the
evangelical creeds.

All these people exemplify the decay of the lofty principles and
noble ideas that they profess, into irrelevance, flippancy, indifference, selfishness, and hatred. Chadband's sermonizing is
nothing but the deliquescence of religion into a self-righteous
substitution of words for deeds of love. 'What is peace?' he
demanded fatuously. 'Is it war? No. Is it strife? No. Is it lovely,
and gentle, and beautiful, and pleasant, and serene, and joyful?
O yes! Therefore, my friends, I wish for peace, upon you and
yours' (ch. 19). But all Chadband thinks of doing for the
crossing-sweeper Jo is to tell him that he is 'in a state of darkness', 'a state of sinfulness', 'a state of bondage', from which if he
chose to profit by this discourse he might emerge into the joy-
fulness of becoming 'a soaring human boy!' (ch. 19). And Mrs
Chadband, once the servant of Esther Summerson's aunt, Miss
Barbary, echoes the relentlessness of that woman, who would tell
a small child that it would have been better if she had never been
born: 'Your mother, Esther, is your disgrace, and you were
hers' (ch. 3). What is Miss Barbary's vengeful rigor but the decay
of religion into ferocity and wrath?

In such a society, where religion degenerates into perversions
of its inspiration, culture into the cheating and cadging of Skimpole, and courtesy into the cold-hearted parental cannibalism of
Turveydrop, mere self-preservation also sinks at its lowest into
the hideous rapacity of Grandfather Smallweed. 'The father of
this pleasant grandfather . . . was a horny-skinned, two-legged,
money-getting species of spider, who spun webs to catch un-
wary flies, and retired into holes until they were entrapped. The
name of this old pagan's god was Compound Interest. He lived

for it, married it, died of it. Meeting with a heavy loss in an honest little enterprise in which all the loss was intended to have been on the other side, he broke something – something necessary to his existence; therefore it couldn't have been his heart – and made an end of his career' (ch. 21).

Cumulatively, these characters make *Bleak House* both an anatomy of society and a fable in which its major influences and institutions are portrayed by means of sharply individualized figures. They are instruments through which the meaning of the story is enlarged and extended to one of the broadest social significance. But everywhere its statements are conveyed not in abstractions but embodied in character and action organically related to the analysis. Archibald MacLeish is wrong in saying that a poem should not mean but be: like any work of literature, it may legitimately both mean and be. Into the very existence of *Bleak House* Dickens has precipitated the understanding of nineteenth-century society that he has achieved.

His method is at the same time realistic and figurative. Mrs Jellyby, never seeing anything nearer than Africa, Mrs Pardiggle, forcing her children to contribute their allowances to the Tockahoopo Indians, are themselves; but they are also the types of a philanthropy that will do nothing to diminish the profitable exploitation of England's poor. Mrs Pardiggle will hand out patronizing little booklets to debased brickmakers who are unable to read; she will not work to obtain them a living wage or decent homes with sanitary facilities. Neither she nor Mrs Jellyby will do a thing to abolish a pestilent slum like Tom-all-Alone's or to help an orphan vagrant like Jo.

'He is not one of Mrs Pardiggle's Tockahoopo Indians', Dickens says bitterly; 'he is not one of Mrs Jellyby's lambs, being wholly unconnected with Borioboola-Gha; he is not softened by distance and unfamiliarity; he is not a genuine foreign-grown savage; he is the ordinary home-made article. Dirty, ugly, disagreeable to all the senses, in body a common creature of the common streets, only in soul a heathen. Homely filth begrimes him, homely parasites devour him, homely sores are in him, homely rags are on him: native ignorance, the growth of English soil and climate, sinks his immortal nature lower than the beasts that perish. Stand forth, Jo, in uncompromising colours! From the sole of thy foot to the crown of thy head, there is nothing interesting about thee' (ch. 47).

Even more marked, however, in *Bleak House* is the use of poetic imagery and symbolism to underline and parallel the meaning of its patterns. The fog of the opening chapter is both literal and allegorical. It is the sooty London fog, but it covers all England, and it is the fog of obstructive procedures and out-moded institutions and selfish interests and obscured thinking as well. Miss Flite's caged birds symbolize the victims of Chancery, and the very names she has given them in her insanity are sig-nificant: 'Hope, Joy, Youth, Peace, Rest, Life, Dust, Ashes, Waste, Want, Ruin, Despair, Madness, Death, Cunning, Folly, Words, Wigs, Rags, Sheepskin, Plunder, Precedent, Jargon, Gammon, and Spinach.' 'That's the whole collection,' adds Krook, the sham Lord Chancellor, 'all cooped up together, by my noble and learned brother' (ch. 14). Later, Miss Flite adds two more birds to the collection, calling them 'the Wards in Jarndyce' (ch. 60). And always outside the cage lurks the cat Lady Jane, waiting, like the lawyers, to seize and tear any that might get free. Lady Jane is sometimes seen as a tiger and some-times as the wolf that cannot be kept from prowling at the door. Mr Vholes, skinning his tight black gloves off his hands as if he were flaying a victim, is constantly described, as are the other lawyers, in metaphors drawn from beasts of prey. And there is a further imagery of spiders spinning their traps, entangling flies within strand upon strand of sticky and imprisoning filaments, hanging their meshes everywhere in gray and dusty clotted webs.

The most elaborately worked out of these symbols is the parallel between Krook and the Lord Chancellor. 'You see I have so many things here,' Krook explains, 'of so many kinds, and all, as the neighbours think (but *they* know nothing), wasting away and going to rack and ruin, that that's why they have given me and my place a christening. And I have so many old parchmentses and papers in my stock. And I have a liking for rust and must and cobwebs. And all's fish that comes to my net. And I can't abear to part with anything I once lay hold of (or so my neighbours think, but what do *they* know?) or to alter anything, or to have any sweeping, nor scouring, nor cleaning, nor repairing going on about me. That's the way I've got the ill name of Chancery. *I* don't mind. I go to see my noble and learned brother pretty well every day when he sits in the Inn. He don't notice me, but I notice him. There's no great odds betwixt us. We both grub on in a muddle' (ch. 5).

And to sharpen the point still more, as Lady Jane, at his bidding, rips a bundle of rags with tigerish claws, he adds, 'I deal in cat-skins among other general matters, and hers was offered me. It's a very fine skin, as you may see, but I didn't have it stripped off! *That* warn't like Chancery practice though, says you!' (ch. 5)

Nor are these sharp and bitter strictures unjustified by the actualities. The Day case, nowhere near settled at the time Dickens wrote, dated from 1834, had always involved seventeen lawyers and sometimes thirty or forty, and had already incurred costs of £70,000. The case of Gridley, the man from Shropshire, was based upon an actual case that had been called to Dickens's attention. Jarndyce and Jarndyce was suggested by the notorious Jennings case, involving the disputed property of an old miser of Acton who had died intestate in 1798, leaving almost £1,500,000. When one of the claimants died *in 1915* the case was still unsettled and the costs amounted to £250,000.

Such facts give cogency to Dickens's conclusions: 'The one great principle of the English law is, to make business for itself. There is no other principle distinctly, certainly, and consistently maintained through all its narrow turnings. Viewed by this light it becomes a coherent scheme, and not the monstrous maze the laity are apt to think it. Let them but once perceive that its grand principle is to make business for itself at their expense, and surely they will cease to grumble.'

'But not perceiving this quite plainly', the laity *do* grumble, and then the 'respectability of Mr Vholes is brought into powerful play against them. "Repeal this statute, my good sir?" says

Mr Kenge to a smarting client, "repeal it, my dear sir? Never,
with my consent. Alter this law, sir, and what will be the effect
of your rash proceeding on a class of practitioners very worthily
represented, allow me to say to you, by the opposite attorney in
the case, Mr Vholes? Sir, that class of practitioners would be
swept from the face of the earth. Now you cannot afford – I will
say, the social system cannot afford – to lose an order of men
like Mr Vholes. Diligent, persevering, steady, acute in business.
My dear sir, I understand your present feelings against the existing state of things, which I grant to be a little hard in your case;
but I can never raise my voice for the demolition of a class of
men like Mr Vholes" ' (ch. 39).

The respectability of Mr Vholes 'has even been cited with
crushing effect before Parliamentary committees' and been no
less reiterated in private conversations affirming 'that these
changes are death to people like Vholes: a man of undoubted
respectability, with a father in the Vale of Taunton, and three
daughters at home. Take a few steps more in this direction, say
they, and what is to become of Vholes's father? Is he to perish?
And of Vholes's daughters? Are they to be shirtmakers, or
governesses? As though, Mr Vholes and his relations being
minor cannibal chiefs, and it being proposed to abolish
cannibalism, indignant champions were to put the case thus:
Make man-eating unlawful, and you starve the Vholeses!'
(ch. 39)

But the law is only the archetype of those vested interests that
plunder society under the guise of being society, that strangle the
general welfare, that grow fat on the miseries of the poor. It is
one of the instruments that give 'monied might the means
abundantly of wearying out the right' (ch. 1), the visible symbol
behind which lurk the forces of greed and privilege spinning
their labyrinthine webs of corruption. Spread out over the fair
English landscape are Chesney Wold, with its noble dignity, its
green garden terraces and stately drawing rooms, Bleak House,
with its orderly comfort and generous master, Rouncewell's,
with its productive and self-respecting industry. But Rouncewell's is no more than part of the whole – a part, too, that will

reveal its own dark evils under the deeper analysis of *Hard Times*. Bleak House, at its best and for all its warm intentions, is itself helplessly enmeshed and can make only frustrated gestures to reach out a helping hand. And Chesney Wold has its corollary and consequence in Tom-all-Alone's and the wretched hovels of the brickmakers: its dignity is built on their degradation.

Chesney Wold and Tom-all-Alone's are thus also symbols in the symbolic structure. For Dickens does not mean that Sir Leicester Dedlock, or even the aristocracy as a class, is personally responsible for social evil, any more than are the Lord Chancellor or Carboy and Kenge or Inspector Bucket. Individually they may all be amiable enough, but they are instruments of a system in which the stately mansion and the rotting slum represent the opposite extremes. Inspector Bucket, officially the bloodhound of the law, is personally a bluff and kind-hearted fellow, Conversation Kenge merely a florid rhetorician, the Lord Chancellor a harmless old gentleman. And to Sir Leicester, who epitomizes the system, Dickens is chivalrously magnanimous.

Sir Leicester is a good feudal landlord, a kind and generous master to his servants, loyal to his family, devoted to his wife. 'He is a gentleman of strict conscience, disdainful of all littleness and meanness, and ready, on the shortest notice, to die any death you may please to mention rather than give occasion for the least impeachment of his integrity. He is an honourable, obstinate, truthful, high-spirited, intensely prejudiced, perfectly unreasonable man' (ch. 2). Beneath his high demeanor and occasional absurdity there is a core of true nobility. When he learns the story of Lady Dedlock's past, and falls moaning to the floor, paralyzed and unable to speak, his devotion to his wife and his distress at her flight are greater than the horror of the revelation, and his faltering hand traces upon a slate the words, 'Full forgiveness. Find——' (ch. 56).

But, for all his private virtues, he has no hesitation about trying to bully or buy a victory in Parliamentary elections, although he bitterly resents the corrupt opposition to his own purposes that makes this expensive course necessary. The 'hundreds of thousands of pounds' required to bring about the triumph of his

own party he blames on the 'implacable description' of the opposition and the 'bad spirit' of the people. His dependent spinster
cousin, the fair Volumnia, with her rouge, her still girlish ways,
and her little scream, is innocently unable to imagine the need
for this enormous outlay; Sir Leicester freezes her with his displeasure: 'It is disgraceful to the electors. But as you, though
inadvertently, and without intending so unreasonable a question
asked me, "what for?" let me reply to you. For necessary ex-
penses' (ch. 11).

The 'implacable' opposition is, of course, merely a rival faction
contending for the spoils of office, and no matter which party
wins, the country is still dominated by wealth and privilege
manipulating all the puppetry of political juntas. This is true
even when the candidates of Mr Rouncewell the ironmaster cap-
ture a few seats, and will continue to be true when they fill the
House, despite Sir Leicester's gasping conviction that 'the floodgates of society are burst open, and the waters have – a – obliterated the landmarks of the framework of the cohesion by which
things are held together!' (ch. 11) All that the rising power of
the industrialists really means is that they too will force their
way into the coalition of exploitation formed by their predecessors, the landed aristocracy, the lawyers and politicians, the
merchants and the bankers.

The political aspects of this situation Dickens conveys with a
wonderful burlesque brilliance. 'His description of our party
system, with its Coodle, Doodle, Foodle, etc.,' writes Bernard
Shaw, 'has never been surpassed for accuracy and for penetration
of superficial pretence.' But Shaw's feeling that Dickens 'had not
dug down to the bedrock of the imposture' is derived from a
failure to notice that Dickens portrayed Tom-all-Alone's and
the brickmakers as much more than a mere indictment of 'individual delinquencies, local plague-spots, negligent authorities'.[2]
In reality Dickens links all these phenomena with each other, the
political bargains and combinations no less so than the slow-
moving chicaneries of law.

Lord Boodle points out to Sir Leicester that the formation of a
new Ministry lies 'between Lord Coodle and Sir Thomas

Doodle – supposing it to be impossible for the Duke of Foodle
to act with Goodle, which may be assumed to be the case in
consequence of the breach arising out of that affair with Hoodle.
Then, giving the Home Department and the Leadership of the
House of Commons to Joodle, the Exchequer to Koodle, the
Colonies to Loodle, and the Foreign Office to Moodle, what are
you to do with Noodle? You can't offer him the Presidency of
the Council; that is reserved for Poodle. You can't put him in the
Woods and Forests; that is hardly good enough for Quoodle.
What follows? That the country is shipwrecked, lost, and gone
to pieces . . . because you can't provide for Noodle!

'On the other hand, the Right Honourable William Buffy,
M.P., contends across the table with some one else, that the ship-
wreck of the country – about which there is no doubt; it is only
the manner of it that is in question – is attributable to Cuffy. If
you had done with Cuffy what you ought to have done when he
first came into Parliament, and had prevented him from going
over to Duffy, you would have got him into alliance with Fuffy,
you would have had with you the weight attaching as a smart
debater to Guffy, and you would have brought to bear upon the
elections the wealth of Huffy, you would have got in for three
counties Juffy, Kuffy, and Luffy, and you would have strengthened your administration by the official knowledge and business habits of Muffy. All this, instead of being as you now are,
dependent upon the mere caprice of Puffy!' (ch. 12)

Beyond their witty parody of the language of political manipulation, these two paragraphs ingeniously exploit the mere
ludicrous rhyming sounds of their alphabetical succession of
names and the derogatory implications of many of those names.
Boodle is not an auspicious name for a politician, nor do Noodle
and Poodle convey the most promising insinuations. Doodle and
Noodle were names of two of the characters in one of the versions
of Fielding's burlesque *Tom Thumb*. And from the time immediately before his reporting days Dickens may well have remembered that the notoriously incompetent Lord Dudley, Secretary
of State for Foreign Affairs under the Duke of Wellington in
1828, was widely known as Lord Doodle,[3] and that 'doodle'

meant to trifle or to make droning noises. Guffy, Huffy, Muffy,
and Puffy may also be made to yield derisive associations, and
possibly even Buffy, Cuffy, and Luffy.

With biting satire Dickens paints the ensuing political corruption. 'England has been in a dreadful state for some weeks.
Lord Coodle would go out, Sir Thomas Doodle wouldn't come
in, and there being nobody in Great Britain (to speak of) except
Coodle and Doodle, there has been no Government. . . . At last
Sir Thomas Doodle has not only condescended to come in, but
has done it handsomely, bringing in with him all his nephews, all
his male cousins, and all his brothers-in-law. So there is hope for
the old ship yet.' In the process, he 'has found that he must
throw himself upon the country – chiefly in the form of
sovereigns and beer', 'in an auriferous and malty shower' while
'mysterious men with no names' rush backward and forward
across the country on secret errands. Meanwhile Britannia is
'occupied in pocketing Doodle in the form of sovereigns and
swallowing Doodle in the form of beer, and in swearing herself
black in the face that she does neither'.

All this structure of venality rises upon a foundation of exploitation, destitution and misery. We are shown the wretched
hovels of the brickmakers at St Alban's, 'with pigsties close to
the broken windows', old tubs 'put to catch the droppings of
rainwater from a roof, or . . . banked up with mud into a little
pond like a large dirt-pie' (ch. 8). Within their damp and musty
rooms we see their dwellers, 'a woman with a black eye nursing
a poor little gasping baby by the fire; a man all stained with clay
and mud, and looking very dissipated, lying at full length on the
ground, smoking a pipe; a powerful young man, fastening a
collar on a dog; and a bold girl, doing some kind of washing in
very dirty water' (ch. 8). As Professor Cazamian points out, contemporary official reports all more than justify the hideous picture.

Into this scene Mrs Pardiggle pushes her way, hectoring its
inhabitants in her loud, authoritative voice and ignoring the
growling resentment of the man on the floor.

'I wants a end of these liberties took with my place. I wants an
end of being drawed like a badger. . . . Is my daughter a-washin?'

Yes, she *is* a-washin. Look at the water. Smell it! That's wot we drinks. How do you like it, and what do you think of gin, instead! Ain't my place dirty? Yes, it is dirty – it's nat'rally dirty, and it's nat'rally onwholesome; and we've had five dirty and onwholesome children, as is all dead infants, and so much the better for them, and for us besides. Have I read the little book wot you left? No, I ain't read the little book wot you left. There ain't nobody here as knows how to read it; and if there wos, it wouldn't be suitable to me. It's a book fit for a babby, and I'm not a babby. If you was to leave me a doll, I shouldn't nuss it. How have I been conducting of myself? Why, I've been drunk for three days, and I'd a been drunk four, if I'd a had the money. Don't I never mean for to go to church? No, I don't never mean for to go to church. I shouldn't be expected there, if I did; the beadle's too gen-teel for me. And how did my wife get that black eye? Why, I giv' it her; and if she says I didn't, she's a Lie!' (ch. 8)

Worse still is the urban slum of Tom-all-Alone's, a black, dilapidated street of crazy houses tumbling down and reeking with foul stains and loathsome smells, dripping with dirty rain, and sheltering within its ruined walls a human vermin that crawls and coils itself to sleep in maggot numbers on the rotting boards of its floors among fetid rags. 'Twice, lately, there has been a crash and a cloud of dust, like the springing of a mine, in Tom-all-Alone's; and each time a house has fallen. These accidents have made a paragraph in the newspapers, and have filled a bed or two in the nearest hospital. The gaps remain, and there are not unpopular lodgings among the rubbish' (ch. 16). There dwells Jo, with his body exuding a stench so horrible that Lady Dedlock cannot bear to have him come close to her; and thence comes Jo, munching his bit of dirty bread and, admiring the structure that houses the Society for the Propagation of the Gospel in Foreign Parts. 'He has no idea, poor wretch, of the spiritual destitution of a coral reef in the Pacific, or what it costs to look up the precious souls among the cocoa-nuts and bread-fruit' (ch. 16). And when Jo lies dead of neglect, malnutrition, and disease, the narrative swells into an organ-toned and accusing dirge: 'Dead, your Majesty. Dead, my lords and gentlemen. Dead,

Right Reverends and Wrong Reverends of every order. Dead, men and women, born with Heavenly compassion in your hearts. And dying thus around us every day' (ch. 47).

Counterpointed with the death of Jo is that of Richard Carstone, for high-spirited and generous youth, with every advantage, is no less prey to the infection of an acquisitive society than helpless ignorance and misery. All Richard's buoyancy and courage, his gentleness and frankness, his quick and brilliant abilities, are not enough to save him. Gradually he becomes entangled in the fatal hope of getting something for nothing, stakes everything on the favorable outcome of the Chancery suit, neglects his capacities, fosters his careless shortcomings, dissipates the little money he has, feverishly drifts into suspicion and distrust of his honorable guardian, argues that Mr Jarndyce's appearance of disinterestedness may be a blind to further his own advantage in the case. How, Richard asks, can he settle down to anything? 'If you were living in an unfinished house, liable to have the roof put on or taken off – to be from top to bottom pulled down or built up – to-morrow, next day, next week, next month, next year, – you would find it hard to rest or settle' (ch. 37). By early manhood his expression is already so worn by weariness and anxiety that his look is 'like ungrown despair' (ch. 45). Not until it is too late, and he is dying, does he speak of 'beginning the world', and confess his mistakes and blindnesses to his wife. Esther Summerson reports his words:

'I have done you many wrongs, my own. I have fallen like a poor stray shadow on your way, I have married you to poverty and trouble, I have scattered your means to the winds. You will forgive me all this, Ada, before I begin the world?'

A smile irradiated his face, as she bent to kiss him. He slowly laid his face down upon her bosom, drew his arms closer round her neck, and with one parting sob, began the world. Not this world. O not this! The world that sets this right.

When all was still, at a late hour, poor crazed Miss Flite came weeping to me, and told me she had given her birds their liberty. (ch. 65)

Richard Carstone and poor Jo, Miss Flite driven insane, Gridley dying broken on the floor of George's shooting gallery and George in the toils of the moneylenders, Mr Tulkinghorn shot through the heart in his Lincoln's Inn Fields chambers beneath the pointing finger of allegory, Sir Leicester humbled, heartbroken, and paralyzed, Lady Dedlock dead, disgraced, and mudstained outside the slimy walls of the pauper graveyard where her lover lies buried – all are swept on to frustration or defeat in the titanic intensity of this dark storm of a story. Everywhere the honest, the generous, the helpless, the simple, and the loving are thwarted and crippled. John Jarndyce, the violently good master of Bleak House, can rescue only a distressingly small number of those he sets out to save. In a life of poverty and struggle imposed by a society where nature itself is deformed and tainted, poor Caddy Jellyby and her husband Prince Turveydrop can give birth only to an enfeebled deaf-and-dumb child. For *Bleak House* (like Shaw's *Heartbreak House*, of which it is a somber forerunner) is in its very core symbolic: *Bleak House* is modern England, it is the world of an acquisitive society, a monetary culture, and its heavy gloom is implied by the very adjective that is a part of its title.

But the mood of *Bleak House* is not one of resignation or despairing sorrow; it is that of indignation and grim fire-eyed defiance. Dickens is no longer, as Shaw points out, merely the liberal reformer who takes it for granted that 'the existing social order' is 'the permanent and natural order of human society, needing reforms now and then and here and there, but essentially good and sane and right and respectable and proper and everlasting'. He has become instead a revolutionist, to whom 'it is transitory, mistaken, dishonest, unhappy, pathological: a social disease to be cured, not endured'.[4] It is this that troubles numbers of readers in Dickens's later books, which are his greatest ones, and makes those readers prefer the earlier stories. It is now the very root-assumptions of that social order that Dickens is attacking and insisting must be destroyed.

One of the forms taken by the discomfort of such readers is the repeated criticism that Dickens could not portray a gentleman. At the time of Sir Mulberry Hawk and Lord Frederick Verisopht this might have been true; by the time of Sir Leicester Dedlock it was so no longer. It should be observed that Thackeray, who was never accused of a failure to understand gentlemen, paints them far more savagely than Dickens does; he makes Sir Pitt Crawley mean, dirty, illiterate, and brutal, and almost the entire aristocracy profligate, sycophantic, ill-bred. But Thackeray took the stability of society for granted, whereas Dickens was by now demanding a radical reconstruction of society. So Thackeray may be smiled upon as a genteel satirist who merely exposed the flaws of the polite world, and Dickens must be thrown out of court as one who had no understanding of the upper classes. 'It would be nearer the mark', Shaw says dryly, 'to say that Dickens knew all that really mattered in the world about Sir Leicester Dedlock', and that Thackeray 'knew nothing that really mattered about him. . . . Thackeray could see Chesney Wold; but Dickens could see through it.'[5]

He could see through Lombard Street and Threadneedle Street and the City, too; and, as he was soon to prove, he could see through Birmingham, Manchester, Leeds, and Preston. He sees the world about him as a conflict between the forces of love and life and those of acquisition, retention, and greed, with pride and cruelty everywhere inflicting the most frightful mutilations upon helplessness. But not without having recoil back upon themselves the inevitable consequences of the system that embodies their working, nor without evils being engendered that spread almost at random everywhere. Sir Leicester cannot protect the woman he loves and honors; the Lord Chancellor himself cannot speed the slow movement of Chancery or prevent it from grinding its victims, of whatever class they may be. Esther Summerson's face cannot be saved from having its beauty ruined as long as there are waifs like Jo and plague spots like Tom-all-Alone's.

In this society of shocking extremes the highest and the lowest are inextricably linked to each other. Dickens had shown this before, in *Barnaby Rudge* with Sir John Chester and Hugh, in

Dombey and Son with Edith Dombey and Alice Marwood, but in *Bleak House* it becomes central to the very structure and meaning of the plot. Tom-all-Alone's, Dickens shows us, has his revenge.

Even the winds are his messengers, and they serve him in these hours of darkness. There is not a drop of Tom's corrupted blood but propagates infection and contagion somewhere. It shall pollute, this very night, the choice stream (in which chemists on analysis would find the genuine nobility) of a Norman house, and his Grace shall not be able to say Nay to the infamous alliance. There is not an atom of Tom's slime, not a cubic inch of any pestilential gas in which he lives, not one obscenity or degradation about him, not an ignorance, not a wickedness, not a brutality of his committing, but shall work its retribution, through every order of society, up to the proudest of the proud, and to the highest of the high. Verily, what with tainting, plundering, and spoiling, Tom has his revenge. (ch. 46)

And just as Tom-all-Alone's sends out its noxious vapors poisoning society, its waifs bearing pollution and infection, its criminals returning evil for the evil that has formed them; just as Tom-all-Alone's slowly and piecemeal crumbles into ruins from the rottenness of its old beams and reeking plaster, now one and now another house crashing down into dust and rubbish: so the internal rottenness of the social structure that not merely tolerates but perpetuates Tom-all-Alone's must inevitably destroy itself in the end, die of its own self-engendered diseases, annihilate itself by its own corruption. Such is the symbol of Krook's death by Spontaneous Combustion:

Here is a small burnt patch of flooring; here is the tinder from a little bundle of burnt paper, but not so light as usual, seeming to be steeped in something; and here is – is it the cinder of a small charred and broken log of wood sprinkled with white ashes, or is it coal? O Horror, he is here! and this from which we run away, striking out the light and overturning one another in the street, is all that represents him.

Help, help, help! come into this house for Heaven's sake!

Plenty will come in, but none can help. The Lord Chancellor

of that Court, true to his title in his last act, has died the death of all Lord Chancellors in all Courts, and of all authorities in all places under all names soever, where false pretences are made, and where injustice is done. Call the death by any name Your Highness will, attribute it to whom you will, or say it might have been prevented how you will, it is the same death eternally – inborn, inbred, engendered in the corrupt humours of the vicious body itself, and that only – Spontaneous Combustion, and none other of all the deaths that can be died. (ch. 32)

It is Dickens speaking with the voice of prophecy. For the sham Lord Chancellor and his shop clearly symbolize not only the real Court of Chancery and all the corruptions of all law, but 'all authorities in all places under all names soever' – all the injustices of an unjust society. And they are no longer subjects for local cure or even amputation. Nothing will do short of the complete annihilation that they will ultimately provide by blowing up of their own corruption.

SOURCE: *Charles Dickens; His Tragedy and Triumph*, 2 vols (1953).

NOTES

1. Morgan MS., Dickens to Miss Coutts 4 Mar 1850: 'I dream of Mrs Chisholm and her housekeeping. The dirty faces of her children are my continual companions.'
2. G. B. Shaw, preface to *Great Expectations* (Edinburgh, 1937).
3. *The Times Literary Supplement*, 28 July 1950, p. 476: 'John Wilson Croker as Gossip, 1' by Alan Lang Strout, quoting a letter of Croker's to Lord Hertford.
4. Shaw, preface to *Great Expectations*.
5. Ibid.

J. Hillis Miller

BLEAK HOUSE AND THE
MORAL LIFE (1958)

I

It is a dull street under the best conditions; where the two long rows of houses stare at each other with that severity, that half-a-dozen of its greatest mansions seem to have been slowly stared into stone, rather than originally built in that material. (ch. 48)

The Temple, Chancery Lane, Serjeants' Inn, and Lincoln's Inn even unto the Fields, are like tidal harbours at low water; where stranded proceedings, offices at anchor, idle clerks lounging on lopsided stools that will not recover their perpendicular until the current of Term sets in, lie high and dry upon the ooze of the long vacation. (ch. 19)

Though the world of *Bleak House* is not, we discover, the sheer atomistic chaos it at first appears to be, the connection, by repetition, of successive moments in isolated locations does not organize this chaos. It does not seem that a truly human existence is possible here – no organization of time into a lived duration, no relation between people making possible significant communication. But we come to see that the inhuman fixity and paralysis which seems to possess things and men in *Bleak House* is not a permanent condition. It is not now in the same stasis it has always maintained. The houses were not originally stone. They were 'slowly stared into stone'. And the ooze and idleness of the long vacation is merely the motionless end point of a progressive withdrawal of the tide of human action and life. Prior to the timeless paralysis of things there was a long process of deceleration and decay. It is impossible to stop the forward movement of things in time. Both an attempt to freeze the present as a repetition of a past time and the eternally repeated moment

of expectation which awaits some definitive event in the future
are essentially a denial of the proper human relation to time and
to the objective world. Both are cut off from the 'moving age'.
But man cannot cut himself off from time and the world. If he
is not related authentically to them, if he does not command
them, they will command him. He will be assimilated into the
inhuman world and become part of a mechanical concatenation
of causes and effects which is a horrible parody of historical
continuity. In the absence of human intervention things will take
matters into their own hands, and initiate a long natural process
of decay and disintegration in which man will become unwittingly involved. The world possesses an immanent tendency
toward decomposition which only the most delicately and reso-
lutely applied constructive force can counteract. And it is just
this force which is almost totally absent in *Bleak House*.

The world of the novel is already, when the story begins, a
kind of junk heap of broken things. This is especially apparent
in the great number of disorderly, dirty, broken-down interiors
in the novel. The Jellyby household is 'nothing but bills, dirt,
waste, noise, tumbles down-stairs, confusion, and wretchedness'
(ch. 14). At the time of the preparations for Caddy Jellyby's
marriage 'nothing belonging to the family, which it had been
possible to break, was unbroken . . . nothing which it had
been possible to spoil in any way, was unspoilt . . . no
domestic object which was capable of collecting dirt, from a dear
child's knee to the door-plate, was without as much dirt as could
well accumulate upon it' (ch. 30). The Jellyby house is perhaps
the extreme case, but Skimpole's home too is 'in a state of dilapi-
dation' (ch. 43), Symond's Inn, where Richard Carstone's lawyer, Vholes, lives, has been made 'of old building materials,
which took kindly to the dry rot and to dirt and all things decaying and dismal' (ch. 39), and Richard himself lives in a room
which is full of 'a great confusion of clothes, tin cases, books,
boots, brushes, and portmanteaus, strewn all about the floor'
(ch. 45). The 'dusty bundles of papers' in his room seem to
Esther 'like dusty mirrors reflecting his own mind' (ch. 51).

These present states of disorder are not simply inorganic form-

lessness; they are the terminal point of an organically inter-
connected series of stages which led naturally and inevitably
from one to another. The present stage of rottenness is the result
of an inverted process of growth, 'like [that] of fungus or any
unwholesome excrescence produced . . . in neglect and impurity'
(ch. 46). Such a process escapes from the discontinuous, but only
to replace it with a mode of continuity which is apparently an
irreversible growth toward death. This death will be defined as
the putrefaction of every organic form and as the pulverization
of every structured inorganic thing. There is here no Spencerian
constructive law immanent in nature and guaranteeing, through
the impersonal operation of causality, the creation of ever finer
and more discriminated forms of life. Rather, it is as though the
generative cause and immanent principle of growth had been
withdrawn altogether, leaving things to fall back to their primal
disorder.

Sometimes this process appears, not as a certain stage which
it has now reached, but in the very midst of its happening. Although the participles in the opening paragraphs of the novel
suggested the present activity of inanimate objects, participial
forms can also express the falling away and disintegration from
moment to moment of things which are collapsing into chaos.
Thus, Esther is painfully aware of 'the musty *rotting* silence of
the house' where Ada and Richard are living (ch. 51), and in
Nemo's room, 'one old mat, trodden to shreds of rope-yarn, lies
perishing upon the hearth' (ch. 10). A description of the beach at
Deal shows it as a kind of wasteland of disunity, and ends with
the apparent metamorphosis of the inhabitants into a lower form
of existence. The heterogeneity gives way at last to a single
substance into which the men seem to be transforming themselves, just as the litter of the beach dissolves into the sea and the
fog: 'The long flat beach, with its little irregular houses, wooden
and brick, and its litter of capstans, and great boats, and sheds,
and bare upright poles with tackle and blocks, and loose gravelly
waste places overgrown with grass and weeds, wore as dull an
appearance as any place I ever saw. The sea was heaving under
a thick white fog; and nothing else was moving but a few early

ropemakers, who, with the yarn twisted round their bodies, looked as if, tired of their present state of existence, they were spinning themselves into cordage' (ch. 45). Perhaps the best example of this disintegration is the initial description of Tom-all-Alone's, which makes an elaborate use of present participles to express an active process of decomposition matching the forward movement of time: 'It is a street of perishing blind houses, with their eyes stoned out; without a pane of glass, without so much as a window-frame, with the bare blank shutters tumbling from their hinges and falling asunder; the iron rails peeling away in flakes of rust; the chimneys sinking in; the stone steps to every door (and every door might be Death's Door) turning stagnant green; the very crutches on which the ruins are propped, decaying' (ch. 8).

One might plot the curve of this approach to maximum entropy by a series of crucial points. There was once evidently, long ago in the past, a time when things were orderly, when everything fitted into its place in an organic structure, and when each individual object was itself a formal unity. From that point things passed eventually to a stage in which they were simply collections of broken objects thrown pell-mell together. Things are then like the wreckage left behind after the destruction of a civilization. Each fragmentary form once had a use and a purpose, but is now merely debris. Such collections form the contents of Krook's rag and bottle shop or of the closets of the Jellyby house:

In all parts of the window, were quantities of dirty bottles: blacking bottles, medicine bottles, ginger-beer and soda-water bottles, pickle bottles, wine bottles, ink bottles. . . . A little way within the shop-door, lay heaps of old crackled parchment scrolls, and discoloured and dog's-eared law-papers. I could have fancied that all the rusty keys, of which there must have been hundreds huddled together as old iron, had once belonged to doors of rooms or strong chests in lawyers' offices. The litter of rags . . . might have been counsellors' bands and gowns torn up. One had only to fancy . . . that yonder bones in a corner, piled together and picked very clean, were the bones of clients, to make the picture complete. (ch. 5)

But such wonderful things came tumbling out of the closets when they were opened – bits of mouldy pie, sour bottles, Mrs Jellyby's caps, letters, tea, forks, odd boots and shoes of children, firewood, wafers, saucepan-lids, damp sugar in odds and ends of paper bags, footstools, blacklead brushes, bread, Mrs Jellyby's bonnets, books with butter sticking to the binding, guttered candle-ends put out by being turned upside down in broken candlesticks, nutshells, heads and tails of shrimps, dinner-mats, gloves, coffee-grounds, umbrellas. . . . (ch. 30)

Not only are things moving in the direction of increasing disorder, they are also moving further and further beyond the limits of human intelligence. Whatever human meaning and order there may have been originally is now obliterated in complexity which defies comprehension: 'This scarecrow of a suit has, in course of time, become so complicated, that no man alive knows what it means' (ch. 1). Even if there were some intelligible purpose in the original impetus which set the case in motion, that purpose has been utterly lost in its own self-proliferating complexity. Now the case runs automatically, without any direction from the thousands of people, suitors and lawyers, who are mere parties to it, mere instruments of its autonomous activity: 'It's about a Will, and the trusts under a Will – or it was, once. It's about nothing but Costs now. We are . . . equitably waltzing ourselves off to dusty death, about Costs. That's the great question. All the rest, by some extraordinary means, has melted away' (ch. 8).

But in the end even this kind of structure, a structure so elaborate that it cannot be understood by the human mind, yields to complete heterogeneity. And a world of complete heterogeneity is, paradoxically, a world of complete homogeneity. Since nothing has any relation to anything else and cannot therefore be understood in terms of a contrast to anything else, everything is, finally, the equivalent of everything else. The contents of Krook's rag and bone shop, like everything involved in Chancery, are transformed at last to mere undifferentiated dust, another form of the fog and mud which dominate the opening scene of the novel. Everything there is 'wasting away and going to rack and ruin', turning into 'rust and must and cobwebs' (ch. 5). The final product is made up of thousands of distinct particles, but each particle is, in the end, no more than another example of the general pulverization. So Tom-all-Alone's is at one stage of its decay like the ruined body of a man half dead and crawling with vermin: 'these tumbling tenements contain, by night, a swarm of misery. As, on the ruined human wretch, vermin parasites appear, so, these ruined shelters have bred a crowd of foul existence that crawls in and out of gaps in walls and boards; and coils itself to sleep, in maggot numbers, where the rain drips in . . .' (ch. 16). But later on even this semblance of life disappears from the scene and Tom-all-Alone's is like the cold and lifeless moon, a 'desert region unfit for life and blasted by volcanic fires' (ch. 46), with a 'stagnant channel of mud' for a main street (ch. 46). In the end, any organic entity, whether human or material, which gets caught up in the process of decomposition becomes nothing but a powdery or pasty substance, without form or life. This process can be either a physical or a spiritual disintegration, either the destruction of the individual through his absorption in the impersonal institution of 'law and equity', or the dissolution of all solid material form in 'that kindred mystery, the street mud, which is made of nobody knows what, and collects about us nobody knows whence or how' (ch. 10). One of the basic symbolic equations of the novel is the suggested parallel between these two forms of disintegration.

The mud and fog of the opening paragraphs of the novel are not, we can see now, the primeval stuff out of which all highly developed forms evolve. They are the symptoms of a general return to the primal slime, a return to chaos which is going on everywhere in the novel and is already nearing its final end when the novel begins.

The human condition of the characters of *Bleak House* is, then, to be thrown into a world which is neither fresh and new nor already highly organized, but is a world which has already gone bad. From the very first moment in which they are aware of themselves at all, the characters find themselves involved in this world. Their dereliction is to be already a suitor in a case which began long before they were born, or already tainted with the quasi-sin of illegitimacy. Their mode of being in the world is to be already committed to a situation which they have not chosen.

This dereliction will never end, as long as the character is alive. It is the permanent condition of human existence in *Bleak House*. The fact that almost all of the characters in the novel are in one way or another engaged in an endless suit in Chancery is much more than a mere device of narrative unity. To be involved in an endless case, a case which can only be concluded by the total using up of both suit and suitor, becomes a symbol in the novel of what it is to be in the world at all. It is because a person is part of a process, because he is born into a case which is going on at his birth and remains unfinished throughout his life, that he cannot settle down, cannot find some definitive formulation of his identity and of his place in the world. But to be unfinished, to be open toward the future, to be evermore about to be, is, for Dickens, to be human. Richard suffers the human situation itself and defines the state of all the characters when he describes himself as living permanently in a 'temporary condition' (ch. 23):

'. . . I am a very unfortunate dog not to be more settled, but how *can* I be more settled? If you lived in an unfinished house, you couldn't settle down in it; if you were condemned to leave everything you undertook, unfinished, you would find it hard to apply yourself to anything; and yet that's my unhappy case. I was born into this unfinished contention with all its chances and changes, and it began to unsettle me before I quite knew the difference between a suit at law and a suit of clothes; and it has gone on unsettling me ever since.' (ch. 23)

Richard's error is not to understand that his case can never be finished, to live in the expectation of an end which will settle his life in a permanent form: 'it can't last for ever. We shall come on for a final hearing, and get judgment in our favour. . . . These proceedings will come to a termination, and then I am provided for' (ch. 23). But the nature of these proceedings is precisely to be interminable, as long as the character is alive.

For many of the characters the determining cause, which has

made of their situations what they irrevocably are, occurred so long before their birth that it assumes a quasi-mythical character. They attempt to trace the series of effects and causes from the present moment back retrogressively to the first cause, only to be lost in the mists and confusions of the past. Long, long ago in the past, so long ago that no one now has any direct contact with what happened then, the chain of causes and effects which has brought things to their present pass was initiated. Such characters seem to be involved in a kind of original sin for which they must innocently suffer: 'How mankind ever came to be afflicted with Wiglomeration, or for whose sins these young people ever fell into a pit of it, I don't know; so it is' (ch. 8).

But for other characters the definitive event which has determined their lives is prior to the beginning of the novel but not prior to their birth. As in Faulkner's novels, we are presented with characters who are when we first meet them already doomed by something which happened long ago in their own lives, something which they hide carefully from the world, but on which their conscious attention is permanently fixed in a kind of retrospective fascination. All their lives are spent attempting unsuccessfully to escape from this determining moment. It is a constantly reënacted failure which only makes their lives all the more permanently attached to a past from which they cannot separate themselves, and which irrevocably defines them as what they are. The secretly obsessed quality of many of the characters in *Bleak House* makes this novel very different from *Martin Chuzzlewit*. In the earlier novel the characters either had no inner lives at all as distinct from their environments, or had subjectivities which were anonymous and empty, mere pure and vivid vision, existing only in the present. In *Bleak House*, some characters are seen as possessing, not this anonymous lucidity, but a concentrated awareness of their pasts and of their destinies. Such consciousnesses are not yet shown from the inside, as they will be in *Little Dorrit*, but their presence is unmistakably implied by the actions of the characters and revealed in occasional glimpses of their interior worlds. Of the tragedy of Boythorn's projected marriage, Jarndyce says: 'That time has had its in-

fluence on all his later life' (ch. 9 and see ch. 43). And Nemo was
living, we realize, in the constant suffering of the tragedy of his
relations to Lady Dedlock, just as George Rouncewell's bluff
exterior hides a secret remorse for having run away from home,
and just as Tulkinghorn lives in a state of quiet desperation. He
is shown for one moment as he is for himself, remembering a
friend of his, obviously a surrogate for himself, a 'man of the
same mould', who 'lived the same kind of life until he was
seventy-five years old', and then hanged himself (ch. 22). But
Lady Dedlock is, of course, the chief example of this theme. Her
boredom hides an intense concentration on her own past, and all
her attempts to cease to be the lover of Captain Hawdon only
carry her more irresistibly toward her final reaffirmation of her
past self. Her tragedy, like that of Racine's characters, of Hardy's,
or of Faulkner's, is the tragedy of the irrevocable. Her fate is to
be the doomed victim of her own past, a past which continues
itself ineluctably into her present state as long as she lives.

But the determining cause which makes impotent victims of
all these characters does not exist solely as a kind of mythical
event occurring so long ago that no direct contact with it is possible, nor does it exist solely as an impersonal force which imposes itself from the outside on people and warps or destroys
them. It may be both of these, but in its most powerful form it is
immanent, present in the contemporary spiritual condition of the
characters, although they may not even be consciously aware of
it. It is able to get inside its victims, and inhabit them as a destructive force. It then no longer needs to exist as an exterior
power, and can withdraw and disappear, leaving the possessed
character to his isolated doom. Everywhere in *Bleak House* we
can see the intrusion into the present of a fatally determining past
from which the characters can in no way free themselves because
it has become part of the very substance of their beings. In *Bleak
House* the present is not really something isolated and without
engagement in the past, but is the preservation of the past and its
continuation in the present. Inhabited by immanent determining
forces tending irreversibly toward their dissolution the characters disintegrate, just as Grandfather Smallweed collapses 'like

some wound-up instrument running down' (ch. 39), and just as
his daughter 'dwindled away like touchwood' (ch. 21).

The self-enclosed life of the characters of *Bleak House* is, then,
not a mechanical repetition. It is a clock that runs down, something organic which has died and decays, the entropy of an
enclosed system approaching the maximum equilibrium of its
forces. As in the 'circumscribed universe' of Poe,[1] since there is
no influx of life, energy, air, or novelty from the outside, there is
a gradual exhaustion of the forces inside, a disaggregation of all
solid forms, as all diversity is slowly transformed into a bland
and motionless homogeneity. Such an enclosed system will, like
a case in Chancery, eventually 'die out of its own vapidity' (ch.
24), or 'lapse and melt away' (ch. 65). Beneath a carapace of
solitude the will, the strength, the life of these characters exhausts
itself, consumes itself in its own internal activity. So Richard, 'the
good consuming and consumed, the life turned sour', is slowly
transformed into 'the one subject that is resolving his existence
into itself' (ch. 39). Wholly enclosed within his own obsession,
such a character experiences a steady decomposition of his life,
an acceleration toward the ultimate disorder and lifelessness of
dust and mud:

'My whole estate . . . has gone in costs. The suit, still undecided,
has fallen into rack, and ruin, and despair, with everything
else. . . . '(ch. 15)

In the meantime [while Tom Jarndyce became absorbed in his
suit], the place became dilapidated, the wind whistled through
the cracked walls, the rain fell through the broken roof, the
weeds choked the passage to the rotting door. (ch. 8)

His voice had faded, with the old expression of his face, with his
strength, with his anger, with his resistance to the wrongs that
had at last subdued him. The faintest shadow of an object full of
form and colour, is such a picture of it, as he was of the man from
Shropshire whom we had spoken with before. (ch. 24)

. . . it is the same death eternally – inborn, inbred, engendered
in the corrupted humours of the vicious body itself, and that only
– Spontaneous Combustion, and none other of all the deaths
that can be died. (ch. 32)

Krook's death by spontaneous combustion, described in the last quotation, is of course the most notorious example of this return to homogeneity in *Bleak House*. Krook is transformed into the basic elements of the world of the novel, fog and mud. The heavy odor in the air, as if bad pork chops were frying, and the 'thick yellow liquor' which forms on the window sill as Krook burns into the circumambient atmosphere, are particularly horrible versions of these elements.

But if the deterioration of the characters in *Bleak House* can appear as the inescapable fulfillment of an inner principle of corruption, it can also appear as a destiny which draws the characters from some prospective point toward their doom. Instead of being pushed from behind or from within, the characters may be attracted from the future. This may appear in the sudden collapse or dissolution of some object or person which has long been secretly mined from within by decay, and goes to pieces in a moment when some artificial foundation or sustaining principle gives way. So the houses in Tom-all-Alone's collapse (ch. 16); so the man from Shropshire 'break[s] down in an hour' (ch. 24); and so the death of Tulkinghorn seems to Lady Dedlock 'but the key-stone of a gloomy arch removed, and now the arch begins to fall in a thousand fragments, each crushing and mangling piecemeal!' (ch. 55) 'It was right,' she says, 'that all that had sustained me should give way at once, and that I should die of terror and my conscience' (ch. 59). Indeed the spontaneous combustion of Krook is just such a rapid fulfillment of a process which has been preparing itself invisibly for a long time, just as the stroke which paralyzes Sir Leicester makes him physically what he spiritually has been all along, a frozen and outmoded form of life, speaking 'mere jumble and jargon' (ch. 56).

In all these cases, it is as though a hidden orientation suddenly revealed itself when, all restraint gone, the character yields at last to a destiny which has been attracting him with ever-increasing intensity. As Bucket says, 'the frost breaks up, and the water runs' (ch. 54). It does not run randomly, however, but toward a center which has all along been exerting its gravitational pull. This pull does not now commence, but only now manifests itself.

And so Miss Flite can speak of the Court of Chancery not as a first cause, but as a final cause drawing men to their ruin by means of its irresistible magnetic attraction:

'There's a cruel attraction in the place. You *can't* leave it. And you *must* expect. . . . It's the Mace and Seal upon the table.'
What could they do, did she think? I mildly asked her.
'Draw,' returned Miss Flite. 'Draw people on, my dear. Draw peace out of them. Sense out of them. Good looks out of them. Good qualities out of them. I have felt them even drawing my rest away in the night. Cold and glittering devils!' (ch. 35)

For many characters their disintegration is not so much the working out of a chain of causes and effects begun long in the past as it is the fatal convergence of their inner lives and their external situations toward a point where both will coincide at their death. Richard had mistakenly believed that 'either the suit must be ended . . . or the suitor' (ch. 51). But he is slowly consumed by his vampire-like lawyer, Vholes, just as the case of Jarndyce and Jarndyce is entirely consumed in costs. When both processes are finally complete, Vholes gives 'one gasp as if he had swallowed the last morsel of his client' (ch. 65). The termination of the interminable case coincides necessarily with the exhaustion of all the money involved in it, and with the simultaneous death of Richard. All of these events inevitably occur together as the vanishing point toward which all the parallel motions have been converging, as toward their final cause. This temporal progression is glimpsed by Esther in a momentary scene which prognosticates Richard's fate. It is a good example of the way scenes in Dickens which are initially merely narrative realism are transformed into symbolic expressions of the entire destiny of a character:

I shall never forget those two seated side by side in the lantern's light; Richard, all flush and fire and laughter, with the reins in his hand; Mr Vholes, quite still, black-gloved, and buttoned up, looking at him as if he were looking at his prey and charming it. I have before me the whole picture of the warm dark night, the summer lightning, the dusty track of road closed in by hedgerows and high trees, the gaunt pale horse with his ears pricked up, and the driving away at speed to Jarndyce and Jarndyce. (ch. 37)

In the same way the life and death of Jo the crossing sweeper are made symbolic. During his life Jo has been continually forced to 'move on'. His death is imaged as the 'breaking down' of a cart that as it disintegrates approaches closer and closer to an end point which will be its total fragmentation: 'For the cart so hard to draw, is near its journey's end, and drags over stony ground. All round the clock it labours up the broken steps, shattered and worn. Not many times can the sun rise, and behold it still upon its weary road' (ch. 47). And so the death of Lady Dedlock is described as a journey which is the slow closing in of her destiny: 'When I saw my Lady yesterday . . . she looked to me . . . as if the step on the Ghost's Walk had almost walked her down' (ch. 58). Like Richard's future, the prospect before and beside the road which she is journeying is getting narrower and narrower. The end point will be her death, the complete extinction of all possibility of choice or movement: 'The dark road I have trodden for so many years will end where it will. I follow it alone to the end, whatever the end be. . . . [Danger] has closed around me, almost as awfully as if these woods of Chesney Wold had closed around the house; but my course through it is the same' (ch. 36).

But this sudden break-up of things when the keystone of the arch has been removed may be imaged not as a narrowing, but as a descent deeper and deeper into the pit of the dark and unformed. When the fragile foundations which have been precariously upholding things give way, there is a sudden drop vertically into infernal depths. The Chancery suit is a 'dead sea' (ch. 37), and Richard 'sink[s] deeper and deeper into difficulty every day, continually hoping and continually disappointed, conscious of change upon change for the worse in [himself]' (ch. 39). Mr Snagsby, being led by Bucket and his colleagues into the heart of Tom-all-Alone's, 'feels as if he were going, every moment deeper and deeper down, into the infernal gulf' (ch. 22). What he sees is like a vision of hell itself. Not the least horrible part of this visionary experience is the way the human dwellers

in Tom-all-Alone's seem to have been transformed into the
elements they live in, the fog and mud: '. . . Mr Snagsby passes
along the middle of a villainous street, undrained, unventilated,
deep in black mud and corrupt water. . . . [T]he crowd flows
round, and from its squalid depths obsequious advice heaves up
to Mr Bucket. Whenever they move, and the angry bull's-eyes
glare, it fades away, and flits about them up the alleys, and in the
ruins, and behind the walls . . .' (ch. 22).

But it is Lady Dedlock's journey to death, after the murder of
Tulkinghorn has revealed her secret, which is the most elaborate
dramatization of this kind of disintegration. The chase after Lady
Dedlock by Bucket and Esther is not simply a Victorian melodrama. It is a subtly symbolic dramatization of the destiny of
Lady Dedlock and of her relation to her daughter. Once her
'freezing mood' is melted, she rapidly becomes, like Poe's
mesmerized man when his trance is broken, what she has really
been all along: dead. The thawing snow, the change of direction
from a centrifugal flight outward from the city to a return to the
center of disintegration and corruption where her dead lover lies
buried, her disguise in the dress of a brickmaker's wife whose
baby has died, all these function symbolically. Here, more intensely than for any other character, we experience the descent
into formlessness which follows inevitably the failure to achieve
a proper relation to the onward motion of time.

Bucket's chase after Lady Dedlock is presented through
Esther's eyes. All that happens has for her a visionary, dreamlike quality: 'I was far from sure that I was not in a dream' (ch.
57); '. . . the stained house fronts put on human shapes and looked
at me . . . great water-gates seemed to be opening and closing in
my head, or in the air . . . the unreal things were more substantial than the real' (ch. 59). The dominant symbol of the whole
sequence is contained here in the image of water-gates opening
and closing. The process of Lady Dedlock's dying after her
freezing mood has broken is mirrored in nature itself in the
melting snow which lies everywhere that night: 'From the por-
tico, from the eaves, from the parapet, from every ledge and
post and pillar, drips the thawed snow. It has crept, as if for

shelter, into the lintels of the great door – under it, into the corners of the windows, into every chink and crevice of retreat, and there wastes and dies' (ch. 58).

At the center of all this melting is perhaps the river, which is reached by a 'labyrinth of streets' (ch. 57). There, Bucket fears, Lady Dedlock may be found: '. . . he gazed into the profound black pit of water, with a face that made my heart die within me. The river had a fearful look, so overcast and secret, creeping away so fast between the low flat lines of shore: so heavy with indistinct and awful shapes, both of substance and shadow: so deathlike and mysterious' (ch. 57). But the real center, reached by 'descending into a deeper complication of such streets' (ch. 59), is the pauper graveyard, the low point into which all things are resolving, the center of anonymity, putrefaction, and formlessness, the point at which Lady Dedlock at last becomes herself at the very moment of her death:

The gate was closed. Beyond it, was a burial-ground – a dreadful spot in which the night was very slowly stirring; but where I could dimly see heaps of dishonoured graves and stones, hemmed in by filthy houses, with a few dull lights in their windows, and on whose walls a thick humidity broke out like a disease. On the step at the gate, drenched in the fearful wet of such a place, which oozed and splashed down everywhere, I saw, with a cry of pity and horror, a woman lying – Jenny, the mother of the dead child. (ch. 59)

But the woman is, of course, really Lady Dedlock, herself the mother of a dead child, the child Esther might have been. That Lady Dedlock's death is in a way a liberation is suggested by her contrary movements during her flight out from the city and then back toward its dark center. At the extremity of her outward flight she sends her surrogate, the brickmaker's wife, on out into the open country to lead her pursuers astray. This woman, in her movement toward freedom and openness, is Lady Dedlock's representative only because Lady Dedlock herself voluntarily chooses to return to her destined death at Nemo's grave, or, rather, to her death at a place where she is still shut off by one final symbolic barrier, the closed gate, from union

with her dead lover. In assuming at last the self she has been
fleeing for so long, Lady Dedlock achieves the only kind of freedom possible in Dickens' world, the freedom to be one's destined
self, the Kierkegaardian freedom to will to accept oneself as what
one already irrevocably is.

But for most of the characters, even such a narrow freedom is
not possible. Their decomposition happens to them, rather than
being chosen, and the image for their final end is not even permitted the hint of life-giving regeneration suggested by Lady
Dedlock's melting from her frozen state. Their lives are single
cases of a vast process of disintegration into dust, and the entire
world of the novel is being transformed into 'ashes . . . falling
on ashes, and dust on dust' (ch. 39):

In his lowering magazine of dust, the universal article into which
his papers and himself, and all his clients, and all things of earth,
animate and inanimate, are resolving, Mr Tulkinghorn sits at one
of the open windows. . . . (ch. 22)

II

I think the business of art is to lay all that ground carefully, not
with the care that conceals itself – to show, by a backward light,
what everything has been working to – but only to *suggest*, until
the fulfilment comes. These are the ways of Providence, of which
ways all art is but a little imitation.

(Letter to Collins)[2]

The world of *Bleak House* at first seemed to be a collection of
unrelated fragments plunged into an ubiquitous fog. Then we
recognized the presence, in isolated centers, of repetitive same-
ness. Now both recognitions have been replaced by the vision of
an omnipresent decomposition, going forward steadily, and, it
seems, irreversibly, everywhere in the world. Is there any 'open
window'? Is there any possibility of escape from this universal
process, or are all the characters, without exception, doomed to
experience no other life but the slow, steady moldering away of
their existences, as they helplessly drift toward a final dissolution?

This process of dissolution is not really, we come to see, the result of the self-enclosure of each individual life or each isolated circle of society. It comes rather from the absence of moral relationship between people in the novel. In one sense this absence leaves the characters isolated in the self-destructive depreciation of their beings, but in another sense it leaves them at the mercy of impersonal, unintentional contact with one another. For Dickens, the world is one unified whole, and if the relations between one man and another and between man and the world are not beneficent, they will be harmful. No man can cut himself off from the world and from other people. At first apparently a world of truncated fragments, *Bleak House* turns out to be a world in which everything is intimately connected with everything else, both temporally and spatially. Even people who seem to be separated by great gulfs of space, time, or social status actually have the most decisive effect on one another's lives. The world of *Bleak House* is a vast interlocking system in which any action or change in one place will have a corresponding and reciprocal effect on every other place:

On the coincidences, resemblances, and surprises of life, Dickens liked especially to dwell, and few things moved his fancy so pleasantly. The world, he would say, was so much smaller than we thought it; we were all so connected by fate without knowing it; people supposed to be far apart were so constantly elbowing each other; and to-morrow bore so close a resemblance to nothing half so much as to yesterday.[3]

. . . the whole bileing of people was mixed up in the same business, and no other. (ch. 59)

What connexion can there be, between the place in Lincoln-shire, the house in town, the Mercury in powder, and the where-about of Jo the outlaw with the broom, who had that distant ray of light upon him when he swept the church-yard-step? What connexion can there have been between many people in the innumerable histories of this world, who, from opposite sides of great gulfs, have, nevertheless, been very curiously brought together! (ch. 16)

This determining contact of people with one another is not abstract and distant, like Mrs Jellyby's 'telescopic philanthropy', or the apparent relation of suitors to the law. It is immediate and intimate, between one person and another, not between person and institution, or between person and person via institution. Mrs Jellyby's real action in the world is her destructive effect on her husband and children, not her charity to the natives of Borrioboola-Gha, just as Skimpole's real action is on his neglected family, and Lady Dedlock's is on the child she has unwittingly abandoned. This unintentional effect on things and people who are near is perfectly imaged in Mrs Pardiggle, who, with her 'rapacious benevolence' (ch. 8), and her 'show that was not conciliatory, of doing charity by wholesale, and of dealing in it to a large extent' (ch. 8), has the strange power of upsetting things in any room she enters: '. . . she knocked down little chairs with her skirts that were quite a great way off' (ch. 8).

Bleak House nevertheless contains many cases of an apparently mechanical and impersonal liaison between people who are either ignorant of one another, or who voluntarily refuse responsibility for one another. Skimpole might be speaking for almost all the characters when he says: 'I never was responsible in my life – I can't be' (ch. 37). The effect of this universal abnegation of responsibility is that many of the characters feel themselves to be caught up in a vast mechanical system of which they are the helpless victims. The system is run by laws, but these laws are unfathomable, and what will happen is altogether unpredictable. So Dickens says of Richard Carstone: '. . . the uncertainties and delays of the Chancery suit had imparted to his nature something of the careless spirit of a gamester, who felt that he was part of a great gaming system' (ch. 17). The alienation of such characters is to be unable to come face to face with the human beings who have caused their plight. They are coerced into a transformation which is more physical than moral and cannot be resisted by human means:

. . . it is in the subtle poison of such abuses to breed such diseases. His blood is infected, and objects lose their natural aspects in his sight. It is not *his* fault. (ch. 35)

The system! I am told, on all hands, it's the system. I mustn't
look to individuals. It's the system. I mustn't go into Court, and
say, 'My Lord, I beg to know this from you – is this right or
wrong? Have you the face to tell me I have received justice, and
therefore am dismissed?' My Lord knows nothing of it. He sits
there, to administer the system. (ch. 15)

This sense of being destroyed by an impersonal system may
make the characters feel that they are destructively involved, as
when Esther in her delirium dreams that 'strung together somewhere in great black space, there was a flaming necklace, or ring,
or starry circle of some kind, of which *I* was one of the beads!'
(ch. 35) Instead of being open to a future of possibility and
hope, such a character's relationship to the world is a narrow
contact with immediate surroundings which absolutely limit and
define. But this enclosure in the world may also appear as the
experience of being wholly cut off from the world, wholly *un-*
involved. Some people seem to have been overlooked by a vast
apparatus of impersonal institutions and fixed social structures.
So, the 'strangeness' of Jo's state is simultaneously to be manipu-
lated, pushed around as though he were an animal, and to be
utterly ignored: 'To be hustled, and jostled, and moved on; and
really to feel that it would appear to be perfectly true that I have
no business, here, or there, or anywhere; and yet to be perplexed
by the consideration that I *am* here somehow, too, and everybody
overlooked me until I became the creature that I am!' (ch. 16);
'He is of no order and no place; neither of the beasts, nor of
humanity' (ch. 47).

The effect of this mechanical involvement in the world, an
involvement which leaves the inner self of the person untouched
and isolated, is a further form of alienation. Such characters lose
the sense of their own existence. They feel separated from themselves, or feel that their experiences do not happen to them, but
merely to 'someone'. A wide gap opens between the selves who
are involved in the world of impersonal institutions, and the
selves they really are, and the latter, lacking all contact with the
world, dissolve and disappear into a profound inner void. It is a
void of which the characters themselves are not even aware. So

Skimpole speaks 'of himself as if he were not at all his own affair,
as if Skimpole were a third person' (ch. 6), 'as if he had been
mentioning a curious little fact about somebody else' (ch. 37).
He divides himself into two persons, and in a 'fantastic way'
'[takes] himself under his own protection and argue[s] about that
curious person' (ch. 43). This self-division is analogous to the
impersonal connection between people involved in the Chancery
suit, or in telescopic philanthropy. To be so separated from oneself that one's experiences seem to happen to someone else is to
be wholly without a proper inherence in the world. And yet such
are the pressures of existence that in sheer self-defense some
characters adopt this mode of presence-absence in the world.
'You talk of yourself as if you were somebody else', says Jarndyce to George Rouncewell, who has been falsely accused of
murder. And George answers, 'I don't see how an innocent
man is to make up his mind to this kind of thing without knock-
ing his head against the walls, unless he takes it in that point of
view' (ch. 52).

But, even if it is only negative evidence, such modes of existence in *Bleak House* are important proof that the disintegrative
process in which so many of the characters are caught is not
necessary, but is the result of the absence of moral relationships.
If people are not related morally, they will be related amorally in
a vast destructive process. The dominating symbol of this unintentional contact between people is disease – the disease which
is bred in the 'poisoned air' (ch. 11) of Tom-all-Alone's, and
spreads from Nemo's graveyard to Jo the crossing sweeper, and
then to Esther, Lady Dedlock's daughter and Nemo's daughter
too. Corruption multiplies itself in the world of *Bleak House*,
and disorder spreads, but only in the absence of a restraining
human principle of order. If the world is going to pieces, it is
man's fault, and the abandoned world will turn on the irrespon-
sible-responsible ones, and take its revenge:

[Tom] has his revenge. Even the winds are his messengers, and
they serve him in these hours of darkness. There is not a drop of
Tom's corrupted blood but propagates infection and contagion
somewhere. . . . There is not an atom of Tom's slime, not a cubic

inch of any pestilential gas in which he lives, not one obscenity or degradation about him, not an ignorance, not a wickedness, not a brutality of his committing, but shall work its retribution, through every order of society, up to the proudest of the proud, and to the highest of the high. (ch. 46)

The world, then, is in man's hands. If its decomposition is his fault, it is possible that he might be able to reverse this decay and put the world back together. But how and where is he going to get the strength for this constructive and life-giving act? By himself he seems powerless to stop the rotting away of the world, a rotting which eventually involves him too, and makes of the whole earth, human and material, a single system of self-destruction.

But for some few characters just such a rescuing reconstruction of the world seems possible. The world organizes itself around such characters as orderly, stable, and clarified, as an integrated circle of which they are the center. 'Everything about you is in perfect order and discipline', says George Rouncewell to his brother the ironmaster (ch. 63), and Richard says of Allan Woodcourt: '. . . the place brightens whenever he comes' (ch. 51). 'You can', he says, 'pursue your art for its own sake; and can put your hand upon the plough, and never turn; and can strike a purpose out of anything' (ch. 51). To Esther all the 'happiness' of her life seems to '[shine] like a light from one central figure' (Jarndyce) (ch. 44). And Caddy Jellyby is able to create a happy home for her husband, 'striking out' 'a natural, wholesome, loving course of industry and perseverance that [is] quite as good as a Mission' (ch. 38). But it is Esther herself who provides the best example of this quasi-magical power to organize and sustain the world. Skimpole describes her as 'intent upon the perfect working of the whole little orderly system of which [she is] the centre' (ch. 37), and she says of herself: 'I thought it best to be as useful as I could, and to render what kind services I could, to those immediately about me; and to try to let that circle of duty gradually and naturally expand itself' (ch. 8). She is able to succeed in this magnificently. 'Ringing' herself into any new situation with a 'merry little peal' of her housekeeping keys, she is able with

apparent ease to organize and control the world, to reduce it to
order. The world yields resistlessly to her volition and action.
She is what Jarndyce calls her: the 'little old woman of the
Child's . . . Rhyme' who 'sweep[s] the cobwebs out of the sky'
(ch. 8).

The world in Esther's presence, to her vision of it, has another
extremely important quality, a quality which it seems altogether
to lack for the other characters. To her it appears to be the
abiding place of a beneficent Providence whose strength she
shares, and who orders all the world and every event of her life
in the kindly manipulation of her destiny. For her, the world
openly reveals its secret spiritual power. This openness, this
depth and clarity, and the visible presence in them of an immanent deity, are the keynotes of the scenic perspectives we see
through her eyes:

We had one favourite spot, deep in moss and last year's leaves,
where there were some felled trees from which the bark was all
stripped off. Seated among these, we looked through a green
vista supported by thousands of natural columns, the whitened
stems of trees, upon a distant prospect made so radiant by its
contrast with the shade in which we sat, and made so precious
by the arched perspective through which we saw it, that it was
like a glimpse of the better land. (ch. 18)

O, the solemn woods over which the light and shadow travelled
swiftly, as if Heavenly wings were sweeping on benignant
errands through the summer air. . . . (ch. 18)

The divine power is not simply there in nature, glimpsed by
Esther as a kind of unattainable transcendence which remains at
a distance. Rather, it is felt as something close and intimate,
present as much in her own life as in nature. It is immanent and
near, and sustains her with its friendly power:

It was grand . . . to hear the solemn thunder, and to see the lightning; and while thinking with awe of the tremendous powers by
which our little lives are encompassed, to consider how beneficent they are, and how upon the smallest flower and leaf there
was already a freshness poured from all this seeming rage, which
seemed to make creation new again. (ch. 18)

This storm is the occasion of Esther's first direct contact with her mother. It is as though God had intended the storm, and had intended the storms of suffering too that are to make Esther a new person, recreate her as a different self. It is not by accident that Esther's visions of openings in the prospect which reveal a providential presence are in many cases views of Chesney Wold. For it is just in her relationship to her mother and to Chesney Wold that Providence seems to be most clearly working in Esther's life: 'I saw very well,' she says, 'how many things had worked together, for my welfare. . . . I knew I was as innocent of my birth as a queen of hers; and that before my Heavenly Father I should not be punished for birth, nor a queen rewarded for it' (ch. 36).

Moreover, Esther is able to draw strength from Providence. She is able through prayer to feel, at crucial moments of her life, that divine grace has descended into her own being, and has made it possible for her to endure her life and carry on her work as a bringer of light and order:

I repeated the old childish prayer in its old childish words, and found that its old peace had not departed from it. (ch. 35)

I opened my grateful heart to Heaven in thankfulness for its Providence to me and its care of me, and fell asleep. (ch. 17)

Esther's power to create a circle of order and meaning around her does not, then, come from herself, but from the God who appears present to her everywhere in the world and in her own life. But does this immanent deity appear in the world to the other characters? Does He appear to the narrator in those times when he withdraws from the human actions he is describing and surveys the world as a totality and as something in which no human consciousness but his own detached awareness is active?

The answer is easy to give. To the cool, uninvolved gaze of the narrator, the world appears again and again as the dwelling place of a light which is rapidly, at this very moment, fading away, withdrawing to an infinite distance, and leaving the world to absolute darkness: 'Darkness rests upon Tom-all-Alone's. Dilating and dilating since the sun went down last night, it has gradually swelled until it fills every void in the place. . . . The blackest nightmare in the infernal stables grazes on Tom-all-Alone's, and Tom is fast asleep' (ch. 46). And, strangely enough, the narrator has this frightening vision of a world being transformed to formless darkness when perceiving the very scene which brought Esther her apprehension of an immanent Providence. This darkness is seen as the emblem of Lady Dedlock's life, not of Esther's:

> . . . the light of the drawing-room seems gradually contracting and dwindling until it shall be no more. (ch. 66)

But the fire of the sun is dying. Even now the floor is dusky and shadow slowly mounts the walls, bringing the Dedlocks down like age and death. And now, upon my lady's picture over the great chimney-piece, a weird shade falls from some old tree, that turns it pale, and flutters it, and looks as if a great arm held a veil or hood, watching an opportunity to draw it over her. Higher and darker rises shadow on the wall – now a red gloom on the ceiling – now the fire is out. (ch. 40)

If the narrator sees the light of a spiritual presence at all, he glimpses it precisely as a transcendence rather than as an immanence. It is seen as an inhumanly distant power which refuses, or is unable, to relate itself to the world, and either hovers motionlessly, tantalizingly unattainable, or is caught momentarily in the very act of withdrawing. 'All that prospect, which from the terrace looked so near, has moved solemnly away, and changed – not the first nor the last of beautiful things that look so near and will so change – into a distant phantom' (ch. 40).

If this receding transcendence enters the human world at all, it enters to renew it by rest, by bringing it a momentary repose. That is to say, to the narrator's eye, it seems that the transcendent light is so incommensurate with the nature of human existence in a corrupt world, that it can only come into this world by bringing a temporary end to that existence, an end of sleep, rest, and forgetfulness which is a rehearsal of death. The world is at peace, it is the presence rather than the absence of God, only when there is no human consciousness left awake to endure awareness of the pain of living, or only a single human consciousness, the consciousness of a watcher who is altogether uninvolved in the world, seeing it in a pure lucidity of perception:

When the moon shines very brilliantly, a solitude and stillness seem to proceed from her, that influence even crowded places full of life. Not only is it a still night on dusty high roads and on hill-summits, whence a wide expanse of country may be seen in repose, quieter and quieter as it spreads away into a fringe of trees against the sky, with the grey ghost of a bloom upon them ... not only is it a still night on the deep, and on the shore where the watcher stands to see the ship with her spread wings cross the path of light that appears to be presented to only him; but even on this stranger's wilderness of London there is some rest. (ch. 48)

But this presence of a repose which emanates from a divine source is also an absence. It is the total absence of ordinary day-light life. God appears only when the world is seen for a moment from the viewpoint of utter solitude, only when the path of light appears to be presented to a single watcher. This solitary watching is as close as any human being can come to seeing the world as it would appear if there were no human consciousness present in it at all. If man is present as involved in the world, as manipulating it for his own ends, God disappears. If man withdraws from the world, God appears, but only as something wholly foreign to man, as something which is frightening proof of man's nonentity. This vision of a world without human presence is seen at Chesney Wold when 'the great house, needing habitation more than ever, is like a body without life' (ch. 40), when there is 'no family to come and go, no visitors to be the souls of pale cold shapes of rooms' (ch. 66). But in the absence of human beings who might give 'souls' to inanimate objects, an inhuman presence appears, a cold light whose life is more disquieting than the complete death of the uninhabited house would have been: 'The clear cold sunshine glances into the brittle woods, and approvingly beholds the sharp wind scattering the leaves and drying the moss. It glides over the park after the moving shadows of the clouds, and chases them, and never catches them, all day. It looks in at the windows, and touches the ancestral portraits with bars and patches of brightness, never contemplated by the painters' (ch. 12). At such a time when the world is seen without a human presence, 'it is . . . awful, stealing through [the house], to think of the live people who have slept in the solitary bedrooms: to say nothing of the dead' (ch. 40). It is awful to think of the live people because, in their absence, one recognizes suddenly that they are in a way absent even when they are present. One sees that the living are, from the point of view of the transcendent light, or of the wholly detached spectator, the exact equivalent of the dead. The nothingness of human existence appears, then, at the very moment when the existence of some transhuman spirit is recognized. Man and God seem to be altogether incompatible, to cancel one another out. So, in a striking passage, Dickens shows us a Chesney Wold without any inhabitant at all but the pictured forms on the walls, and suggests that the presence of a living Sir Leicester would not change the scene. For a moment the small difference that a human presence seems to make dissolves into complete nothingness. If men 'leave no blank to miss them' when they die, are they not really that same blank when they are alive?

Dreary and solemn the old house looks, with so many appliances of habitation, and with no inhabitants except the pictured forms upon the walls. So did these come and go, a Dedlock in possession might have ruminated passing along; so did they see this gallery hushed and quiet, as I see it now; so think, as I think, of the gap that they would make in this domain when they were gone; so find it, as I find it, difficult to believe that it could be, without them; so pass from my world, as I pass from theirs, now closing the reverberating door; so leave no blank to miss them, and so die. (ch. 40)

The narrator's detached observation of the world leads in *Bleak House*, as in *Martin Chuzzlewit*, but in a different way, to a discovery of the essential nothingness of the human spirit. Here the discovery is posited on the idea of death, a death which somehow moves from its position as the end point of a long life, and undermines, hollows out, that life itself.

Does this mean that Esther's sense of an intimate contact between her life and Providence is a fiction, that she merely thinks she sees something which is not really there at all? Does this mean that the presence of Esther to a world which she makes orderly is necessarily dependent on the absence of God from all that she does? Is it wholly impossible for human action to install God in the world, to bring Him into the world and to keep Him there as its foundation and justification? Apparently so.

And yet the narrator, precisely because of his solitude, is not only able to see the brightness of the divine presence; he is also able to see the human world of the novel in its light. He can identify himself with its perspective, as when he praises Sir Leicester for his fidelity to Lady Dedlock:

His noble earnestness, his fidelity, his gallant shielding of her, his generous conquest of his own wrong, and his own pride for her sake, are simply honourable, manly, and true. Nothing less worthy can be seen through the lustre of such qualities in the commonest mechanic, nothing less worthy can be seen in the best-born gentleman. In such a light both aspire alike, both rise alike, both children of the dust shine equally. (ch. 58)

To see a human action or event from this point of view is to see it in terms of the nullity of all social distinctions, of all worldly values. If it is not to see the divine transcendence as inherent in the social world, it is at least to see that human actions may have some value for this transcendence. It is to see the world from the viewpoint of a total disengagement from all earthly aims and expectations, a disengagement which allows true values suddenly to appear. Are there any characters in *Bleak House* who achieve this disengagement and this clarification?

Just such clarifications occur for Jo and for Richard Carstone at the moment of their deaths. '. . . he is', Chadband says of Jo, 'devoid of the light that shines in upon some of us. What is that light? What is it? I ask you what is that light?' (ch. 25) This light, Dickens tells us, is what would appear 'if the Chadbands, removing their own persons from the light, would but show it thee in simple reverence' (ch. 25). As he lies dying Jo says, 'It's turned wery dark, sir', and asks, 'Is there any light a-comin?' And at the moment of Jo's death, when he has left this obscure world altogether, Dickens says of him: 'The light is come upon the dark benighted way' (ch. 47).

For Richard Carstone, this clarification comes just before his death, while he is still momentarily in the human world. His blindness has been precisely his infatuation, 'the clouded, eager, seeking look' (ch. 37) that went with having 'no care, no mind, no heart, no soul, but for one thing' (ch. 45). But, like Racine's Phèdre, Richard is permitted a few moments of clear vision just before he dies, moments which are possible only because he has been liberated from his infatuation by the fatal ending of the suit. Now he can see that his life has been 'a troubled dream' (ch. 65), and Jarndyce can say for him: '. . . the clouds have cleared away, and it is bright now. We can see now. We were all bewildered . . . more or less' (ch. 65). Richard feels that he is now at last able to 'begin the world', but of course it is too late, and the world he begins is 'not this world'. It is 'the world that sets this right' (ch. 65).

The light, we recognize, appears only to those people who for some reason have abandoned all hope in an earthly judgment. Only such people can relate themselves to the true Justice, can make that Justice come into being for this world. This reversal is a double one. By being disabused of a narrow, enclosed faith in the world, the characters achieve a clarification, a breadth of view which is in a sense an appropriation of the world. It is Esther's good fortune to be already, at the beginning of her life, because of the social alienation of her illegitimacy (strongly impressed upon her by her foster mother), disengaged from the social world and unblinded by any false expectations from it.

In *Bleak House*, then, Dickens shows the possibility of a truly moral life. In the early novels the choices were passive expectancy or selfish activity. To act was, except for semi-divine human providences, like Mr Brownlow or old Martin Chuzzlewit, inevitably to act immorally, to impose a rigorous and

coercive form on the world and on other people. It was to deceive
them, and to be either self-deceived or consciously deceiving.
Now, in *Bleak House*, Dickens goes beyond this. He sees that
there is something between these two extremes, that there is a
way in which human beings can act morally. Between the two
extremes of a passivity which allows the world to return to
primeval slime, or a rigid and coercive will which imposes an
inhuman fixity on the world, there is glimpsed the possibility of
a voluntary action which constitutes the world as an order. The
premise for this possibility is the idea that human beings inhere
in the world, that man and the world participate in one another.
It is only because human beings are detached from the world
that it appears fragmentary and disconnected. Moreover, if
human beings detach themselves from the world, it will become
more and more disordered and fragmentary.

And there is a true Providence in *Bleak House*. It does not,
however, work within things, nor does it work within all men,
nor in any man all of the time. It appears to be intermittent, even
though it may secretly be continuous. It is only after this grace
and the responsibility someone takes to accept it have permitted
the creation of a limited circle of duty that this enclosed place
can be seen as orderly and intelligible, can be seen as providential.
Providence is powerless to work in things for man, and can only
work through the heart of man himself. God has withdrawn himself from the world of *Bleak House*. He apparently does not exist
immanently within things as an ubiquitous Providence ordering
all events for good in mysterious ways. He does not exist in
many events at all. He has left the human world and the objective world to human beings. It is their responsibility.

But what sort of voluntary action will succeed in bringing
God to earth? It is not a question of forming a rigid plan and
coercively carrying it out by forceful action. It is much easier to
misuse the will than to use it correctly. The will, for Dickens,
must always act in accordance with the nature of things as they
already are. Each person is thrown into a world and into a situation in the world which he has not chosen. All his attempts to
deny this, to reject the nature of the world as it is, are doomed

to failure. Too much will, the inhumanly fixed will of Lady Dedlock and Tulkinghorn or of Sir Leicester's conservatism,
attempts to hold the world to an inhuman permanence. The will
cannot act in this positive way. On the other hand, the alternative of no will, of mere passive expectation, such as we find in
Miss Flite, Skimpole, or Richard Carstone, is no more effective.
Richard's failure is a failure, precisely, of will. 'I shall have to
work my own way', he says, echoing Jarndyce, who had said,
'. . . he must make some choice for himself' (ch. 8). But instead
of choosing and acting he 'build[s] as many castles in the air as
would man the great wall of China' (ch. 14). He is continually
wiping the slate clean of all that he has done so far, and continually deciding to 'make a clear beginning altogether' (ch. 24).
He is like Mr Jellyby, who 'sometimes half took his coat off, as if
with an intention of helping by a great exertion; but he never got
any further. His sole occupation was to sit with his head against
the wall . . .' (ch. 50). But, just as it is fatal to expect a judgment
from the human court, so it is equally fatal to expect God to do
it all. God helps those who help themselves. 'Trust in nothing',
says Jarndyce, 'but in Providence and your own efforts' (ch. 13).
To trust either of these separately will fail. God's grace can oper-
ate only through those who, like Esther and Jarndyce, take
matters into their own hands.

The extremes of violent frontal attack and passive expectancy
inevitably fail. Just what form, then, must this shouldering of
responsibility take to be successful? It is not machinery, not the
actual doing or making of anything. Esther's creation of a small
area of order and significance around her is primarily a spiritual
act. The human will must accept the fact that its action must be
continuous and perpetual. The world must be held together from
moment to moment. Esther's success comes from the fact that
she submits to the human condition which she so vividly imagines in her delirious dream: '. . . I laboured up colossal staircases,
ever striving to reach the top, and ever turned, as I have seen a
worm in a garden path, by some obstruction, and labouring
again' (ch. 35). The human will must act negatively rather than
coercively and positively. It must act by a yielding to time and to

tradition, rather than through an attempt to freeze the former or break from the latter.

The nature and results of this yielding can be seen in the good households in the novel. The good household possesses the orderly multiplicity and diversity of Bleak House, with its many rooms and passages, its 'quaint variety' (ch. 6), its continual surprises: 'It was one of those delightfully irregular houses where you go up and down steps out of one room into another, and where you come upon more rooms when you think you have seen all there are, and where there is a bountiful provision of little halls and passages, and where you find still older cottage-rooms in unexpected places, with lattice windows and green growth pressing through them' (ch. 6). Such a 'pleasantly irregular' house allows full room for the freedom and privacy of those living there. And yet, though there is no sense of a mechanical regimen, everything is orderly and planned.

The temporal existence of such a household will be like that of Boythorn's dwelling, which is very unlike Boythorn himself. His milieu is a world of repose, but not of paralyzed fixity. Its temporal duration is a slow maturing which is the very opposite of the process of disintegration accelerating toward death which is so nearly ubiquitous in *Bleak House*. Rather than being the loss of utility and value in the part and of structure in the whole, it is a progressive enrichment through time. Nothing of the past is lost. The past still exists as the enhancement of the present, and the present therefore contains an inexhaustible multiplicity and abundance. The temporal dimension of Boythorn's house is an almost organic growth in which the past exists not only as the outward signs of fruitfulness and life, but as an inward warmth which is the stored up vitality of long years. It is a world of mellowness and plenitude:

He lived in a pretty house, formerly the Parsonage-house, with a lawn in front, a bright flower-garden at the side, and a well-stocked orchard and kitchen-garden in the rear, enclosed with a venerable wall that had of itself a ripened ruddy look. But, indeed, everything about the place wore an aspect of maturity and abundance. . . . [T]he very shadows of the cherry-trees and

apple-trees were heavy with fruit, the gooseberry-bushes were
so laden that their branches arched and rested on the earth, the
strawberries and raspberries grew in like profusion, and the
peaches basked by the hundred on the wall. . . . [T]here were
such heaps of drooping pods, and marrows, and cucumbers, that
every foot of ground appeared a vegetable treasury. . . . [T]he
wall had such a ripening influence that where, here and there
high up, a disused nail and scrap of list still clung to it, it was
easy to fancy that they had mellowed with the changing seasons,
and that they had rusted and decayed according to the common
fate. (ch. 18)

But the 'common fate' here is not, like the fate of the suitors in
Chancery, to be slowly used up and destroyed. Even the rusting
of nails and the decay of wood is, within Boythorn's precincts,
the accretion of value, an organic growth and maturing, rather
than a dissolution.

With such a yielding to time's maturing movement goes a
reverence for the past which makes of the present a living repetition of the past. Such are the celebrations of Mrs Bagnet's birthdays. These celebrations are a repeated ceremony through which
value is gained rather than emptied out: 'The auspicious event is
always commemorated according to certain forms, settled and
prescribed by Mr Bagnet some years since' (ch. 49). Mrs Bagnet
herself, like the family community of which she is the center, 'is
like a thoroughly fine day. Gets finer as she gets on' (ch. 27).
And the entire Bagnet household, as the result of a constant
maintaining of 'discipline', the continual renewal of a constructive activity which is based on family love and solidarity,
is a model of order and cleanliness (ch. 27).

But for Esther the moral and orderly world must be created
rather than accepted from the past. In the necessary conditions
of this creation we can see another form of the theme of repetition after an intervening gap which we found to be so important
in *Oliver Twist* and *Martin Chuzzlewit*. Nothing is more striking
in Dickens than the way many characters who are freed from
traditional morality or from a determined place in society simply
reaffirm a traditional and narrow morality. Their only freedom

is to have chosen this morality rather than having had it imposed upon them by force. The simplicity, the timidity, the conservatism, the domesticity, of the moral life of many of Dickens' good characters, all testify to Dickens' fear of a moral life of breadth, imagination, or novelty. Dickens sometimes seems to believe that only with this narrowness is the moral life likely to be successful. In a way Esther is, like Tom Pinch in *Martin Chuzzlewit*, seen from the outside by someone who recognizes her as an ideal, but as a limited ideal. It is an ideal which is impossible for the narrator because he is not so innocent as she is, because he is able to juxtapose her world against all the other worlds of the other characters, and against his own neutral, fragmented, optic world. There is, then, a subtle irony in Dickens' attitude toward Esther as narrator. He does not wholly identify himself with her experience or judgment. The acceptance of the bourgeois Protestant ethical principles of duty, public service, domesticity, responsibility, frugality, thrift, cleanliness, orderliness, and self-discipline is qualified and in a way undermined by the juxtaposition of the two modes of narration. The suggestion is that the world can only be seen as Esther sees it, as moral, as containing an immanent Providence, through her eyes. The narrator cannot see the world in this way through his own neutral point of view. Moreover, in Lady Dedlock, Dickens presents someone who has had a chance at the broad, imaginative moral life with all its complexities. But Lady Dedlock's struggles with the kind of moral problems which will command the center of Henry James' novels, and even of Meredith's, are only at the periphery of *Bleak House*. Her real decision has taken place long before the novel begins. And she is, of course, destroyed by the ambiguous moral position into which she has put herself by first becoming the lover of Captain Hawdon and then marrying Sir Leicester. For Esther, the moral life is simpler, the world yields more easily to spirit, than is shown to be the case by the novel as a whole. For Esther duty, kindness, self-sacrifice make the world orderly, and in the end everything she has given up is given back to her. But for Lady Dedlock, who has made a breakthrough to a complex, ambiguous, moral world, things are not so easy. Things are for her impossible of solution. To Dickens the fear of a broad, imaginative, daring moral life seems to have presented itself as a sense that the will would find great difficulty in operating at all, or in operating other than destructively, once it was liberated into self-consciousness. Therefore the unself-conscious, instinctive goodness of Esther seemed to him the only possibility.

But it was absolutely necessary, for Dickens, that Esther should be free to reaffirm this narrow and conventional morality. Against the dead duration of the Smallweeds, which is a hypnotized repetition, or the progressive duration of Richard or Gridley, which is a single curve of descent deeper and deeper into the pit of darkness, or the reaffirmation of her true self by Lady Dedlock, which necessarily coincides with her death, there is the radically transforming discovery of her true self by Esther. As opposed to the other characters, Esther's historical existence is a truly dramatic progression with a climax centering on the reversal of her orientation when she discovers her origin, and on her liberation into an authentic life when she chooses to accept the self she finds herself to be. Her 'reiteration' of herself, like Oliver's and Martin's, is broken by a long interval of separation from herself, a separation which is not like, Lady Dedlock's, voluntary, but is caused by her real ignorance of who she is.

But Esther is not wholly self-sufficient. Her final happiness depends on the existence of two people who are, as she is, free from any faith in society and ,its values, and who choose to act morally toward her. The marriage of Allan and Esther is the marriage of two people who have no imposed ties with one another, and who freely choose one another. Final happiness for Esther can come not through her own efforts alone, but through Allan Woodcourt's voluntary surrender of all social determination of his choice of a wife. It is the liberating act of love. But even love does not break the law of Dickens' moral world which says that there is no ceasing to be the self one already is, no transformation with impunity into an entirely new self. Allan's love transforms Esther not by making her cease to be illegitimate and therefore socially alienated, but by choosing her as she is. The novel ends with a scene in which Allan tells Esther that the disfiguration of her face, caused by her illness, and the symbolic sign of her illegitimacy, has made her 'prettier than [she] ever [was]' (ch. 67). The full presentation of this theme is, however, obscured by the role of Jarndyce. He sacrifices his claim on Esther, and, like old Martin Chuzzlewit, gives the lovers to one another, and sets them up in a new Bleak House which is an exact repetition of the old. He thus makes it unnecessary for the lovers to accept full responsibility for their asocial act. But Woodcourt's choice of Esther, like Lady Dedlock's and Esther's choice of themselves, is an act of free volition. Dickens has now come to recognize that salvation cannot possibly come through mere passive waiting and the eventual acceptance of an identity and a place in the world given from the outside. It comes, Dickens sees now, only through an act of voluntary liberation. But this all-important act of will may turn out to be extremely difficult, as *Little Dorrit* is brilliantly to show.

SOURCE: *Charles Dickens: The World of his Novels* (1959).

NOTES

1. See Georges Poulet, 'L'Univers circonscrit d'Edgar Poe', in *Les Temps Modernes*, CXIV, CXV (1955) 2179–2204.
2. *The Letters of Charles Dickens*, ed. Walter Dexter, 3 vols (1938, the Nonesuch Dickens) III 125.
3. John Forster, *Life of Dickens*, 3 vols (Philadelphia, 1873–4) I (1873) 112. This passage is discussed by T. S. Eliot in his excellent essay on melodrama in Dickens and Collins: 'Wilkie Collins and Dickens', in *Selected Essays: 1917–1932* (New York, 1947) p. 378.

Monroe Engel

BLEAK HOUSE:
DEATH AND REALITY (1959)

IN *Bleak House*, as in *Dombey and Son*, death functions as a touchstone of reality. It is a measure of the wretchedness of man's earthly sojourn, awful and profound, but – and this is much to the point – more kindly than the torments imposed by society. One of Esther Summerson's earlier memories is of a sombre birthday, the only recognition of which was her godmother's remark after dinner: 'It would have been far better, little Esther, that you had had no birthday; that you had never been born!' When Caddy Jellyby gives her first confidence to Esther, her misery bursts from her uncontrollably: 'I wish I was dead! . . . I wish we were all dead. It would be a great deal better for us!' The bricklayer's wife, Liz, thinking of her friend Jenny's dead baby, says: 'Ah, Jenny, Jenny! . . . better so. Much better to think of dead than alive, Jenny! Much better!' And of her own child, sleeping, she says: 'If he should be turned bad, 'spite of all I could do, and the time should come when I should sit by him in his sleep, made hard and changed, an't it likely I should think of him as he lies in my lap now, and wish he had died as Jenny's child died!' Mr Jarndyce, horrified to find that Richard has based all his expectations on the outcome of the chancery suit, says: 'Whatever you do on this side the grave, never give one lingering glance towards the horrible phantom that has haunted us so many years. Better to borrow, better to beg, better to die!' Poor Mr Jellyby tells Caddy that she and her brothers and sisters have been allowed to grow up like Indians, without care or teaching, and that 'the best thing that could happen to them was, their being all Tomahawked together'. Esther again, when she discovers the secret of her parentage, feels and knows 'it would have been better and happier for many people, if indeed I had never breathed'. And Jo, when he is caught by Allan Woodcourt and Jenny, says:

'Can't you never let such an unfortnet as me alone? An't I unfortnet enough for you yet? How unfortnet do you want me fur to be? I've been a chivied and a chivied, fust by one on you and nixt by another on you, till I'm worritted to skins and bones. The Inkwhich warn't *my* fault. *I* done nothink. He wos wery good to me, he wos; he was the only one I knowed to speak to, as ever come across my crossing. It ain't wery likely I should want him to be Inkwhich'd. I only wish I wos, myself. I don't know why I don't go and make a hole in the water, I'm sure I don't.'

Jo is an extreme example of a recurrent type in Dickens' novels: the child already old with knowledge of the ways and miseries of the world. Guppy and Smallweed are repellent examples of the same type. But Jo, a far more extreme version, though repellent too, also stirs our compassion. Among many other things, Jo knows about dying. When Charley tells him he shouldn't sleep at the brick kiln, because people die there, he says: 'They dies everywheres. . . . They dies more than they lives, according to what *I* see.' And when it comes Jo's time to die, the fears he has are not of death. His only fear is of being taken back to Tom-All-Alone's. He thinks of death as being 'moved on as fur as ever I could go and couldn't be moved no furder'. It is peace for him, quiet, the end of the need to move on. Just before the end he starts up, afraid that he will not get to the paupers' burying ground in time – or that, once there, he will not be allowed to get in, that they will not unlock it for him. But at last:

The light is come upon the dark benighted way. Dead!

Dead, your Majesty. Dead, my lords and gentlemen. Dead, Right Reverends and Wrong Reverends of every order. Dead, men and women, born with Heavenly compassion in your hearts. And dying thus around us every day.

Jo is a central character in *Bleak House.* He might, in fact, be called *the* central character. In his notes for chapter 29, Dickens wrote: 'Then connect Esther and Jo.' And by one means or another, Jo is 'connected' with virtually all the characters of importance in *Bleak House*. This is not accident, nor even the story-maker's simple and inevitable extension of coincidence to tie his story together. The notes to *Bleak House* begin with several lists of possible titles for the novel. Every list but the final and deciding one starts with the title 'Tom-All-Alone's'. And in his notes for chapter 16, Dickens indicated that Tom-All-Alone's was 'the ruined property in Jarndyce and Jarndyce, already described by Mr Jarndyce'.

Mr Jarndyce does describe the property which he prophesies quite correctly will no longer be anything but the means to pay the lawyers' costs in the case.

It is a street of perishing blind houses, with their eyes stoned out; without a pane of glass, without so much as a window-frame, with the bare blank shutters tumbling from their hinges and falling asunder; the iron rails peeling away in flakes of rust; the chimneys sinking in; the stone steps to every door (and every door might be Death's Door) turning stagnant green; the very crutches on which the ruins are propped, decaying. These are the Great Seal's impressions . . . all over England – the children know them!'

Dickens is vehement against that moneyed world of fashion which is 'wrapped up in too much jeweller's cotton and fine wool, and cannot hear the rushing of the larger worlds, and cannot see them as they circle round the sun'. He insists that this ignorance does not just befall the well-to-do but that it is actually willed by them, that part of the *status quo* they wish to preserve is the *status quo* of their own ignorance, the peculiar ignorance of 'ladies and gentlemen . . . who have agreed to put a smooth glaze on the world, and to keep down all its realities. . . . Who have found out the perpetual stoppage.'

Such a 'perpetual stoppage' is, of course, as impossible as Dombey's 'double door of gold' to 'shut out all the world'. Truth has terrible ways to assert itself, and not even wealth, though it has many protections, is a barrier to infection. Tom-All-Alone's will have its revenge.

Even the winds are his messengers, and they serve him in these hours of darkness. There is not a drop of Tom's corrupted blood but propagates infection and contagion somewhere. It shall pollute, this very night, the choice stream ... of a Norman house, and his Grace shall not be able to say Nay to the infamous alliance. There is not an atom of Tom's slime, not a cubic inch of any pestilential gas in which he lives, not one obscenity or degradation about him, not an ignorance, not a wickedness, not a brutality of his committing, but shall work its retribution, through every order of society, up to the proudest of the proud, and to the highest of the high. Verily, what with tainting, plundering, and spoiling, Tom has his revenge.

Jo carries his fever about with him as he is hounded around the country. Charley catches it from him, and Esther Summerson catches it from Charley. They have been kind to Jo, but the realist Dickens knows that the fruits of social injustice are not distributed in any strict accordance with deserving. And at Jo's bedside, when he is dying, both Mr Jarndyce and Allan Woodcourt think 'how strangely Fate has entangled this rough outcast in the web of very different lives'.

Epidemic is nature's counterpart for revolution. In Dickens' mind, disease and oppression were closely linked. In 1854, the year after he finished *Bleak House*, he warned Lady Burdett-Coutts of the danger the government faced if it did not take proper measures to control cholera:

Let it [the cholera] come twice again, severely – the people advancing all the while in the knowledge that, humanly speaking, it is, like Typhus Fever in the mass, a preventible disease – and you will see such a shake in this country as never was seen on Earth since Sampson pulled the Temple down upon his head.[1]

The misery that makes people long for death also and similarly breeds violence. By this time in the fifties, revolution seemed a dreadful and present possibility to Dickens. It is surely the possibility that lurks in the fog and mire of *Bleak House*.

When Richard asks Krook why his shop is called Chancery, the old man starts to explain directly; then is diverted by Ada's hair, and says he has three sacks of ladies' hair below in his shop; then finally does explain that he and the Lord Chancellor 'both grub on in a muddle'. By this time and through his inadvertence, we suspect what the human consequences of this grubbing and muddling are. When Krook dissolves of spontaneous combustion, Dickens tells us that this is the death 'of all Lord Chancellors in all Courts, and of all authorities in all places under all names soever, where false pretenses are made, and where injustice is done . . . [a death] inborn, inbred, engendered in the corrupted humours of the vicious body itself'.

A kind of inevitable dissolution is the hope, but how much is invested in this hope? Will the Dedlocks (surely the name is symbolic: dead-lock) break up or must they be broken up? Toward the end of *Bleak House* it is the suit of Jarndyce and Jarndyce that 'lapses and melts away', but not Chancery, and it is clear that Dickens has grave doubts that enough will happen by peaceful process. When Esther and Ada visit the bricklayers' house with Mrs Pardiggle, they both feel 'painfully sensible that between us and these people there [is] an iron barrier'. Miss Flite, who in her own flighty way is a social realist too, expects a judgment on the Day of Judgment when she will release or give flight to those birds, Hope, Joy, etc., which symbolize all that is frustrate and imprisoned in the hell of the world. Mr Boythorn says that the only possible way to reform Chancery is to blow it to atoms 'with ten thousand hundred-weight of gunpowder', and in the next instant he calls Sir Leicester Dedlock 'the most stiff-necked, arrogant, imbecile, pig-headed numskull, ever, by some inexplicable mistake of Nature, born in any station of life but a walking-stick's'.

It is the obduracy of the old bad system that makes the hope for gradual or peaceful improvement seem so small to Dickens – this obduracy, and terrible ignorance too, for the fog and mire of *Bleak House* are the fog and mire of ignorance. The willful ignorance of the upper classes is based on a limited concept of self-interest; but middle-class ignorance is something else. Mr Turveydrop – in whose name the dropping that is a bow or curtsey and the dropping that is animal excrement become inextricably combined – is a genteelly impoverished and hypocritical worshipper of the upper classes, a gentlemen's gentleman, part of that middle class that Dickens describes as no class at all, but only a fringe on the mantle of the upper class. Mr Bayham Badger, another member of this no-class, prides himself ridiculously on the gentility of his wife's former husbands.

This pretentious ignorance, amounting to a failure of self-interest, is specially galling to Dickens, for he feels that there is nothing to hope for from a man who fails to recognize even his own needs and reasonable claims, whose pretensions cause him to be ignorant of his own interests. In this cataloguing of kinds of ignorance, there is the self-deluding ignorance too of the Mrs Jellybys and Mrs Pardiggles, who find it easier to do good deeds at a distance than to do their duty close by. And there is Krook, who has his own brand of ignorance – the stubborn, self-destroying, and vicious but still comic ignorance of craft – and won't ask anyone to teach him to read because they might teach him wrong.

The most dangerous ignorance of all, though, is the ignorance of those too down-trodden in the world to know or care. A couple of years later, Dickens was to tell a friend that 'the alienation of the people from their own public affairs' was 'extremely like the general mind of France before the breaking out of the first Revolution'.[2] To every question addressed to him, Jo says, '*I* don't know nothink [no-think?].' Dickens compares Jo to a vagabond dog, and says: 'Turn that dog's descendants wild . . . and in a very few years they will so degenerate that they will lose even their bark – but not their bite.' The logic of the drama scarcely requires Dickens' explanation.

Bleak House confronts authority – the authority of office, and of money, and of family – with the misery of the world. Mr Gridley asks who is responsible, and Esther tells Mr Skimpole that she fears 'everybody is obliged to be' responsible. Responsibility is part of Esther Summerson's great and revolting virtue. Most of the other impossible young women in Dickens' novels spring from the usual source for perfect young women in fiction, the area of erotic wish-fulfillment. But Esther stirs no chord of desire, and it is more likely that Dickens has created her as some

kind of *alter ego* for himself, deprived of his aggressive force
and talent but made kind and lovable instead. Lovable, too, for
herself – not for her beauty, which for a time she loses, nor for
her wealth and influence, which she never has. She starts as an
unloved child, as Dickens at least fancied that he was himself,
and there are certain aspects of her childhood that remind us of
Pip and David Copperfield, the only other first-person narrators
in Dickens' novels, and each in some sense a self-portrait. But
Dickens had to take back all that he thought the world owed
him for his lost childhood, and more, by the force of his own
hand, whereas everything comes back to Esther Summerson
through love. Yet it requires none of this speculation to see that
Esther has a schematic place in the novel by being responsible: as
John Jarndyce is, as Charley is, as Mrs Bagnet is, as Allan Woodcourt is, as Bucket is, as the Rouncewell family are; and as Skimpole, and Mrs Jellyby, and Mrs Pardiggle, and Mr Chadband are
not. As Sir Leicester Dedlock is only by his own insufficient
lights.

The attack on Chancery, and on the law and legal process, is
an attack on irresponsibility. The law, we are told, takes no
responsibility for anything but itself. Its first principle is 'to make
business for itself'. It makes hypocritical claims, of course, to
much more: Mr Tulkinghorn talks of his devotion to Sir
Leicester Dedlock, and Vholes talks always of putting his
shoulder to the wheel, and of his responsibility to his growing
daughters, and to his old father in the Vale of Taunton. But all
this is mere sham, and what the legal gentlemen really intend is
to enrich and dignify themselves. There are, too, many kinds of
responsibility. Attractive responsibilities are easy, but it is the
unattractive ones that are the real test. The poor, Dickens
knows and shows, are unattractive, like Jo:

Dirty, ugly, disagreeable to all the senses, in body a common
creature of the common streets. . . . Homely filth begrimes him,
homely parasites devour him, homely sores are in him, homely
rags are on him: native ignorance, the growth of English soil
and climate, sinks his immortal nature lower than the beasts
that perish. Stand forth, Jo, in uncompromising colours! From

the sole of thy foot to the crown of thy head, there is nothing interesting about thee.

It is easy to be responsible for pretty Rosa, or rosy Mrs Rouncewell. But who will be responsible for Jo, or for Nemo, the wretched nobody that Captain Hawdon becomes after he has failed in responsibility. For Esther's illegitimacy too is regarded in the light of responsibility, not of sexual morality, and both her father and her mother are made to pay a final price for their irresponsibility toward her.

The very point being made, and that helps substantiate this novel's realism, is that responsibility is difficult, indirect, often very obscure, but that the price of irresponsibility must be paid nonetheless. This is conveyed obviously by the fog–law analogy; less obviously but perhaps more tellingly by the indirect exactions made by disease, epidemic. Only when we have paid the price for our irresponsibilities – secret or unclear as they may be – can we 'begin the world'. Chancery is the set theme of this novel, death is the reality against which the foggy irresponsibility of legal process is assessed, and epidemic – moving by terrible indirection – symbolizes all too realistically the disaster that continued irresponsibility will bring.

SOURCE: *The Maturity of Dickens* (1959).

NOTES

1. *Letters from Charles Dickens to Angela Burdett-Coutts*, selected and edited by Edgar Johnson (1953) p. 273.

2. *The Letters of Charles Dickens* (in the Nonesuch Dickens, 1938) II 651; to Layard, 10 Apr 1855.

C. B. Cox

A DICKENS LANDSCAPE (1960)

My Lady Dedlock has been down at what she calls, in familiar
conversation, her 'place' in Lincolnshire. The waters are out in
Lincolnshire. An arch of the bridge in the park has been sapped
and sopped away. The adjacent low-lying ground, for half a
mile in breadth, is a stagnant river, with melancholy trees for
islands in it, and a surface punctured all over, all day long, with
falling rain. My Lady Dedlock's 'place' has been extremely
dreary. The weather, for many a day and night, has been so wet
that the trees seem wet through, and the soft loppings and prun-
ings of the woodman's axe can make no crash or crackle as they
fall. The deer, looking soaked, leave quagmires, where they pass.
The shot of a rifle loses its sharpness in the moist air, and its
smoke moves in a tardy little cloud towards the green rise,
coppice-topped, that makes a background for the falling rain.
The view from my Lady Dedlock's own windows is alternately
a lead-coloured view, and a view in Indian ink. The vases on the
stone terrace in the foreground catch the rain all day; and the
heavy drops fall, drip, drip, drip, upon the broad flagged pave-
ment, called, from old time, the Ghost's Walk, all night. On
Sundays, the little church in the park is mouldy; the oaken
pulpit breaks out into a cold sweat; and there is a general smell
and taste as of the ancient Dedlocks in their graves. My Lady
Dedlock (who is childless), looking out in the early twilight
from her boudoir at a keeper's lodge, and seeing the light of a
fire upon the latticed panes, and smoke rising from the chimney,
and a child, chased by a woman, running out into the rain to
meet the shining figure of a wrapped-up man coming through
the gate, has been put quite out of temper. My Lady Dedlock
says she has been 'bored to death'. (ch. 2)

The conventional view of Dickens has often been of a man who
could not resist facts, whose curiosity concerning the odd and the
eccentric poured itself abundantly into his novels. In the last

decades, the work of Edmund Wilson in particular has shown that Dickens never merely listed interesting facts. His great descriptions of places and people attain their peculiar hold upon our minds because every detail fits into an imaginative pattern. Much attention has been given to Dickens's psychological problems, and the ways these affect his selection of material; but there are many other sources for his striking originality.

In spite of the thousands of text-books written by psychologists, consciousness is still a mystery, and its nature is often best expressed in imaginative symbols, rather than by analytical description. Dickens knew that the state of an individual mind depends upon a quality of movement, quick or slow in apprehension; precision, clarifying its awareness or leaving all issues blurred; will-power, forcing an action onwards or shifting according to every wind of opinion; focus, relating events to particular needs or prevailing ideas. He recognised that when a character looks outwards, these factors and many others determine what he sees. Landscapes in his novels thus become projections of the mind, expressing by their tones and qualities the whole personality of one of his characters. The details of skies, fields and woods cannot describe a character going through a process of thought, or reacting in time to experience, but they can reveal profoundly a total response to life, the general attitude which defines a person whatever he may do. In Dickens's novels, adults do not often develop radically once they have settled down into some routine. His characters are defined by their surroundings, every detail of town or countryside representing some aspect of consciousness.

The extract from *Bleak House* describes Lady Dedlock's view of her 'place' in Lincolnshire. Her marriage into the Dedlock family has broken her down, until for her all experiences have lost their significance. She has retained no sense of purpose, nothing firm and definite which can give meaning to her life. As in her mind, so in the Lincolnshire scene everything has lost precision and sharpness. The trees are wet through; they make no crash or crackle as they fall. Even a rifle shot has lost its sharpness. An arch of the bridge has been sapped and sopped

away. Every image describes a breakdown of creative effort;
there is no hardness, firmness, energy or order, for everything
in Nature is being softened by the rain.

Men have a fundamental psychological need to deal with
objects which are firm and precise; this provides one reason why
extroverts in particular enjoy making things with wood, or
giving a hard blow with a hammer. The hardness of exterior
objects, against which we struggle, gives proof of a firmness in
ourselves. Nothing for Lady Dedlock has such definiteness; the
view from her windows is alternately a lead-coloured view, and
a view in Indian ink. She is moving away from life, with its
colour and vitality and purposes, towards the dulling of the
faculties which precedes death; so the passage moves towards the
church of the Dedlocks, whose odours seem to be rising from
the grave to engulf Lady Dedlock, and to drag her down with
the family ancestors.

The passage thus begins with a series of impressions of stag-
nation and frustration. The 'melancholy' trees recall the past
beauty and uprightness of summer, now undermined by the
water. The unending drip, drop of the rain forces Lady Dedlock
to remain indoors, trapped in a sophisticated boredom which has
lost all real contact with life. Only at the end does her gaze focus
on a precise scene. Suddenly there is movement, as the child,
chased by the woman, runs out into the rain; there is warmth,
with the light of the fire; and the man returning home after his
work is not frustrated by the rain. Another view of the landscape
is offered, that of the countryman whose life has the purpose and
order of Nature itself.

Lady Dedlock has placed herself outside this world; she has
reached a condition of mind when all activity seems pointless,
when the hills and valleys of her life have flattened out into
meaninglessness. This description is one of the best examples of
Dickens's poetic technique, his use of images of fog, rivers,
cities or Nature to define the complex factors which make up a
particular consciousness. In one sentence he can convey a
frightening picture of Lady Dedlock's total apathy and depres-
sion:

The adjacent low-lying ground, for half a mile in breadth, is a stagnant river, with melancholy trees for islands in it, and a surface punctured all over, all day long, with falling rain.

SOURCE: *Critical Quarterly*, II i (1960).

Mark Spilka

RELIGIOUS FOLLY (1963)

BOTH Dickens and Kafka began their adult careers in law. After leaving school, Dickens worked as an office boy for lawyers, then turned to law reporting in Doctors' Commons. These legal cloisters lay in a shady nook beside St Paul's; the courts were ecclesiastical, and, for Dickens, the courtroom seemed like a chapel where 'monkish attorneys' muddled wills and testaments. Kafka studied the law directly, took his doctorate in 1906, then served his year of clerkship. In *Bleak House* and *The Trial*, both writers fashioned oddly religious Courts, and used them to exemplify the adult world; and again there are signs that Kafka followed Dickens' lead. Admittedly, Kafka himself makes no remarks on *Bleak House*; it does not appear among his books, and none of his friends record it in his reading. Yet, as Rudolf Vašata observes:

The similarity between *The Trial and Bleak House* is obvious. . . . The central theme of both novels is the machinery of law crushing everybody and everything which comes under its wheels, the victim realising all its horrors without understanding its mechanism. And it is equally obvious that, in both cases, the legal system and its workings are used merely as a symbol for the society which they are serving.[1]

Vašata's insistence on the social parallel seems arbitrary and exclusive. One might agree more readily with George Ford, that 'Kafka is primarily concerned with the apparent muddle of Divine Law, and Dickens with the actual muddle of human law.'[2] Or one might even go beyond this, to suggest that Dickens gives a pseudo-religious cast to the law which magnifies its horrors. But whatever its form, the legal metaphor is central in both novels, and the similarity between them is decidedly strong.

When it comes to point of view, moreover, a more subtle relation develops than either Ford or Vašata suggests. Consider the legal scheme in *Bleak House* as it appears to children. A pseudo-religious Court would appeal to Kafka, but a childhood view of that Court, especially the view of Esther Summerson, the outcast Jo, and the desperate litigant Richard Carstone, would appeal with striking force. For children lack a comprehensive grasp of complicated systems; they convert their complexities into immediate effects of absurdity and confusion; they respond, as it were, from below, with emotional immediacy and concreteness, but without those speculative and synthetic powers which make for clarity, scope and fullness of perception: and Kafka, for all his intellectual sophistication, for all his legalistic and Talmudic sense of contradictions and alternatives, was as confined as Dickens by the child's emotional outlook. By following up these figures, then, we can perhaps explain how *Bleak House* might have influenced *The Trial* or, at the least, prefigured its appearance; in either case, the important fact is continuity of vision.

First, Esther Summerson. Like Pip and David Copperfield, she tells her portion of the novel directly, while Dickens covers the broader scene in alternating chapters. Through these narrative shifts the author presents his theme from two perspectives. With Dickens we view the fogs of Chancery from above, with ironic severity; with Esther we see them from within, as a sensitive and tender child might see them, or more accurately, a woman reviewing youth and childhood. Esther's name suggests her narrative function: she is the 'summer sun', a bright, sustaining force for those around her, in contrast to the darkening blight of Chancery. Unfortunately, she seems colorless and dull in the middle chapters, though radiant enough in describing childhood and her later pursuit of a sinful mother. For Esther is an illegitimate child, a shameful outcast, and seems able to speak best of matters which resemble Dickens' life. Her godmother, Miss Barbary, is a severely religious woman who treats her as a pariah, suppresses the facts of her parentage, and keeps her away from other children. In consequence, her birthdays are always glum occasions. Dickens himself was sent to the warehouse on his twelfth birthday,[3] and Esther receives a similar shock on hers. Frightened by her godmother's somber face, which seems to imply her guilt in being born, she forces her to speak out plainly:

'Your mother, Esther, is your disgrace, and you were hers. . . . Unfortunate girl, orphaned and degraded from the first of these evil anniversaries, pray daily that the sins of others be not visited upon your head, according to what is written. . . .

'Submission, self-denial, diligent work, are the preparation for a life begun with such a shadow on it. You are different from other children, Esther, because you were not born, like them, in common sinfulness and wrath. You are set apart.' (ch. 3)

So too was Dickens 'set apart' and forced to do hard, depleting labor. Accordingly, he could invest these scenes with deepfelt needs, or with characteristic emblems for those needs, like Esther's doll, which carries the psychic charge of Barkis' box, Cuttle's hat, or Miss Mowcher's ambulant umbrella. Esther begins her story, for instance, by mentioning her lonely talks with 'Dolly', who faithfully waits her return from school each day and listens to her account of childhood woes. The doll replaces the missing mother here, and provides the girl with her only source of comfort. Thus, when Esther learns of her disgraceful birth, she runs to her room, holds 'that solitary friend' against her bosom, and repeats the story of her birthday:

I . . . confided to her that I would try, as hard as ever I could, to repair the fault I had been born with (of which I confusedly felt guilty and yet innocent), and would strive as I grew up to be industrious, contented, and kind-hearted, and to do some good to some one, and win some love to myself if I could. (ch. 3)

Two years later Esther is able to win herself some love. Her godmother dies, and she is sent by an unknown guardian to a boarding school, where she speedily wins the hearts of all around her. Before leaving for school, however, she wraps her doll in a shawl ('I am half ashamed to tell it') and buries her in the garden below her window. About six years afterwards, she receives a comic proposal from the bumptious Mr Guppy, one of the law clerks from Kenge and Carboy, which stirs up painful memories: she again goes to her room, begins to laugh and cry, and feels 'as if an old chord had been more coarsely touched than it ever had been since the days of the dear old doll, long buried in the garden' (ch. 9). So the doll is strongly connected with the absence, on the one hand, of a mother's love, and with marriage on the other. It suggests the sense of exclusion and inadequacy, or of dreams gone wrong, which Dickens himself might have felt in these connections, and which he seems to associate with the search for love.

At twenty Esther is called to her guardian's house to serve as governess to an adopted ward. When she arrives in London, the city is so full of dense brown smoke (the fog of Chancery) that Esther feels bewildered:

We drove slowly through the dirtiest and darkest streets that ever were seen in the world (I thought), and in such a distracting state of confusion that I wondered how the people kept their senses, until we passed into sudden quietude under an old gateway, and drove on through a silent square until we came to an odd nook in a corner, where there was an entrance up a steep, broad flight of stairs, like an entrance to a church. And there really was a church-yard, outside under some cloisters, for I saw the gravestones from the staircase window. (ch. 3)

The converted church (for what else can we call it?) is Kenge and Carboy's law office. In the same location, but around the corner, under a colonnade, and in at a side door, is the Lord High Chancellor's office, where Esther meets the wards in Chancery, Miss Ada Clare and her cousin Richard Carstone. All three of them are orphans; all meet together, for the first time, before a roaring fire in the outer room; and together all face his lordship, who sits in an armchair in the next room, dressed in black. Esther is touched that this dry official place is 'home' for the lovely Ada: 'The Lord High Chancellor, at his best, appeared so poor a substitute for the love and pride of parents.' Esther herself is supposedly 'not related to any party in the cause'; but she

is actually related to the cause, illegitimately, through her mother,
Lady Dedlock, and perhaps to the parties in it too, since Richard
Carstone is allied to Lady Dedlock 'by remote consanguinity'.
Thus the three young people – Ada, Richard and Esther – really
stand together as wards of the court; their 'father' is the Lord
High Chancellor; and just as Ada is later called a 'child of the
universe', so are they all 'children of the universe'. At present
they are baffled by the events which bring them to the Chancellor's office. But before they leave, their bafflement turns to
sudden alarm:

We looked at one another, half laughing at our being like the
children in the wood, when a curious little old woman in a
squeezed bonnet, and carrying a reticule, came curtseying and
smiling up to us, with an air of great ceremony.
　'O!' said she. 'The wards in Jarndyce! Very happy, I am sure,
to have the honour! It is a good omen for youth, and hope, and
beauty, when they find themselves in this place, and don't know
what's to come of it.'
　'Mad!' whispered Richard, not thinking she could hear him.
　'Right! Mad, young gentleman,' she returned so quickly that
he was quite abashed. 'I was a ward myself. I was not mad at that
time,' curtseying low, and smiling between every little sentence.
'I had youth, and hope. I believe, beauty. It matters very little
now. Neither of the three served, or saved me. I have the
honour to attend Court regularly. With my documents. I expect
a judgment. Shortly. On the Day of Judgment.' (ch. 3)

　The little madwoman is Miss Flite. Along with the frenzied
Mr Gridley, who later dies through defending his legal interest,
she represents the fate of Richard Carstone, and of all other
wards in Chancery who would assert their claims before the
Court. Through such hints, alarms and portents, Dickens gives
a religious cast to the law in *Bleak House*. In a single chapter,
his heroine is first impressed with her sinfulness, then plunged
through a squalid urban scene to reach a churchlike nook in a
quiet square; soon she stands, along with other children of the
universe, before the Lord High Chancellor, their common
'father' – and afterwards receives a hint of Judgment Day. To

her the world *appears* to be very like the world which Kafka's heroes actually inhabit. Indeed, her guardian, John Jarndyce, is involved in a lawsuit which suggests a number of Kafkan metaphors, like the punishment scheme in 'The Penal Colony' or the unfinished wall in 'The Great Wall of China':

A certain Jarndyce, in an evil hour, made a great fortune, and made a great Will. In the question how the trusts under that Will are to be administered, the fortune left by the Will is squandered away; the legatees under the Will are reduced to such a miserable condition that they would be sufficiently punished, if they had committed an enormous crime in having money left them; and the Will itself is made a dead letter. . . . And thus, through years and years, and lives and lives, everything goes on, constantly beginning over and over again, and nothing ever ends. And we can't get out of the suit on any terms, for we are made parties to it, and *must be* parties to it, whether we like it or not. (ch. 8)

So the three orphans and their guardian are involved in a legal muddle which suggests Original Sin. Even Ada senses this, as she speaks of herself as the enemy of 'a great number of relations and others', who are also her enemies, all 'ruining one another, without knowing how or why . . . in constant doubt and discord all our lives. It seems very strange, as there must be right somewhere, that an honest judge in real earnest has not been able to find out through all these years where it is' (ch. 5). Ada says this as the orphans leave the dark and airless apartment of Miss Flite, which is located above an old rag and bottle warehouse. The owner of the warehouse, Mr Krook, is called the Lord Chancellor by his neighbors. His shop is called the Court of Chancery, because of the tremendous collection of old ink bottles, law books and legal papers hoarded there. Krook admits to the comparison ('We both grub on in a muddle'), and his congested shop, which is located in the squalid district around the Court, suggests the pervasiveness of the legal blight. It also helps to reveal the inner nature of the system, through the corruptness of Krook and the bleak, hopeless lives of his tenants, in the dark rooms above.

In *The Trial* the artist's garret performs a similar function.

Like Kafka's supernatural Court, it is located in a dirty tenement house, though in another section of town; yet it is directly connected with law offices, as if the entire city were a sprawling Court, constantly in session, even in the most unexpected places, and sitting in perpetual judgment on Joseph K. On the stairs leading up to the garret, moreover, there are leering adolescent girls who 'belong to the Court' (*Trial*). K has already run into flocks of children in the tenement where his first interrogation is held, and the woman who then directs him to the courtroom is washing children's clothes. Scenes like these play an important part in *Bleak House*. At Mrs Jellyby's, children sprawl about the house in a welter of confusion, falling down stairs, getting their heads stuck through the outer railings, pushing their faces into the orphans' bedroom. In the country, at the cottage of a poor family, five children have died and a sixth succumbs at Ada's touch. Near the Court itself, three orphans are locked in a cold, barren room, while their adolescent sister takes in washing to support them. Their father, recently dead, has been connected with the Court in a minor capacity, and this connection suggests what is true of all these children: they are all wards in Chancery, either as victims of social neglect and commercial hardheartedness, or of the false and ineffectual philanthropy of the middle class. For in *Bleak House*, as in *The Trial*, 'everything belongs to the Court'; in fact, life even *begins* under its jurisdiction.

As many critics remark, the legal metaphor extends to social, economic and political realms, in *Bleak House*, from the rich manor at Chesney Wold through the muddle of Parliament and of the commercial middle class, down to the crashing tenements in Tom-All-Alone's. More pertinently, it also extends to sexual realms, though always in connection with the social problem. George Santayana notes, for example, that Lady Dedlock's secret is treated 'as if it were the sin of Adam, remote, mysterious, inexpiable'.[4] In terms of dramatic tension, this means that the whole novel is grounded in socio-sexual mystery – or in the sin of Lady Dedlock and Captain Hawdon, of which Esther is the illegitimate fruit. From Esther's childhood guilt through

Hawdon's mysterious death to Lady Dedlock's fatal collapse in the snow, the sexual crime informs the social muddle and provides it with a personal context. Hence Edmund Wilson's comment:

At the bottom of the whole gloomy edifice is the body of Lady Dedlock's lover and Esther Summerson's father, Captain Hawdon, the reckless soldier, adored by his men, beloved by women, the image of the old life-loving England, whose epitaph Dickens is now writing. Captain Hawdon has failed in that world, has perished as a friendless and penniless man, and has been buried in the pauper's graveyard in one of the foulest quarters of London, but the loyalties felt for him by the living will endure and prove so strong, after his death, that they will pull that world apart.[5]

Lady Dedlock's crime, then, is to betray Hawdon's love (and by that act, to betray the lower classes) by marrying for social position. Yet their common crime is illicit love, which Dickens treats as the sin of Adam. Thus, as Hawdon dies, he lies above Krook's shop in a dark, foul filthy room, the shutters of which are pierced by two gaunt holes, resembling giant staring eyes. Dickens calls them the eyes of famine, but Hawdon's immediate death is caused by opium, a drug which Dickens elsewhere connects with sexual passion.* If these giant eyes admonish sexual as well as social crimes, then the scene combines some of the harshest memories of Dickens' past with growing marital tensions. He seems to align himself with Hawdon here: he too had been rejected, by the family of Maria Beadnell, for lack of money and social position; and as Edmund Wilson observes, he too had spent his life without any clear-cut social rank, a member of no respectable class, and an enemy of all fashionable pomp and snobbery. But more than this, he was on the verge of experiments in sexual license, along with his young friend Wilkie Collins, which were foreign to his nature. In Hawdon's betrayal of the moral code he seems to convict himself of real or impending lapses. His sense of guilt and inadequacy, which began with

* See *The Mystery of Edwin Drood*, where John Jasper's opium dreams are connected with dancing girls, and with his passionate desire to possess Rosa Budd.

the warehouse episode and which was deepened by the Beadnell fiasco, is now connected with forbidden love.

Kafka may have sensed this element in *Bleak House*. He seems to borrow the staring eyes, for example, when Joseph K and his uncle visit Advocate Huld 'in the very suburb where the Law Court had its attic offices':

Behind a grille in the door two great dark eyes appeared, gazed at the two visitors for a moment, and then vanished again; yet the door did not open. K and his uncle assured each other that they had really seen a pair of eyes. 'A new maid, probably afraid of strangers,' said K's uncle and knocked again. Once more the eyes appeared and now they seemed almost somber, yet that might have been an illusion created by the naked gas-jet which burned just over their heads and kept hissing shrilly but gave little light. 'Open the door!' shouted K's uncle, banging upon it with his fists, 'we're friends of the Herr Advocate's.' 'The Herr Advocate is ill,' came a whisper from behind them. A door had opened at the other end of the little passage and a man in a dressing-gown was standing there imparting this information in a hushed voice.

When the door is finally opened, K recognizes the dark protuberant eyes in the girl Leni, with whom he later makes love, to the detriment of his case before the Court. Now Leni stands in the entrance hall with a candle in her hand:

'The Herr Advocate is ill,' said the girl, as K's uncle without any hesitation, made towards an inner door. . . . 'Is it his heart?' [he asked]. 'I think so,' said the girl, she had now found time to precede him with the candle and open the door of a room. In one corner, which the candlelight had not yet reached, a face with a long beard attached rose from a pillow.

Compare this with the scene in *Bleak House* where the aged lawyer, Tulkinghorn, who is the legal representative for Lady Dedlock's husband, enters Hawdon's room. When he comes to the dark door, he 'knocks, receives no answer, opens it, and accidentally extinguishes his candle'. On a low bed opposite the fire, 'a confusion of dirty patchwork, lean-ribbed ticking, and coarse sacking', he sees a spectral bearded figure. Crying 'Hallo', he rattles on the door and strikes it with his iron candle-stick. The candle in the room goes out, 'and leaves him in the dark; with the gaunt eyes in the shutters staring down upon the bed'. A touch from behind makes the lawyer start; Krook whispers in his ear, and the two go in together, whispering, after Krook returns with a lighted candle. 'As the light goes in, the great eyes in the shutters, darkening, seem to close. Not so the eyes upon the bed' (chs. 10–11).

In the turmoil which follows, a young surgeon, Allan Wood-court, appears suddenly on one side of Hawdon's bed, as if from nowhere (even as Inspector Bucket will materialize, more auspiciously, in a later scene). On the other side stands Krook, the mock High Chancellor, while the lawyer Tulkinghorn stands silently in the background, near an old portmanteau. In *The Trial*, as K and his uncle converse with the ailing Advocate, a form begins to stir in a dark corner of the room, and the Chief Clerk of the Court appears there, at a little table. Mood, theme, and arrangement are thus similar in each scene: there are mysterious staring eyes, to suggest the sin of Adam; there are loud rappings at the door, hushed voices, and sudden interruptions from behind; there are sick-beds and legal figures in faltering candlelight, and dark forms which materialize from nowhere; and finally, there is a mock or substitute Chancellor from the Court, to lend an air of judgment to the entire tableau. The parallels run rather thick for mere coincidence.

If the expiation theme appealed to Kafka, he might have liked its superbly-told completion, in the final chapters, where Lady Dedlock pays for her share in sexual crime. Stricken by guilt, she has approached her daughter humbly, embraced her for the first and last time, and asked her forgiveness. She believes, however, that she has earned her 'earthly punishment' and must bear it. When Tulkinghorn, the legal keeper of aristocratic secrets, is murdered, her husband learns of her sexual sins, and the house of Dedlock falls. Aware of her exposure, and falsely accused of murder, she flees the house on foot, pursued by Esther and Inspector Bucket with a futile message of forgiveness. Here

Esther re-emerges, with renewed vitality, as an innocent point
of view in a darkened world. Her dreamlike account of the search
through squalid urban scenes, along snow-filled country roads,
then back again to Chancery Lane, becomes a psychological
journey in which houses put on human shapes and water-gates
close and open in her mind. The journey ends at her father's
grave, where her mother lies dead, dressed in the garb of the
poor, the class she had deserted. In Kafka's novel, *Amerika*,
another illegitimate child, the servant girl Therese (whose name
resemble's Esther's), tells of her mother's death in dreamlike
fashion – a self-inflicted death involving sexual and economic
betrayal and wanderings through urban streets in winter. The
parallel seems worth mentioning, since it helps to establish
Kafka's possible interest in this sequence, where the sin of Adam
gives tension and significance to the legal metaphor.*

II

Next Jo, the sweeping boy, whom Dickens characterizes as being
'of no order and no place; neither of the beasts nor of humanity'
(ch. 47). Jo is another point of view, another lonely child of the
universe; he stands at the very bottom of society, as the representative of the slum, Tom-All-Alone's, the site of crime, pollution and abject poverty in nineteenth-century London. Through
the eyes of Jo, then, Dickens is able to present the bewildering
hopeless quality of life among the ignorant poor:

It must be a strange state to be like Jo! To shuffle through the
streets, unfamiliar with the shapes, and in utter darkness as to

* Therese's story differs circumstantially from Esther's. Perhaps she
descends from Dickens's Nell (in *The Old Curiosity Shop*) through
Dostoevsky's Nellie (in *The Insulted and Injured*), another illegitimate
child who walks through wintry streets with a dying mother. The
imitation may be twice-removed; yet, as E. W. Tedlock observes,
Therese's story, 'in its quality of grotesquely pathetic pantomime, is
straight Dickens' (E. W. Tedlock, Jr, 'Kafka's Imitation of *David
Copperfield*', in *Comparative Literature*, VII (Winter 1955) 58). If so,
it may derive from *Bleak House*, at least in theme (sexual and economic betrayal) and texture.

the meaning, of those mysterious symbols, so abundant over the shops, and at the corners of the streets, and on the doors, and in the windows! To see people read and to see people write, and to see the postman deliver letters, and not to have the least idea of all that language – to be, to every scrap of it, stone blind and dumb! It must be very puzzling to see the good company going to the church on Sundays, with their books in their hands, and to think (for perhaps Jo *does* think, at odd times) what does it all mean, and if it means anything to anybody, how comes it that it means nothing to me? To be hustled, and jostled, and moved on; and really to feel that it would appear to be perfectly true that I have no business, here, or there, or anywhere; and yet to be perplexed by the consideration that I *am* here somehow, too, and everybody overlooked me until I became the creature that I am! It must be a strange state, not merely to be told that I am scarcely human . . . , but to feel it of my own knowledge all my life! To see the horses, dogs, and cattle, go by me, and to know that in ignorance I belong to them, and not to the superior beings in my shape, whose delicacy I offend! Jo's ideas of a Criminal Trial, or a Judge, or a Bishop . . . should be strange! His whole material and immaterial life is wonderfully strange; his death the strangest thing of all. (ch. 16)

It seems interesting that Dickens slips quickly into the first person here. His easy identification with Jo suggests another identification, by a later writer. That leading supposition, for instance – 'It must be a strange state to be like Jo' – and the closing supposition – 'Jo's ideas of a Criminal Trial, or a Judge, or a Bishop . . . should be strange' – sound almost like an invitation to write *The Trial*, to take Dickens up on his suppositions, as they affect an older Jo, or (without insisting on the name), a Joseph K, at a higher level of bewilderment. Some of the lines which follow, moreover, suggest another parallel:

The town awakes . . . Jo, and the other lower animals, get on in the unintelligible mess as they can. . . . A band of music comes, and plays. Jo listens to it. So does a dog – a drover's dog, waiting for his master outside a butcher's shop, and evidently thinking about those sheep he has had upon his mind for some hours, and is happily rid of. . . . A thoroughly vagabond dog, accustomed to

low company and public-houses . . . but an educated, improved,
developed dog, who has been taught his duties and knows how
to discharge them. He and Jo listen to the music, probably with
much the same amount of animal satisfaction; likewise, as to
awakened association, aspiration or regret, melancholy or joyful
reference to things beyond the senses, they are probably on a
par. But otherwise, how far beyond the human listener is the
brute!

The dog who stops to listen to music, the 'educated, improved, developed dog', who is on a par with Jo 'as to . . .
melancholy or joyful reference to things beyond the senses',
suggests the Kafka fable, 'Investigations of a Dog', which was
written in conjunction with *The Trial*. Here Kafka too creates
the image of an old but childlike dog, who prides himself on the
preservation of his childish qualities and on the astonishing
things which can be seen through children's eyes, and who tries
to puzzle out the meaning of mysterious music. Of course, the
fable is ingeniously and elaborately developed as religious
allegory; yet the parallel with Dickens' sketch, in conjunction
with those previous lines on little Jo, baffled at signs and portents in the world around him, most baffled of all by the workings of a monstrous (and for the first time) *Criminal* Court, seems
more than coincidental. Indeed, whenever Jo appears, there is
this same connection with a court, his plight, and a religion which
fails to give his life significance. At the death of Hawdon, for
example, Jo is brought before the court of inquest to answer
questions about the deceased. But when he proves vague about
the hereafter, the Coroner rejects him as a witness. Later, he is
hauled off the streets by a constable and brought before a higher
authority, the Reverend Mr Chadband. The policeman has
merely asked the boy to 'move on', but Dickens amplifies the
meaning of such orders: 'The one grand recipe remains for you –
the profound philosophical prescription – the be-all and the
end-all of your strange existence upon earth. Move on! You are
by no means to move off, Jo. . . . Move on!' Then, after a brief
cross-examination of the boy by the ubiquitous Mr Guppy, the
Reverend Chadband expands upon his earthly state:

'You are a human boy, my young friend. A human boy. . . .

> O running stream of sparkling joy
> To be a soaring human boy!

And do you cool yourself in that stream now, my young friend? No. Why do you not cool yourself in that stream now? Because you are in a state of darkness, because you are in a state of obscurity, because you are in a state of sinfulness, because you are in a state of bondage. My young friend, what *is* bondage? Let us, in a spirit of love, inquire.' (ch. 19)

Jo yawns at this sanctimonious outburst, and is called 'a limb of the arch-fiend' by pious Mrs Snagsby. Later he escapes to the city, with some food from gentler Mr Snagsby, and 'moves on' to Blackfriars Bridge:

And there he sits, munching and gnawing, and looking up at the great Cross on the summit of St Paul's Cathedral, glittering above a red and violet-tinted cloud of smoke. From the boy's face one might suppose that sacred emblem to be, in his eyes, the crowning confusion of the great, confused city; so golden, so high up, so far out of his reach. . . .

The cathedral dome is as far beyond Jo as the source of celestial music is beyond the dog in Kafka's fable. Again and again, Dickens satirizes the senselessness and futility of contemporary faith, always in conjunction with a powerful, smothering, all-pervasive Court, and with the lives of children caught within its jurisdiction. His purpose is to present the social muddle, through children's eyes, as seemingly inevitable and foreordained; but at the same time, to expose its source in conditions man might alter. Thus Jo, as symbol of the slums, is a source of pollution which compassionate men might remedy; yet, as dramatic go-between, he appears at first to affirm Original Sin. Befriended by Captain Hawdon, who is an outcast like himself, he is later sought out by Lady Dedlock, whom he guides to the Captain's grave. This supposedly Christian burial ground is itself a source of malignant disease, so that Jo's later illness might stem as much from the grave as from the slum. The point is never made clear, but the illness itself is passed by the driven

Jo to Esther Summerson, who is stricken blind for a time and whose face is marred by it – and in this sense the sins of others are literally visited upon her head. But if Jo is the carrier of sexual blight, Dickens means us to see his 'crime' in social terms. Through Jo, that is, he re-enacts the *social* crime committed by Lady Dedlock against Captain Hawdon. While Hawdon is kind to Jo and attempts to help him, Lady Dedlock shrinks back from the filthy boy, as she had deserted Hawdon before him; and the implication of social neglect accounts for Esther's illness. We can see this, at the end, when the collusion of wealth and legal power has failed, and Esther's beauty is gradually restored. In the meantime Jo has died, and Dickens has stepped before his readers to insist upon the avoidability of his death: 'Dead, your Majesty. Dead, my lords and gentlemen. Dead, Right Reverends and Wrong Reverends of every order. Dead, men and women, born with Heavenly compassion in your hearts. And dying thus around us, every day' (ch. 47). Of course, compassion alone will neither save Jo nor restore Esther's beauty; the eloquent rightness here comes from our sense of human waste, however we avoid it. Curiously enough, that same sense of waste informs the ending of *The Trial*, as Joseph K compares his death with that of a dog – 'it was as if he meant the shame of it to outlive him', Kafka adds, implying that the hero's worth outweighs his guilt.

III

Finally there is Richard Carstone, an actual ward in Chancery, whose predicament comes closest to that of Joseph K. As his guardian observes, 'Jarndyce and Jarndyce was the curtain of Rick's cradle' (ch. 35). His sweetheart also speaks of 'the shadow in which we both were born' (ch. 37), and Richard himself holds forth in Kafkan metaphors:

My dear Esther, I am a very unfortunate dog not to be more settled, but how *can* I be more settled? If you lived in an unfinished house, you couldn't settle down in it; if you were condemned to leave everything you undertook, unfinished, you would find it hard to apply yourself to anything; and yet that's my unhappy case. I was born into this unfinished contention with all its chances and changes, and it began to unsettle me before I quite knew the difference between a suit at law and a suit of clothes; and it has gone on unsettling me ever since; and here I am, conscious sometimes that I am but a worthless fellow to love my confiding cousin Ada. (ch. 23)

Here are some of the most basic elements in *The Trial*: the inherited condition, its unsettling effects, and the sense of unworthiness with regard to marriage. Through his connection with Chancery, Richard develops a habit of putting things off, and moves restlessly from profession to profession. First he tries to be a surgeon; but since he is chiefly interested in his legal suit, he soon decides to switch to law:

'If I went into Kenge's office,' said Richard, 'and if I were placed under articles to Kenge, I should have my eye on the – hum! – the forbidden ground – and should be able to study it, and master it, and to satisfy myself that it was not neglected, and was being properly conducted. I should be able to look after Ada's interests, and my own interests (the same thing!); and I should peg away at Blackstone and all those fellows with the most tremendous ardour.' (ch. 17)

Richard's decision is like K's determination to 'look after' his own interests, rather than trust his lawyer. He resembles K still further as he quickly abandons the law, *per se*, to study his own case. He is forever poring over papers, getting 'at the core of the mystery', haunting the Court itself, and consulting with Miss Flite like an expert client, without seeing 'what a fatal link was riveting between his fresh youth and her faded age; between his free hopes and her caged birds, and her hungry garret, and her wandering mind' (ch. 23). So too the commercial traveler Block, in his doglike servility before the law, suggests the ultimate fate of Joseph K.

Having neglected his law studies, Richard is forced to enter another profession. He begins to work toward a commission in the army. By now he suspects his legal guardian, John Jarndyce, of working against him to protect his own interests. The suit 'taints everybody', he tells Esther, '. . . why should *he* escape?'

As for himself, the case will be his life-pursuit; there is 'truth and justice' in it somewhere, and he will devote his youth and energy to finding it. In the meantime he discovers a 'friend and legal adviser' in Mr Vholes, a sallow, thin-lipped, lifeless man who resembles Kafka's Advocate Huld. This lawyer devotes himself to Richard's case, for example, in spite of his bad digestion; he insists on being his sole legal representative, and he prides himself on professional thoroughness. Indeed, as George Ford observes, 'we have the same *kind* of feeling in listening to Mr Vholes as we have in listening to Kafka's priest or to the lawyers who reply to K's enquiries':[6]

'Again nothing done!' says Richard. 'Nothing, nothing done!'
'Don't say nothing done, sir,' returns the placid Vholes. 'That is scarcely fair, sir, scarcely fair!'
'Why, what *is* done?' says Richard, turning gloomily upon him.
'That may not be the whole question,' returns Vholes. 'The question may branch off into what is doing, what is doing?'
'And what is doing?' asks the moody client.
Vholes, sitting with his arms on his desk, quietly bringing the tips of his five right fingers to meet the tips of his five left fingers, and quietly separating them again, and fixedly and slowly looking at his client, replies:
'A good deal is doing, sir. We have put our shoulders to the wheel, Mr Carstone, and the wheel is going round.'
'Yes, with Ixion on it. How am I to get through the next four or five accursed months?' exclaims the young man, rising from his chair and walking about the room.
'Mr C,' returns Vholes, following him close with his eyes wherever he goes, 'your spirits are hasty, and I am sorry for it on your account. Excuse me if I recommend you not to chafe so much, not to be so impetuous, not to wear yourself out so. You should have more patience. . . . If you had asked me what I was to do, during the vacation, I could have answered you more readily. I am to attend to your interests. . . . Other professional men go out of town. I don't. Not that I blame them for going; I merely say, I don't go. This desk is your rock, sir!'
Mr Vholes gives it a rap, and it sounds as hollow as a coffin.
(ch. 39)

In *The Trial* Advocate Huld chides K for impatience and lack of confidence; Huld 'sacrifices' his health to the case, gives K preferred treatment and expects it in return, and prides himself on devotion to his work. For his part, K sinks deeper and deeper into the legal muddle, with no change for the better in sight and with nothing tangible accomplished – as with Richard Carstone, or 'Mr C', as Vholes repeatedly calls him, though again there is no need to insist on verbal parallels. One need only note that Dickens used abbreviated names, like 'Jo' and 'C' and Captain 'Nemo' (meaning 'No One'), to suggest suppression of personality, and that Kafka might have used them for that purpose.

There are other similarities. Most notably, Richard loves his case more than he loves his sweetheart Ada. They are engaged early in the book, but, as Richard vacillates through life, the engagement dissolves. The immediate cause of the break is Richard's guardian, who disapproves of his instability. Richard never forgives him, though he has already expressed the same idea himself, in stronger terms: 'I know what the thought of Ada ought to do for me, but it doesn't do it. I am too unsettled even for that. I love her most devotedly; and yet I do her wrong, in doing myself wrong, every day and hour' (ch. 23). If Kafka had read this novel, he could scarcely have missed its bearing on his own predicament. Accused by his father of instability and unmanliness, he had resented the charge and at the same time recognized its truth. Like Richard, he was engaged to a young girl in his early manhood, but 'unsettled' feelings kept him from the point of marriage. Again like Richard, he was more in love with his 'case' than his sweetheart, yet felt guilty about wronging her in his self-absorption. In *The Trial*, moreover, he seems to identify the Court with paternal disapproval, while in *Bleak House* (and this, I think, is the most striking parallel) young Carstone comes to identify his legal guardian, or his substitute father, as 'the embodiment of the suit', so that 'every new delay and every new disappointment, is only a new injury from John Jarndyce's hand' (ch. 39). Once more, this looks like a standing invitation to write *The Trial*.

Of course, there are striking differences too. Richard's trial is ostensibly a matter of property; K's, of Original Sin; and Richard finally marries Ada, while K is never able to push his suit with Fräulein Bürstner, who appears at both ends of the novel as a goal beyond his reach. Yet Richard's case is presented in religious terms, as if he had actually inherited an accumulated burden of sin; and his marriage to Ada is kept subordinate to his case, so that it is founded in mental and spiritual dissolution – like K's relation to Frieda in *The Castle*. Thus Richard and Ada take up quarters a few doors from Vholes' office; their rooms are sunless and unhealthy, and Richard sinks disastrously under his double burden. He becomes thin and languid, slovenly in dress, and abstracted in manner. His eyes become wan and restless: 'I cannot use the expression that he looked old', writes Esther. 'There is a ruin of youth which is not like age; and into such a ruin, Richard's youth and youthful beauty had all fallen away' (ch. 60). One is reminded here of Kafka's perennial youthfulness, accompanied by inward dissolution.

The young wife suffers along with Richard, and though she pretends to cheerfulness before him, she is afraid he will never live to see their coming child. Her prediction is borne out when the case is absorbed in costs, and Richard suffers a stroke while rising to accost the judge. Before his death there is a scene which might have attracted Kafka's interest:

'It was all a troubled dream?' said Richard, clasping both my Guardian's hands eagerly.

'Nothing more, Rick; nothing more.'

'And you, being a good man, can pass it as such, and forgive and pity the dreamer, and be lenient and encouraging when he wakes?'

'Indeed I can. What am I but another dreamer, Rick?'

'I will begin the world!' said Richard, with a light in his eyes.

At this point Richard calls to his wife:

'I have done you many wrongs, my own. I have fallen like a poor stray shadow on your way, I have married you to poverty and trouble, I have scattered your means to the winds. You will forgive me all this, my Ada, before I begin the world?' (ch. 65)

With the forgiveness of both wife and guardian, Richard begins the world – not this one, Dickens adds, but 'The world that sets this right.' It was a sentiment which Kafka might have sharèd, even in his bitter tale of a man who moves in troubled dreams. Beyond this, he might have taken a personal interest in Richard's death and in the sufferings of his wife; he might have found reinforcement here for his own decision to reject his sweetheart, Felice Bauer, who is the prototype for Fräulein Bürstner in *The Trial*. Out of this predicament comes the guilt of Joseph K, and his trial before a Court which, in its baffling and distinctly religious nature, resembles the Court of Chancery in *Bleak House*.

SOURCE: *Dickens and Kafka* (1963).

NOTES

1. Rudolf Vašata, '*Amerika* and Charles Dickens', in *The Kafka Problem*, ed. Angel Flores (New York, 1946) p. 135.

2. George Ford, *Dickens and His Readers* (Princeton, 1955; paperback, New York, 1965) pp. 255–6.

3. Jack Lindsay, *Charles Dickens: A Biographical and Critical Study* (1930) pp. 59–64.

4. George Santayana, 'Dickens', in *Soliloquies in England* (New York, 1923) p. 61.

5. Edmund Wilson, 'Dickens: The Two Scrooges', in *Eight Essays* (New York, 1954) p. 42, and *The Wound and the Bow* (paperback, 1961).

6. Ford, *Dickens and His Readers*, p. 255.

W. J. Harvey

BLEAK HOUSE:
THE DOUBLE NARRATIVE (1965)

ONE way of stating the failure of *The Princess Casamassima*
would be to say that James is no Dickens, while this is the most
Dickensian of his novels. And it is to Dickens and *Bleak House*
that we may finally turn to examine a quite different set of
problems involved in the relation of character to narrator.

Dickens has often been likened to a Jacobean dramatist both
for his vivid, exuberant, 'poetic' use of language and for his
methods of characterization. There is a third point of likeness.
Critics frequently discuss Jacobean plays in terms of 'episodic
intensification'. By this they mean the impulse to exploit to the full
the possibilities of any particular scene, situation or action without too much regard for the relevance of such local intensities to
the total work of art. Clearly much of Dickens's fiction is of the
same order. To admit this is to risk the displeasure of much
modern criticism of fiction which, largely deriving from James,
lays great stress on the organic unity of the novel and demands
that no part shall be allowed autonomy if this threatens the
integrity of the whole.

We can defend in four ways the novel of episodic intensification from such criticism. First, we may admit that in some cases
the work may fail as a whole while succeeding in some part. The
result may be a dead or crippled work which yet intermittently
achieves the vigour of a masterpiece. We may admire what we
can and regret the waste of so much else. This, I think, is true of
Barnaby Rudge. Second, we may deny the fiat of organic unity
and maintain that in *some* cases a novel achieves no more than
episodic intensification and yet possesses so much vitality that
we are content simply to accept its greatness. In James's terms

there must be room in the house of fiction for such 'loose, baggy monsters'. With much less certainty I would place *Pickwick Papers* in this category. Third, we may accept the idea of organic unity and yet maintain that by its standards Dickens's novels are entirely successful. Sometimes he achieves an economy, firmness, and clean-cut clarity of control that can only be called classical. This is surely true of *Great Expectations*. Finally, we may accept the idea of organic unity but argue that the criteria by which we judge its presence or absence have been too narrowly conceived and that there exist conventions and methods of organization which are non-Jamesian but still appropriate and effective. (James, unlike some more recent critics, admitted as much.) *Bleak House* is here a relevant example. Indeed, I would say that one of the reasons for its greatness is the extreme tension set up between the centrifugal vigour of its parts and the centripetal demands of the whole. It is a tension between the impulse to intensify each local detail or particular episode and the impulse to subordinate, arrange and discipline. The final impression is one of immense and potentially anarchic energy being brought – but only just – under control. The fact that the equipoise between part and whole is so precariously maintained is in itself a tribute to the energy here being harnessed.

How well does an examination of the novel's structure support this general view? *Bleak House* is for Dickens a unique and elaborate experiment in narration and plot composition. It is divided into two intermingled and roughly concurrent stories; Esther Summerson's first-person narrative and an omniscient narrative told consistently in the historic present. The latter takes up thirty-four chapters; Esther has one less. Her story, however, occupies a good deal more than half the novel. The reader who checks the distribution of these two narratives against the original part issues will hardly discern any significant pattern or correlation. Most parts contain a mixture of the two stories; one part is narrated entirely by Esther and five parts entirely by the omniscient author. Such a check does, however, support the view that Dickens did not, as is sometimes supposed, use serial publication in the interest of crude suspense. A sensational novelist, for example, might well have ended a part issue with chapter 31; Dickens subdues the drama by adding another chapter to the number. The obvious exception to this only proves the rule; in the final double number the suspense of Bucket's search for Lady Dedlock is heightened by cutting back to the omniscient narrative and the stricken Sir Leicester. In general, however, Dickens's control of the double narrative is far richer and subtler than this. Through this technique, as I shall try to show, he controls the immense, turbulent and potentially confusing material of his novel. Indeed, the narrative method seems to me to be part of the very substance of *Bleak House*, expressive of what, in the widest and deepest sense, the novel is about.

Let us first examine the structural functions of Esther Summerson and her narrative. Esther has generally been dismissed as insipid, one of Dickens's flat, non-comic good characters, innocent of imaginative life, more of a moral signpost than a person. Even if we accept this general judgment we may still find good reasons why Dickens had necessarily to sacrifice vitality or complexity here in order to elaborate or intensify other parts of his novel. If Dickens, far from failing to create a lively Esther, is deliberately suppressing his natural exuberance in order to create a flat Esther, then we may properly consider one of Esther's functions to be that of a brake, controlling the runaway tendency of Dickens's imagination – controlling, in other words, the impulse to episodic intensification.

Can we possibly accept this view? The contrasting styles of the two narratives, while they offer the reader relief and variety, also seem to me evidence of Dickens's control in making Esther what she is, even at the risk of insipidity and dullness. The omniscient style has all the liveliness, fantastication and poetic density of texture that we typically associate with Dickens. Esther's narrative is plain, matter-of-fact, conscientiously plodding. Only very rarely does her style slip and allow us to glimpse Dickens guiding her pen – as when, for instance, she observes 'Mr Kenge, standing with his back to the fire, and casting his eyes over the dusty hearthrug as if it were Mrs Jellyby's biography' (ch. 4), or when, as Turveydrop bows to her, she could 'almost believe I saw creases come into the white of his eyes' (ch. 14). Here one may glimpse Dickens chafing at his self-imposed discipline. Such moments apart, any stylistic vivacity or idiosyncrasy in Esther's prose comes from the oddities and foibles of other characters. Dickens imagines them; Esther merely reports them. Even when, at moments of emotional stress, her prose strays into the purple patch, one still feels that this is the rhetoric of an amateur, not to be compared, for instance, with the controlled crescendo of Jo's death. Similarly, whenever the straightforward flow of Esther's narratives falters – as in her over-casual mention of Allan Woodcourt at the end of chapter 14 – we prefer to see this as appropriate to her character rather than to spot Dickens signalling a new relationship to us behind her back. That, of course, is precisely what he is doing, but the disguise of style persuades us to focus on Esther and not on her creator. (There is, I think, a corresponding and quite remarkable impersonality about the omniscient narrative. The general impression is of a vast, collective choric voice brilliantly mimicking the varied life it describes, yet able to generalize and comment without lapsing into the idiom of one man, of Dickens himself. Obviously the style exploits and manipulates our sympathies; yet surprisingly rarely do we feel that Dickens is directly buttonholing us.)

As I have said, the two narratives are *roughly* concurrent. Deliberately so; Dickens juggles the two chronologies by keeping the details sufficiently vague. Only rarely do we feel any awkwardness in this temporal matching together and any obvious discontinuity generally has a specific narrative or dramatic point. Esther's tale, taken in isolation, plods forward in the simplest kind of sequence. Yet, being autobiographical, it is retrospective and was written, so we are told, at the very end, seven years after the main events. This simplicity is rarely disturbed; only occasionally does Esther sound the note of 'If I had known then what I know now'; only occasionally does she throw an anticipatory light forward into the shadowy future of her tale, as, for example, she does at the end of chapter 37. The reason is that, despite the retrospective nature of her story, Esther must *seem* to be living in a dramatic present, ignorant of the plot's ramifications. Dickens is *really* omniscient in the other narrative; god-like he surveys time as though it were an eternal present and Esther must seem to belong to that present. It is a convention most readers readily accept.

In what ways does Esther's tale throw light on its teller? During his later period Dickens showed considerable interest in the possibilities of the first-person narrative. In some cases – *David Copperfield, Great Expectations* – the adult narrator judges, implicitly or explicitly, his growth towards maturity. Esther is clearly not in this category; she swiftly advances from child to woman and scarcely changes at all. We feel that she was 'born old' – a feeling reflected in the nicknames given her, though in fact she is little older than Ada Clare. On the other hand, she cannot be classed with Miss Wade, of *Little Dorrit*, whose story is taken by some critics as an early exercise in that kind of point-of-view technique which dramatizes a limited or crippled consciousness so that what is conveyed to the reader differs radically from the intention of the narrator. Clearly, we are meant to take Esther on trust. If what she tells us is wrong or limited this signifies no moral blindspot in her, no flaw in her sensibility but only her necessary innocence of the full ramifications of the plot. Dickens's treatment of Esther is devoid of irony. We have only to imagine what narrative would have resulted if the teller had been Skimpole – or even Richard Carstone – to see that Esther's responses, attitudes, and actions are never qualified or criticized. She is, in short, thoroughly idealized.

One result of the idealizing process is the static nature of Esther's character, the essentials of which we quickly come to know. These never change; her story merely exhibits them in a variety of situations in which she is generally the patient rather than the agent. That is, Esther *does* very little in the sense of initiating a chain of actions by a deliberate choice. Things are done to her or because of her rather than by her. Devastating things happen to Esther from the moment of her birth, but she generally emerges with her usual placidity and acceptance of duty. Indeed, at times Dickens takes care to subdue the effect on the reader of these crises through which Esther as patient must pass. The chapter which deals, for example, with the recognition scene between Esther and her mother closes in fact with Esther's reunion with Ada. The curious thing is the feelings aroused by the Esther–Ada relationship seem more intense – and intensely rendered – than those aroused by the Esther–Lady Dedlock encounter.

Esther then is static, consistent, passive. She is also good. The difficulties of combining these qualities to produce a compelling character are so immense that we should wonder not that Dickens fails, but that his failure is so slight. Still, he does fail. The exigencies of the narrative force him to reveal Esther's goodness in a coy and repellent manner; she is, for instance, continually imputing to others qualities which the author transparently wishes us to transfer to her. Esther's goodness is most acceptable when she is least conscious of its effects radiating out to impinge on others. Similarly, her narrative is most acceptable when she is pushed from the centre of the stage by the typical inhabitants of the Dickens world. Happily, this is usually so. In other words, Dickens has to reconcile in Esther the demands of a narrator and a main character and he chooses to subdue Esther as a character in the interests of her narrative function. We do not, so to speak, look *at* Esther; we look *through* her at the teeming Dickensian world. This viewpoint is no Jamesian dramatization of a particular consciousness; Esther is as lucid and neutral as a clear window. We look through at a human landscape but we are not, as with James, constantly aware that the window is limited by its frame or that it has a scratch here and an opaque spot there. The penalty Dickens pays for this is the insipidity of Esther's character. But then, *Bleak House* is a thickly populated novel; each character claims his own share of attention and all are connected by a complicated series of interlocking actions. There is no single centre, no Jamesian *disponible*; rather we have a complex field of force, of interacting stresses and strains. Given this complication it would be too much to ask of the reader that he concentrate on the perceiver as well as the perceived. Were

Esther to be complicated the novel would have to be corre-
spondingly simplified and the Dickens world depopulated. Who
would wish it so? If the real subject-matter of a novel is a subtly
dramatized consciousness then the objects of that consciousness
will tend to the sparse refinements of the closet drama. Dickens
is the opposite of this; he is to Shakespeare as James is to
Racine.

While this, I hope, explains the necessary limitations of
Esther's character, it only pushes the real problem one stage
further back. Why was it necessary to have a narrator of this
kind at all? Any adequate answer must also take into account the
omniscient narrative as well. The two narratives are the systole
and diastole of the novel and between them they produce the
distinctive effect of *Bleak House*; something that I can only call,
in a crudely impressionistic manner, the effect of *pulsation*, of
constant expansion and contraction, radiation and convergence.

The famous first chapter of *Bleak House* has had more than
its fair share of critical attention; at the risk of tedium, therefore,
I wish to isolate two striking features of Dickens's method. The
omniscient eye which surveys the scene is like the lens of a film
camera in its mobility. It may encompass a large panoramic view
or, within a sentence, it may swoop down to a close scrutiny of
some character or local detail. Closely related to this mobility is
the constant expansion and contraction from the omniscient
eye to Esther's single viewpoint. Closely related again is the
constant expansion and contraction of the total narrative; now
concentrating at great length on some episode, now hustling the
plot along with a rapid parade of characters. Dickens's narrative
skill is nowhere more evident than in his control of tempo.

All this I mean by *pulsation*. But chapter 1 displays yet another
related effect. The scene contracts to the Court of Chancery
at the heart of the fog, but suddenly this process is reversed;
Chancery monstrously expands to encompass the whole
country:

This is the Court of Chancery; which has its decaying houses and
its blighted lands in every shire; which has its worn-out lunatic
in every madhouse, and its dead in every churchyard. . . .

The heart of Chancery in this respect is Tom All Alone's the breeding-ground of disease (again the radiation of infection). The two are appropriately linked, for Chancery *is* a disease and is constantly described in these terms.

This theme is, of course, abundantly worked out in the novel – in Miss Flite, in Gridley, and above all, in Richard Carstone. The idea of corruption radiating out from a rotten centre (Chancery *and* Tom All Alone's) is reflected, in geographical terms, in the constant to-and-fro movement between London, Bleak House, and Chesney Wold. But this idea is counterpointed, in plot terms, by the sense one has of convergence, especially the sense of something closing-in on Lady Dedlock. Geography and plot coalesce in the final constriction of the chase and the discovery of Lady Dedlock dead near her lover's tomb.

This pulsation, this interaction of radiation and convergence, is also temporal. The case of Jarndyce and Jarndyce does not merely fan out in the present to enmesh innocent and remote people; it also has a terrible history:

Innumerable children have been born into the cause; innumerable young people have married into it; innumerable old people have died out of it. Scores of persons have deliriously found themselves made parties in Jarndyce and Jarndyce, without knowing how or why; whole families have inherited legendary hatreds with the suit.

Diverse pressures from the past converge to mould the present; Jarndyce and Jarndyce bears down on Richard Carstone; the past catches up with Esther and finally with her mother. This temporal convergence is reflected in the structure of the novel as a whole and locally, in its parts. Thus the first chapter given to Esther (ch. 3) quickly brings us from her childhood back to the dramatic present already described in the omniscient first chapter. Sometimes the dramatic present is illuminated by a shaft driven back into the past; thus both Boythorn and Miss Barbary are in some sense enlarged by the revelation of their abortive love long ago. Or again, the dramatic present will be left unexplained until time has passed and many pages have been turned; thus, on a small scale, the mystery of Jo's disappearance from Bleak House or, on a large scale, Bucket's uncovering of Tulkinghorn's murderess.

Granted the extremely complicated tangle of effects I have labelled *pulsation*, the desirability of a simple, lucid, straightforward narrative such as Esther's should be obvious. It offers us stability, a point of rest in a flickering and bewildering world, the promise of some guidance through the labyrinth. The usual novel may be compared to a pebble thrown into a pool; we watch the ripples spread. But in *Bleak House* Dickens has thrown in a whole handful of pebbles and what we have to discern is the immensely complicated tracery of half-a-dozen circles expanding, meeting, interacting. Esther – to change the metaphor – has the stability of a gyroscope; by her we chart our way.

She is, of course, much more than this. She is, as well, a moral touchstone; her judgments are rarely emphatic but we accept them. She can see Richard more clearly than Ada; through her Skimpole is revealed in his true colours and the Growlery becomes a sign of Jarndyce's obtuseness. She is also the known constant by which we judge all the other variables of character. Through her we can see the horrifyingly vivid notation of decay and infection that signals the slow process of Richard's destruction. (Among other things, the intertwining of the two narratives enables Dickens drastically to foreshorten and mould the *apparent* time sequence here.) Again, by her consistency Esther contributes to the wonderfully skilful characterization of Sir Leicester and Guppy, who change by fits and starts throughout the novel. Because these characters demand very different reactions from us at different times we impute complexity and development to them. In fact they are not so much complex as discontinuous. Dickens's art lies in masking this discontinuity and Esther in large part provides a convincing façade; because she is a simple unity we are conjured into believing that the heterogeneity of Guppy or Sir Leicester is a unified complexity.

Finally – and perhaps most important – by intertwining the two narratives Dickens compels us to a double vision of the teeming, fantastic world of *Bleak House*. We – and Esther – are within; we – and the omniscient author – are outside. This double perspective forces us as readers to make connections which as I have said, because *we* make them have more validity than if Dickens had made them for us. The most crucial instance is Esther's ignorance of so much that surrounds her. What she sees she sees clearly; but she cannot see more than a fraction of the whole. In this she is not alone; one of the triumphs of the novel is the delicacy with which Dickens handles the knowledge, suspicions, guesses, and mistakes of the various characters. Some of them are limited to one or other of the narrative streams; Esther is never seen by the omniscient eye, nor does Tulkinghorn ever appear personally in Esther's narrative. This corresponds to their limited knowledge; Tulkinghorn, for all his plotting, never knows of Esther's relation to Lady Dedlock while there is no substantial evidence that Esther knows anything of her father until after her mother's death.

Granted this, the opportunities for dramatic irony are clearly enormous and it is to Dickens's credit as an artist that with great tact he refuses many of the chances for irony offered by the interlocking narratives. How close – all unknowing – is Esther to meeting her father during her first visit to Krook's? Yet we scarcely perceive this, even on a re-reading of the novel. A lesser artist would have wrung dry the irony of such an incident, but Dickens is sound in his refusal to do so. For the novel, as it stands, is so taut, so potentially explosive, that to expatiate on, or to underline, its implications would make it quite intolerable. Of course the irony is there but it is kept latent and, so to speak, subcritical; it does not explode in the reader's conscious attention. In this, of course, its effect is almost the opposite of that which may be detected in *Death in Venice*. Mann's story depends largely on its insistently schematic nature, whereas Dickens's problem – like that of most novelists – is to avoid over-schematization, to control the complex and manifold life of the novel without drawing too much attention to the art involved. In this he is again helped by his chosen mode of narration. Through the double narrative Dickens refracts, reflects, varies, distorts,

reiterates his major themes, and the disturbing resonance thus
set up is expressive of his deepest sense of what life is like.
Bleak House is so dense with examples of this process that I will
quote only one, very minor example. In chapter 25, Mrs Snagsby
is suspicious:

Mrs Snagsby screws a watchful glance on Jo, as he is brought
into the little drawing-room by Guster. He looks at Mr Snagsby
the moment he comes in. Aha! Why does he look at Mr Snagsby?
Mr Snagsby looks at him. Why should he do that, but that Mrs
Snagsby sees it all? Why else should that look pass between
them; why else should Mr Snagsby be confused, and cough a
signal cough behind his hand. It is as clear as crystal that Mr
Snagsby is that boy's father.

Mrs Snagsby's magnificent illogicality is a comic analogue, a
parody of the dominant atmosphere of the book, that of hints,
guesses, suspicions, conspiracies. It is also a distorted echo of one
of the novel's major themes, that of parents and children. Even
here, in an insignificant corner of the book, its major concerns
are repeated and echoed in a different key; this abundance of
doubling, paralleling, contrasting, this constant modulation
from sinister to pathetic or comic, serves to create a density of
life providing a context for those vivid scenes of episodic intensification. We accept these, take them on trust as more than
brilliant but isolated moments, because we know they mesh with
that complicated web of human affairs which entangles all the
characters, even the most trivial. We weave this web, this
pattern, as the tale shuttles to and fro between its two tellers and,
of course, it is a pattern which gradually and continuously
develops and emerges.

SOURCE: *Character and the Novel* (1965).

Taylor Stoehr

BLEAK HOUSE:
THE NOVEL AS DREAM (1965)

THE prominent fact of *Bleak House* is the division of the novel into two parallel narratives, one told in the third person, present tense, by an unnamed and 'uninvolved' narrator, the other in the first person, past tense, by the heroine Esther Summerson. This division is the extreme example of the splitting into two plots found in all Dickens' later novels except *Great Expectations* and the unfinished *Mystery of Edwin Drood*. These novels written after 1850 tend toward greater unity of structure and a more direct expression of the dream content, with therefore less need to hold the novels together by melodramatic coincidence or any heavy-handed insistence on thematic parallels, repetition, and similar devices of secondary elaboration. *Bleak House*, as the first* of the dark novels, combined the most deeply divided of the plots with the most elaborately constructed network of superficial interconnections designed to bridge the gap. The gap is such and the interconnections are so many that critics who want to complain of Dickens' 'incurable love of labyrinthine mystification' are likely to single out *Bleak House* as a hideous example, even while arguing on the other hand that its plot goes 'all to pieces'.[1]

The most important effect of the split narrative and the devices of secondary elaboration which lace across its surface is their obscuring of the dream meaning of the stories of Esther Summerson and Richard Carstone, the heroine and hero. The double plot is Dickens' major means of camouflaging the basic emotional contents of these novels, for it allows him to present the

---

* Before *Bleak House* there are traces of the typical line of action and the doubled narrative, but nowhere are they developed to the extent that they constitute the formal structure.

elements of sex, class, and violence and at the same time to keep them safely isolated from each other. The doubling of the plot may be compared to the use, at another level, of hidden and apparent strands, a separation that also works against confrontation until the crucial scene of discovery. With the doubled plot, however, there is no equivalent to this scene of discovery, for the two narratives are not alternative accounts of the same set of circumstances; rather, two completely different sets of circumstances are connected on the surface by patterns of secondary elaboration, and beneath the surface by the emotional congruities which the division in plot tends formally to obscure.

In the following analysis of *Bleak House* I shall concentrate on the effects of the split narrative rather than on the concomitant devices of secondary elaboration; for although critics have shown how the various patterns of repetition and parallelism give the novel a superficial unity, no one has attempted to sort out the distortions and displacements imposed on Dickens' materials by the double plot.

The dual point of view keeps the two stories apart in an odd, 'inverted' way, for Esther's story is largely told not in her own narrative, but in the present-tense narrative, while she in turn tells most of Richard's story. This is made possible by the use of a representative or stand-in heroine – a typically dreamlike displacement. Lady Dedlock, Esther's mother, is also a surrogate for her. The apparent and hidden strands of her action, her reversal and discovery, and so on, are the mirror in which we see reflected (from the present-tense narrative) Esther's own story. The discovery, for both mother and child, is just that familial relation between them, of which they are both unaware. It is the secret that Tulkinghorn ferrets out and threatens to reveal to Sir Leicester; it is the guilty knowledge withheld from Esther by her aunt Miss Barbary. For Lady Dedlock the moment of discovery is at the end of chapter 29 in the present-tense narrative:

O my child, my child! Not dead in the first hours of her life, as my cruel sister told me; but sternly nurtured by her, after she had renounced me and my name! O my child, O my child!

For Esther the discovery is withheld for several chapters and is finally revealed by Lady Dedlock herself in the scene between them at Chesney Wold:

I looked at her; but I could not see her, I could not hear her, I could not draw my breath. The beating of my heart was so violent and wild, that I felt as if my life were breaking from me. But when she caught me to her breast, kissed me, wept over me, compassionated me, and called me back to myself; when she fell down on her knees and cried to me, 'O my child, my child, I am your wicked and unhappy mother! O try to forgive me!' – when I saw her at my feet on the bare earth in her great agony of mind, I felt, through all my tumult of emotion, a burst of gratitude to the providence of God that I was so changed as that I never could disgrace her by any trace of likeness; as that nobody could ever now look at me, and look at her, and remotely think of any near tie between us. (ch. 36)

That Esther's first thought is of her recent illness and the scars it has left, a mask to hide her mother's disgrace, is perhaps not so surprising when we realize that that illness has represented Esther's reversal, often in Dickens a warning of discovery to come. Just before her first exposure to the disease, Esther has a typical dreamlike premonition of this reversal and discovery:

I had no thought, that night – none, I am quite sure – of what was soon to happen to me. But I have always remembered since, that when we had stopped at the garden-gate to look up at the sky, and when we went upon our way, I had for a moment an undefinable impression of myself as being something different from what I then was. I know it was then, and there, that I had it. I have ever since connected the feeling with that spot and time, and with everything associated with that spot and time. (ch. 31)

The connection between Esther's scars and her mother's disgrace goes very deep; it is in fact the essence of the discovery, though the full recognition is delayed, as usual in Dickens, until the secondary discovery. The illness, contracted from Esther's maid Charley, who has contracted it from the sweep Jo, is a symbol of the secret and guilty connections between the high and low in society – that is, between Jo and Lady Dedlock,

between Lady Dedlock and Esther, and finally and most dis-
gracefully between Lady Dedlock and Captain Hawdon, Esther's
father, the wretched Nemo. The third-person narrator particularly dwells on these guilty relationships:

What connexion can there be, between the place in Lincolnshire,
the house in town, the Mercury in powder, and the whereabout
of Jo the outlaw with the broom, who had that distant ray of light
upon him when he swept the churchyard-step? What connexion
can there have been between many people in the innumerable
histories of this world, who, from opposite sides of great gulfs,
have, nevertheless, been very curiously brought together!
(ch. 16)

Dickens was fascinated with this idea, that secret, devious,
multitudinous threads of connection run between the high and
low in society. *Bleak House* is full of such threads and knots, and
he makes one strand into the veritable spinal cord of an entire
plot. Esther's lineage is such a bundle of vital connections, and
much of her share of the plot consists in its slow laying bare by a
series of patient anatomists – Tulkinghorn, Guppy, the Smallweeds, Bucket, the third-person narrator, even Esther herself.
The ultimate anatomist is Dickens, who regards his heroine's
lineage as diseased to the core, and uses the metaphors of pestilence and contagion to convey a sense of the hidden channels
of corruption which connect high and low, respectability and
bestiality, Chesney Wold and Tom-all-Alone's. As we slowly
come to see, the connection at which Dickens hints is not limited
to the coincidental collision of Lady Dedlock and Jo, but
involves many other characters as well. Everyone is infected;
society is corrupt. Dickens does not specify the exact place where
Jo picks up the smallpox which he passes on to Charley, and
through her to Esther, but the gruesome cemetery to which Lady
Dedlock pays her secret visit, guided by Jo, is described as a
source of both moral and physical infection:

... A hemmed-in churchyard, pestiferous and obscene, whence
malignant diseases are communicated to the bodies of our dear
brothers and sisters who have not departed; while our dear
brothers and sisters who hang about official backstairs – would

to Heaven they *had* departed! – are very complacent and agreeable. Into a beastly scrap of ground which a Turk would reject as a savage abomination, and a Caffre would shudder at, they bring our dear brother here departed, to receive Christian burial.

With houses looking on, on every side, save where a reeking little tunnel of a court gives access to the iron gate – with every villainy of life in action close on death, and every poisonous element of death in action close on life – here, they lower our dear brother down a foot or two: here, sow him in corruption, to be raised in corruption: an avenging ghost at many a sick bedside: a shameful testimony to future ages, how civilisation and barbarism walked this boastful island together. (ch. 11)

Tom-all-Alone's, itself in Chancery and perhaps named after 'the original plaintiff or defendant in Jarndyce and Jarndyce' (ch. 16), is a similar festering in the landscape of London; it was Captain Hawdon's haunt while he lived as Nemo, and it is Jo's home, or the closest thing he has to a home. Again in the descriptions of this slum, Dickens dwells on the subtle and pervasive implication of a guilt that knows no boundaries of rank or privilege. The metaphor remains that of disease, and Tom-all-Alone, the area personified, is no less likely a candidate for the source of Esther's sickness, both literally and symbolically, than the graveyard where her father lies:

[Tom] has his revenge. Even the winds are his messengers, and they serve him in these hours of darkness. There is not a drop of Tom's corrupted blood but propagates infection and contagion somewhere. It shall pollute, this very night, the choice stream (in which chemists on analysis would find the genuine nobility) of a Norman house, and his Grace shall not be able to say Nay to the infamous alliance. There is not an atom of Tom's slime, not a cubic inch of any pestilential gas in which he lives, not one obscenity or degradation about him, not an ignorance, not a wickedness, not a brutality of his committing, but shall work its retribution, through every order of society, up to the proudest of the proud, and to the highest of the high. Verily, what with tainting, plundering, and spoiling, Tom has his revenge. (ch. 46)

The imagery here, in addition to the already familiar corruption and plague, has also the touch of moral evil, and particularly of

sexual transgression, which is also hinted at by the conclusion of
the love affair between Esther's parents in the filthy cemetery.
Tom-all-Alone's disease seems to be a 'social' one, in both senses
of that term: there is mixed blood here, an 'infamous alliance',
infection 'propagated', all in a context of 'obscenity', 'degradation', and 'brutality'.

The notion of the poor taking revenge for their sufferings by
spreading disease is a familiar one in Dickens. We find it in
Dombey and Son, for instance:

Those who study the physical sciences, and bring them to bear
upon the health of Man, tell us that if the noxious particles that
rise from vitiated air were palpable to the sight, we should see
them lowering in a dense black cloud above such haunts, and
rolling slowly on to corrupt the better portions of a town. But
if the moral pestilence that rises with them, and in the eternal
laws of outraged Nature, is inseparable from them, could be
made discernible too, how terrible the revelation! (ch. 47)

But this idea stems from a larger and deeper conviction running
throughout the novels, namely that any relation, especially a
sexual one, between the high and the low in society is to be
regarded as filthy and diseased, as somehow immoral and unclean. Thus the bond between Lady Dedlock and Esther is set
in the context of illness; and even more strikingly, the illicit love
of Lady Dedlock and Captain Hawdon is symbolized by the
gruesome image of the burial ground where Lady Dedlock
comes to view her lover's grave. That the marriage of high and
low in the liaison of Lady Dedlock and Captain Hawdon is
guilty and unclean – this is the real discovery toward which
Esther is impelled. The flight of Lady Dedlock (and of Esther,
who in pursuing her mother is also in a sense fleeing with her) is
away from this recognition, away from London, away from the
burial ground; but the flight ends, nevertheless, at that very
place:

At last we stood under a dark and miserable covered way, where
one lamp was burning over an iron gate, and where the morning
faintly struggled in. The gate was closed. Beyond it, was a

burial-ground – a dreadful spot in which the night was very slowly stirring; but where I could dimly see heaps of dishonoured graves and stones, hemmed in by filthy houses, with a few dull lights in their windows, and on whose walls a thick humidity broke out like a disease. On the step at the gate, drenched in the fearful wet of such a place, which oozed and splashed down everywhere, I saw, with a cry of pity and horror, a woman lying – Jenny, the mother of the dead child. (ch. 59)

But it is Lady Dedlock dressed in Jenny's clothes; it is the *dead mother of the child*:

I passed on to the gate, and stooped down. I lifted the heavy head, put the long dank hair aside, and turned the face. And it was my mother cold and dead.

This is Esther's secondary discovery, the climax of her story. What is left out is only the explicit recognition that the burial ground, with its contagion and corruption, is the symbol of her mother's relations with Hawdon, and also the symbol of the taint in Esther's own life.

Esther cannot entertain any lover herself because of this taint. When Guppy (a suitor too ludicrously 'low' for her) proposes marriage, Esther rejects him not only because she does not love him, or because he is too common for her, but also because she is tainted. In one of the most affecting scenes in her narrative, she gives us a symbolic clue to this motive, by means of another graveyard image. In early life she had had a doll which was her only comfort. Her aunt, Miss Barbary, was accustomed to harangue the child Esther:

'Submission, self-denial, diligent work, are the preparations for a life begun with such a shadow on it. You are different from other children, Esther, because you were not born, like them, in common sinfulness and wrath. You are set apart.' (ch. 3)

Esther describes her reaction:

I went up to my room, and crept to bed, and laid my doll's cheek against mine wet with tears; and holding that solitary friend upon my bosom, cried myself to sleep. Imperfect as my understanding of my sorrow was, I knew that I had brought no joy, at any time, to anybody's heart, and that I was to no one upon earth what Dolly was to me.

Dear, dear, to think how much time we passed alone together afterwards, and how often I repeated to the doll the story of my birthday, and confided to her that I would try, as hard as ever I could, to repair the fault I had been born with (of which I confessedly felt guilty and yet innocent), and would strive as I grew up to be industrious, contented, and kind-hearted, and to do some good to some one, and win some love to myself if I could.

When she finally left Miss Barbary's, after that lady's death, Esther had buried the old doll in the garden. Now, having rejected Guppy,

I sat there for another hour or more, finishing my books and payments, and getting through plenty of business. Then, I arranged my desk, and put everything away, and was so composed and cheerful that I thought I had quite dismissed this unexpected incident. But, when I went up-stairs to my own room, I surprised myself by beginning to laugh about it, and then surprised myself still more by beginning to cry about it. In short, I was in a flutter for a little while; and felt as if an old chord had been more coarsely touched than it ever had been since the days of the dear old doll, long buried in the garden. (ch. 9)

Again, Esther's other suitors, her guardian John Jarndyce and her true love Allan Woodcourt, also suffer from the perverse caprice of Esther's guilty morality. Woodcourt – to spell out Dickens' pun – would court Esther if he could; but several obstacles prevent him: his mother's snobbism (she thinks Allan's Welsh ancestors too good for Esther, and even tells her so, indirectly); and Esther's sense of guilt. Esther agrees that she is not good enough for Allan; after her illness she is grateful for an excuse to forget about him as a potential lover:

But how much better it was now, that this had never happened! What should I have suffered, if I had had to write to him, and tell him that the poor face he had known as mine was quite gone from me, and that I freely released him from his bondage to one whom he had never seen! (ch. 35)

In this excuse (that she is scarred) we can read her real fear (that she is tainted). The connection comes out even more explicitly in her decision to accept Jarndyce's proposal:

But he did not hint to me, that when I had been better-looking, he had had this same proceeding in his thoughts, and had refrained from it. That when my old face was gone from me, and I had no attractions, he could love me just as well as in my fairer days. That the discovery of my birth gave him no shock. That his generosity rose above my disfigurement, and my inheritance of shame. (ch. 44)

Her acceptance of Jarndyce is possible because it is not really a lovers' union he proposes:

It was not a love letter though it expressed so much love, but was written just as he would at any time have spoken to me. . . . It told me that I would gain nothing by such a marriage, and lose nothing by rejecting it; for no new relation could enhance the tenderness in which he held me, and whatever my decision was, he was certain it would be right.

Indeed, Esther's acceptance of Jarndyce is really a renunciation of love, since she thereby gives up Woodcourt. It is a kind of punishment for her mother's sin. She is finally allowed (by the benevolent Jarndyce) to have her lover, only because once Lady Dedlock is herself brought low in the burial-yard scene, the punishment is over and the guilt has been expiated; we hear no more of barriers of class or family between Esther and Woodcourt, and Mrs Woodcourt is miraculously converted to become a doting mother-in-law.

SOURCE: *Dickens: The Dreamer's Stance* (1965).

NOTE

1. Percy Lubbock, *The Craft of Fiction* (London, 1929; New York, 1957).

A. E. Dyson

BLEAK HOUSE: ESTHER BETTER NOT BORN? (1969)

I

'In *Bleak House* I have purposely dwelt upon the romantic side of familiar things.' So Dickens tells us in his 1853 preface. The wording recalls Wordsworth's ambitions for his part in *Lyrical Ballads*, but *Bleak House* is 'romantic' in an older sense. Its heroine, cheerfully sane and domestic, and much loved by those nearest to her, is surrounded by unsolved riddles concerning her birth. Who is she? How important are the gloomy words remembered so sadly from childhood: 'It would have been far better, little Esther, that you had had no birthday; that you had never been born!'? Lady Dedlock, proud, haughty, riding high above the great world of fashion five miles round, is strangely threatened: by a legal document, whose handwriting disturbs her; by footfalls on the Ghost's Walk at her place in Lincolnshire; by a portrait, fascinating to the young man of the name of Guppy; by a family solicitor, whom she increasingly fears. We stumble on other characters no less mysterious, tucked away in back streets or in legal chambers, or looming suddenly through the fog. Who is Krook, the sinister illiterate nicknamed Lord Chancellor? Who is Krook's mysterious lodger, Nemo? Who are Mr George and his friend Phil? – Tulkinghorn and Bucket? Who is Jo? – our worry as well as Mrs Snagsby's, Dickens assures us. There are further mysteries in *Bleak House* of 'why?' Why is Esther disapproved of, Jo hounded, Sir Leicester deferred to? Why does Tulkinghorn behave so – well, unprofessionally? What professional ethic does Bucket observe? No one in the novel has a safe or stable place in society; not Jo, who is very well aware of this, not Sir Leicester, to whom the discovery will come as a shock. Several of the characters spend their lives rummaging among dust and debris for secrets; Tulkinghorn in his chambers, Krook in his shop; Grandfather Smallweed in 'a rather ill-favoured and ill-savoured neighbourhood', the Lord Chancellor in his High Court of Chancery among the great of the land. Nearly everyone is searching for meanings not easy to come by. *Bleak House* is pervaded from its magnificent opening chapter by the London Particular, as we watch ghostly suitors suing for justice in a world of ghosts.

A romantic setting, and a romantic plot; the plot is particularly important to *Bleak House*. Dickens's new friend, the young Wilkie Collins, must have been fascinated by this forerunner of his own genre. With its shameful secret, its beautiful victim, its implacable blackmailer and its vintage detective, *Bleak House* is a tale of crime and detection. We are obliged therefore to pay the closest attention to Dickens's plot and structure in the novel, as well as to his intentionally transparent hints. This is truer indeed of *Bleak House* than it is of any of the other novels, with the obvious and tantalising exception of *Edwin Drood*. Dickens's early plots from *Pickwick* to *Chuzzlewit* are mainly picaresque in character, and guided by the fortunes of their hero or heroine towards aesthetic shape. The plot of *Barnaby Rudge*, of course, is more complex, but still essentially linear and, like *A Tale of Two Cities* later, controlled by actual historical events. *Dombey and Son*, though no longer picaresque, proceeds chronologically through a fairly straightforward story, with its mysteries clustering around the affairs of Good Mrs Brown. *David Copperfield* is in the form of pseudo-autobiography, and regresses, in plot technique, to the earlier mode.

The plot of *Little Dorrit*, in contrast, is of very great complexity, but is so far from being at the heart of the novel's greatness that even Dickens was hard put to it to unravel the strands. Much the same could be said of *Our Mutual Friend*, where complexities of plot and symbolism are closely wedded, but the plot counts for little on its own. *Bleak House* stands out from all of these in having a plot which is so central and fundamental that if the reader loses his way with it in *this* novel, he is lost indeed. He is left, in fact, in bewildered fellowship with the unfortunate Snagsby, making very Kafkaesque going of the entire affair.

The reader who attends closely is less totally fogbound, in that he engages in the first place not with a metaphysical riddle but with a mystery story, a romance. A mystery story, however, with metaphysical overtones; the formula of *Bleak House* has its truest progeny neither in *The Castle* and *The Trial*, nor in the modern detective story, influential though it was in both these directions, but in such intriguing if comparatively minor master-pieces as Rex Warner's *The Aerodrome* and Graham Greene's *The Ministry of Fear*. A seeming nightmare is created and then in the end resolved by plot logic, but certain unresolved suggestions tease the mind. The plot has explained much, but it has not explained everything; and the novel's power is somewhere in the gap. The word 'identity' is useful as a pointer to the gap in this particular instance. Esther's identity is a mystery raised, and then solved, at plot level, but profounder mysteries of identity per-vade the whole.

'. . . the romantic side of familiar things.' The formula draws attention to Dickens's insertion of grim social realities and soar-ing moral challenges into a story which would have pleased the old writers of romance. But should the 'romantic side' of Chan-cery, or Tom-All-Alone's, or Lady Dedlock's guilt be so familiar? – the words are not innocent of an ironic twist. Yet 'romantic' hints, nonetheless, a promise that unless the reader is to be wholly misled the author's treatment, or his conclusion, will not be unremittingly grim. Many accounts of *Bleak House* make it sound as sombre as its immediate sequel *Hard Times*, but this is far from being true. On the contrary, I would even call this an optimistic novel, given the nature of its material and its themes. The optimism may be felt in a certain expansiveness and humour – mainly Esther's – but more particularly in moments of explicitly religious hope. Jo dies with the unfamiliar words of the Lord's Prayer on his lips, Richard Carstone starts a new world which sets this world to rights. The optimism of such passages is too clear to be doubted, unless we miss the 'strangers and pilgrims' theme so omnipresent in Dickens and absentmindedly ascribe all his religious passages to cant. At the same time, *Bleak House* develops the encouraging symbolism of its title. For one Bleak House blighted by Chancery and fully deserving its name we receive two Bleak Houses, both created by Jarndyce and irradiated by Esther, both calm and fruitful, with 'delightful irregularities' enhancing order and charm.

Bleak House is, moreover, a novel with an astonishing number of virtuous characters, far more than Dickens presented in such numbers elsewhere. To the roll-call of Jarndyce, Esther and Ada we must add Miss Flite, Allan Woodcourt, Charley, Mrs Rouncewell, Mr Boythorn, George and Phil, Mr Snagsby, Mr and Mrs Bagnet, Caddy Jellyby, Rosa and Walter, and, in their hopeless ways, Guster, Jenny and her friend, Mrs Blinder – the poor who are 'so much to the poor'. These characters achieve by their concerted goodness an effect of radiance akin to Esther's serene good humour in 'her' prose. There are also many characters from Lord and Lady Dedlock down through Richard, Jo, Prince, even to Guppy, who on balance, with whatever admixture of weakness or absurdity, strike us as more good than evil at heart. If we turn to the evil characters, they include several in whom Dickens's transforming zest is richly at work. Skimpole and old Mr Turveydrop create themselves in the manner of Pecksniff and Micawber, not only atrocious but atrociously attractive, while Mrs Jellyby and Mrs Pardiggle are softened, for all their awfulness, by Esther's eye. The really vile characters are by Dickens's standards few: Krook, Vholes, Grandfather Small-weed, Hortense, Mrs Snagsby (perhaps) and, of course, Tul-kinghorn. There is also the fascinating enigma of Mr Bucket – surely good at heart? – yet more like Tulkinghorn than we might expect.

II

But, it will be urged, is this not precisely the dividing line in Dickens's work between 'evil' which is associated chiefly with evil men, and 'evil' which invades the texture of society itself? If the characters in *Bleak House* are often demonstrably virtuous, why is there more actual suffering here than ever before? In place of great individual villains like Ralph Nickleby, Fagin and Quilp, we now have Chancery, Tom-All-Alone's and a darkened world. 'The system! I am told on all hands it's the system!' Mr Gridley shouts, in his passionate and futile rage.

This account of Dickens's development is now highly familiar, but more dubious than familiarity might suggest. Like all other attempts to simplify him, it is highly selective. *Barnaby Rudge* and *Dombey and Son* are disregarded, and there is some degree of distortion everywhere else. In early Dickens, for instance, we frequently sense a world in the grip of nightmare, where terrible faces peer out at us, Fagin over Oliver's shoulder, Quilp over Little Nell's, more like exhalations of evil than its original cause. At the same time, it is plainly untrue to say that *Bleak House* lacks spectacular villains: Tulkinghorn is among the two or three most sinister figures that Dickens ever drew. Can we overlook, for that matter, Grandfather Smallweed and his horrible family, or the vampire lawyer Vholes who drinks Richard's blood?

It is important, then, to stress continuities as well as discontinuities, yet one must allow some definite change in Dickens in the late 1840s and early 1850s, towards a more pervasive sense of evils rooted in impersonal things. The sinister villains are joined now by such urbane and kindly souls as the Lord Chancellor, and by the just and honourable Sir Leicester and the whole of his class. It can be argued that Dickens became more conscious in the Great Exhibition era than he had been even at the time of *Dombey* that his society was nearer to the jungle, in its daily realities, than to Christian ideals. Richard is killed, so are Jo, Nemo and the man from Shropshire; so, with the assistance of Tulkinghorn's strange vendetta, is Lady Dedlock. Miss Flite has become deranged by suffering before we meet her, and shares honours with Krook as choric commentator on the Lord Chancellor's Court. Jenny and her friend exist in fear and squalor, and their babies live or die as though nineteen hundred years of Christianity had never been:

'Why, what age do you call that little creature?' says Bucket. 'It looks as if it was born yesterday.' He is not at all rough about it; and as he turns his light gently upon the infant, Mr Snagsby is strangely reminded of another infant, encircled with light, that he has seen in pictures.

Even Jarndyce and Esther withdraw from any large involvement with their society in favour of the domestic but still threatened sphere of private life. Meanwhile, the poor rot in Tom-All-Alone's and men die in Chancery; systems seem indeed more powerful than men. Is it not apparent that traditional privilege and the new capitalism between them are breaking the human spirit and breeding despair?

Some such implications were detected, certainly, and no less certainly resented, by Trollope and other Victorians of Dickens's time. They resented the gloom and savagery of Dickens's social picture, when *laissez faire* and the Great Exhibition seemed to promise so much. (It was a different story when Trollope came to write *The Way We Live Now* in the mid-1870s, but economic optimism by then was starting to ebb.) Modern critics have agreed with Dickens's contemporaries in noting the gloom of his picture; yet the gloom is balanced by powerful forces on the other side. Just as Jo and Richard die with religious hope surrounding them, so Jarndyce proves that Miss Flite's theory of mystical *compulsion* in the Chancellor's mace is not true. Esther dispels the notion that the bastard child of an aristocratic lady need necessarily be warped by her misfortunes or grow up to lament her dubious identity and her uncertain fate. She survives illegitimacy, unrequited love, smallpox, and the terrible knowledge that her very existence is her mother's nightmare, to exist triumphantly in a world of good. The depressing perversions of private charity witnessed to in Mrs Jellyby and Mrs Pardiggle are more than counterbalanced by the constructive charity of Jarndyce, Esther, Mr Snagsby, George, Mr and Mrs Bagnet, Mrs Blinder and Guster. At the same time, *Bleak House* is itself a factor in *Bleak House*, a sufficient reminder that the author, at least, had not succumbed to impotent despair. He went on fighting, in fiction and elsewhere, for that ideal of social responsibility later embodied in the welfare state. In the twentieth century no one lives in Tom-All-Alone's in utter hopelessness, dies like

Jo in the London streets, suffers the law's delay quite as Jarndyce
did. Other evils, yes, and Dickens would have expected them,
but these particular evils have been removed.

III

Nonetheless, *Bleak House* presents evils in abundance, as modern
critics rightly underline. If Dame Durden is there to 'sweep the
cobwebs out of the sky' there is ample work for her broom.
Nowhere else does Dickens survey society so comprehensively
and on the whole so gloomily, from the heights of Chesney
Wold down to the burying-yard to which Lady Dedlock
descends. The brickmakers, Nemo, Coavinses and his children,
Guster and Jo belong to the world of extreme poverty, driven by
the absolute neglect of society towards their death. From this
abyss, we rise through the genteel poverty of Miss Flite, the
honest, hard-working poverty of George and Phil, the self-
respecting near-poverty of Mr and Mrs Bagnet, to the proudly
independent poverty (perhaps this is no longer the word, however) of Mrs Rouncewell, loyal to her employers, and in many
true ways really one of the family at Chesney Wold. Then, rising
again in worldly prospects, though not in attractiveness, we pass
through the lower-middle-class world of the Snagsbys (genteel
vulgarity pointing forward to Mrs Wilfer's tragic stage in Hollo-
way), the eye-to-the-main-chance opportunism of Guppy and
Tony Jobling, the stomach-turning self-imposed squalor of the
Smallweeds, the shabby-elegant *ménage* of Skimpole, the extraordinary manifestations of old Mr Turveydrop's Deportment,
the deplorable Jellyby home. Above these scenes, we emerge into
the world of the prosperous middle classes – Boythorn and Jarndyce prosperous on inherited wealth, the Iron Gentleman on the
wealth of self-made business success – and upwards, again, to
the splendours of Chesney Wold. (Where, however, even amid the
splendour, poor Volumnia broods in the nightwatches on what
is to become of her if her rich relations die, or become bored with
her, or simply forget that she is there.)

In most places and in various patterns and combinations

Dickens sees money as a curse. At the top of the hierarchy it is unproductive. Sir Leicester despises people who earn money, and ascribes his own pre-eminence to immutable laws. Lady Dedlock is bored to death chiefly because her exaltation above society leaves her with nothing to do. Rather worse, money at the top of the hierarchy is irresponsible. Sir Leicester may attend to his devotions at Chesney Wold with all sincerity, but neither the spirit nor even the letter reaches Jo. In Chancery, inherited wealth is the pretext for large-scale and horrible parasitism, which Dickens characteristically embodies in bizarre images: the vampire lawyer Vholes who drinks Richard's blood, Miss Flite's fantastic roll-call of birds. There is also the parasitism of the Smallweed family, and the parasitism of Skimpole, whose pretence to know nothing about money is yet one more mode of vicious misuse.

Where else is money influential? In the North Country, of course, where the Iron Gentleman produces wealth for himself and for his country (yet his factory has sacrificed beauty and cleanliness, and Dickens had never taken kindly to industrial towns). Meanwhile, Guster has her fits in the Snagsby establishment; and Jenny is beaten by her drunken husband; and Nemo dies by inches in Krook's chambers. And Jo is moved on, and on, and on in the London streets, until his mind darkens with bewilderment and his body falls prey to fever; and, after offering a few small gems of insight – about Mr Chadband, and about life; and after communicating his plague unknowingly and much to his sorrow to Esther; and after destroying or helping to destroy, unknowingly, Lady Dedlock; he comes to the end predicted for him all along:

Dead, your Majesty. Dead, my lords and gentlemen. Dead, Right Reverends and Wrong Reverends of every order. Dead, men and women, born with Heavenly compassion in your hearts. And dying thus around us every day.

Money is entwined with most of these evils as it was in *Dombey and Son*, but is money their root? 'Dead, men and women, born with Heavenly compassion in your hearts.' The savagery of this famous stroke of irony is that Dickens believed it to be the truth. In all the perversions of society around him he saw greed, apathy, cruelty, often (and here was a role for literature) simple failure of imagination, but these were familiar consequences of the Fall. 'The good that I would I do not, the evil that I would not that I do.' Behind man's fallen nature another nature survived, if only fitfully – the original heavenly compassion in his heart. It is from *this* conviction that Dickens's creative energy drew so much inspiration that even *Bleak House* could be infused with hope. Other evils he would have expected to arise in human history, and these too would need hope in their turn. But the here-and-now evils could be exposed, despite all obstacles – despite even Parliament, dedicated as it seemed to an evil *status quo*.

Perhaps it is to reinforce these insights that Tulkinghorn is so important in the novel: Tulkinghorn, an extreme but by that token exceptional example of the human *malaise*. A man of power, infinitely malign and corrupt yet in no direct sense motivated by money, he is the presiding genius of evil in *Bleak House*. There are two great cobwebs in the novel, woven by no directing intelligence yet entangling their victims – Chancery, where Richard, the man from Shropshire and Miss Flite flounder, and Tom-All-Alone's, where Jo and Nemo come to their deaths. The two webs meet – Tom-All-Alone's is in Chancery – but no malign creature has fashioned the threads. But in the centre of *Bleak House* there is another web, woven by Tulkinghorn, to catch and destroy one person whom he hates. Hates? – his motive indeed remains hidden, but the end is never in doubt. Like Iago, Tulkinghorn admires and is fascinated by his victim; like Iago, he relishes his power to entangle to destruction, until there seems creative satisfaction, almost, in what he does. Some critics have complained that Tulkinghorn behaves unlike a normal solicitor – an insight that Dickens's ironic heart would surely have enjoyed. We may safely concede that Tulkinghorn's behaviour is surprising, and unprofessional, and that whatever its outcome he could hardly have survived as the trusted solicitor of the great. Whether acknowledged or not, self-destruction seems part of his plotting: it is when Dickens is reminding us that Tulkinghorn, the guardian of mysteries, is himself a mystery, that we learn of the one bachelor friend he has had:

... a man of the same mould and a lawyer too, who lived the same kind of life until he was seventy-five years old, and then suddenly conceiving (as it is supposed) an impression that it was too monotonous, gave his gold watch to his hairdresser one summer evening and walked leisurely home to the Temple and hanged himself.

In Tulkinghorn, Dickens is presenting a study of highly abnormal psychology, yet not too remote for flashes of recognition to light the scene. He is familiar in the peculiarly frightening way that Iago is familiar, not as daily phenomenon, but as something glimpsed, inwards and downwards, in some private abyss. He is like Iago in that he becomes an ultimate image, at one of those extreme points where the ultimate may sometimes take flesh. Does he probe his motives also, like Iago, trying explanations, plausible though shifting, which never fully explain? We feel something wrong in him from his first appearance in Chesney Wold – musty, respectable, almost 'retainer-like' to Sir Leicester's admiring perception (far removed indeed from the Wat Tylerish image of doom in the baronet's mind). What does he feel about the aristocrats and other exalted beings who depend on his services? His thoughts on these matters are not revealed. Yet Dickens conveys that Tulkinghorn in his respected old age walks a tight-rope; needs something to snap merely, some long habit of restraint to be relinquished, some tug, resisted possibly for a lifetime, to be given its way. Some men break when a rational appraisal of them might least anticipate this, and Dickens records many such moments in his work. In *Dombey and Son* it happens to Carker. After a career of careful and successful fraud he risks everything on a reckless elopement, doomed from the start. It happens to Bradley Headstone in *Our Mutual Friend* when, after a painful and unnatural climb to respectability, he succumbs to a madness always waiting close, it seems, behind his back. It happens surely – though the full implications remain permanently

inaccessible – to John Jasper, the respected choirmaster of
Cloisterham. Tulkinghorn fits into the abnormal yet frighteningly understandable pattern of a man – old or young, it might
be either – giving his most destructive compulsions their head.
At a certain moment he abandons himself to evil. By choice? We
no more discern this clearly than he does himself. But he begins
to weave a web which will be fatal to Lady Dedlock, and fatal
in one manner or another to himself. When does he finally
decide to destroy his victim? We find him speculating that 'she
cannot be spared'. He wonders resentfully how she can show
mercy to her maid Rosa, when no mercy is to be shown to her.
Clearly he has to goad her almost beyond endurance, puzzled and
elated by the courage she shows. Must she break before his eyes
for some metaphysical reason – to prove, perhaps, that even an
aristocrat is mortal and evil, like himself? Or is it nourishment he
seeks on a victim's fearfulness, all the richer for a season of
courage and peculiar restraint? Whatever his motives, the result
is nightmare, and gives its distinctive colour to the book. The
webs of Chancery and Tom-All-Alone's become embued with
his evil: yet clearly *he* is no ordinary blackmailer motivated by
money, and there is no heavenly compassion in *his* heart. Some
impulse to power, irrational and murderous, is incarnate in
Tulkinghorn, and its mystery reaches deep in *Bleak House*.

IV

Bleak House is a novel, then, of romantic themes and highly
disparate characters whose destiny is reconciled in the symbol of
a web. As John Harvey has noted, the novel introduces us to
groups of characters who at first seem wholly divorced from
each other. It is when we begin to perceive links in their destiny
that the web comes to be felt.

It is important to notice, however, that the web is not wholly
evil; there are threads of brotherhood and sanity, too, in the
book. Charley and Esther both contract smallpox as the price of
compassion, of their acknowledged responsibilities towards each
other and towards Jo. Lady Dedlock lies frozen to death outside

the foul graveyard where her lover rots, but she is drawn by
nature, as well as pursued, to this place. It is highly appropriate
that Guster should be the last person to encounter Lady Dedlock before her death, and that the Lady from Chesney Wold
should offer her dying blessing to one so wholly removed, in all
social intercourse, from herself. It is characteristic and fitting,
again, that though Lady Dedlock dies and the tragedy moves to
the sombre irony of her final tableau – the great lady become, in
fact, the pauper whose dress she wears – this final meeting with
Guster, and Sir Leicester's forgiveness, should strike us as a
marvellous victory for good. 'Am I my brother's keeper?' Those
who answer 'yes' in *Bleak House* suffer, but they are not crushed.
'And so I took it from her' (says Guster, of Lady Dedlock's last
letter), 'and she said she had nothing to give me, and I said I was
poor myself and consequently wanted nothing. And so she said
God bless you, and went.' Sir Leicester, who functions for much
of the novel as a butt for searching social satire, emerges in
tragic affliction as a truly good man.

It is also appropriate that coincidence should play a very large
part in this work. Throughout Dickens's novels, coincidences
are frequent, usually in the measure that we recognise as 'realistic' for drama on so vast a scale. By which I mean that Dickens's
usual coincidences have the hallmark of coincidences in normal
life: they are unpredictable in that they happen by accident, but
imbued by hindsight with suggestions of poetic justice or unmerited grace. Such suggestions may be arbitrary and in defiance
of logic, but there is ample repository for them in the reservoir
of our wishes and fears. Given the circumstances (we say) things
might have happened so; even *should* have happened so?: even
would have happened so?: given Providence or Justice, or a lucky,
or an unlucky, star. The mind broods hopefully or tormentingly
in the nightwatches, and a novelist defies no canons of realism in
depicting such thoughts.

In *Bleak House*, however, coincidence plays a somewhat larger
part than we might anticipate, yet this is congruous with our
sense of men and women caught in a web. The coincidences turn
out, after all, to be not unqualified, in that chains of probability,

however tenuous, may be perceived. This is nothing like the experience of coincidence in (for instance) Hardy's later novels, where we sense extraneous pressures – the author's temperamental pessimism, his debt to Greek tragedy – behind the scenes. And certainly it is not like the coincidences of lesser novelists, who might resort to such measures at desperate junctures of their plot. Dickens, by mingling good and evil in his coincidences, keeps close to one of the delicate yet elusive mysteries of human destiny, our sense of irrational aspects haunting the most 'ordinary' life. Consider, for instance, Lady Dedlock's recognition of her former lover's handwriting: unexpected, yes, but not unprecedented; and the Tulkinghorns of life look for and build on such things. Guppy visits Chesney Wold and is reminded, by Lady Dedlock's picture, of Esther; but Guppy has dealings both with Esther and with Lady Dedlock through the Jarndyce connection; and who has not been teased by family likenesses in old pictures and prints? Esther and Lady Dedlock meet in church because Esther's host, Mr Boythorn, is a near neighbour of the Dedlocks; but Boythorn is Jarndyce's friend, we may infer, through the Chancery web. Mrs Rachel turns up again as Mrs Chadband and re-enters Esther's history; but then, she is one of the few people who really knows about Esther, and she and her husband are not without a holy eye to the main chance. Mr Allan Woodcourt lands at Deal just as Esther arrives there to reason with Richard. This is 'pure' coincidence, yet people do meet at odd and unexpected times. Charley is maid to the Smallweeds before her rescue by Esther: but her father's profession would have brought him in touch with people like the Smallweeds just as it brings him in touch with Skimpole, and so with Esther herself. Richard borrows money from Grandfather Smallweed and chooses Mr George's establishment for his military training: but Grandfather Smallweed is not unknown in the Chancery circles Richard chooses to move in, and Mr George has his own good reasons for haunting Lincoln's Inn. Mr Bucket's lodger turns out to be Hortense; but, as Bucket supposes, this is Hortense's deliberate attempt to bamboozle him.

What else have we in the way of coincidence? George was the

one confidant of Captain Hawdon as well as being the long-lost
son of Chesney Wold's housekeeper; the two people who are
'wery good' to Jo are Esther's unknown father and Esther herself. Jo, in turn, becomes involved both with Esther, whom he
unwittingly infects with smallpox, and with Lady Dedlock,
whom he unwittingly helps to destroy. These are perhaps again
'pure' coincidences, though they are not without associative
threads. It is because Nemo is very good to him that Jo gets
dragged into the Inquest, and it is because he gets dragged into
it that Lady Dedlock seeks him out. At the same time, the community of Nemo and Jo in poverty is sufficiently probable, given
Nemo's fellow-feeling for one worse off than himself.

The claim to be made about these coincidences is hard to for-
mulate but it ought, to my mind, to be high. The notion that
coincidences should not be permitted in a novel belongs presumably to a theory that characters in fiction should interact only
through patterns of logic and fitness inherent in some artistic
purpose or design. This is to push the novel away from realism
towards pure artifice, where laws, whether of the artist's intention or of art itself, hold unchallenged sway. But if coincidences
are possible in life there should be a place for them in fiction,
however this requires to be subsumed to aesthetic tact. Certain
negative laws of tact, indeed, immediately suggest themselves.
We should not feel that the author is using coincidence to mani-
pulate our responses more than the whole action and concept
sanction; we should not feel strains upon either the credibility of
the subject-matter or the homogeneity of art. But such demands
suggest a more positive test, which Dickens very readily passes:
coincidences in fiction should be happily translated into the texture of art. In *Bleak House*, the coincidences do not weight the
novel towards any precise philosophy or genre commitment, yet
they do not strike us merely as an easy way out. They release the
characters into mutual interaction of the kind we sense as
plausible, and artistically fitting; and they reinforce the manifold
indications of a web. The manner in which the characters react
to coincidences is invariably plausible, and the mingled good and
evil which runs through the coincidences accord with the sense

of reality operative in the book. It may be, however, that Dickens is hinting at certain values inescapably binding people together in the social universe, beyond whatever nets Chancery, Tom-All-Alone's and Tulkinghorn may spread. Despite their diversity, the characters are all one with another: in the social dangers and challenges of disease and poverty; and in that intangible sphere where the bell tolls for us all.

One further facet of the novel's web-like quality may be pinpointed in the marvellous conjunction of Tulkinghorn and Bucket in a single book. Like Jaggers, Bucket poses problems which clearly teased Dickens. What are the ethics proper to a detective? When (if ever) can lying and treachery serve higher truth? How far need a man's profession commit him to guile? Bucket is a man of natural friendliness and good nature who uses these qualities most unscrupulously in his work. To all appearance they become, therefore, their diabolical opposites, a proof that warmth and good nature can never be 'known'. Bucket is like Tulkinghorn in that he enjoys his power over the people he probes, and is not above playing cat and mouse. Even if George's arrest *is* justified by some higher expediency, can we really accept Bucket's disingenuous account of the actual arrest? Three of the novel's stalwart innocents are much imposed upon; and Bucket is more or less sure (we learn later) that George is not really his game. Bucket, again, is chiefly responsible for Sir Leicester's stroke, by his method of breaking his news. The mystifications, which in a lesser detective tale might be *frissons* intended solely and permissibly for the reader, become psychological torture in a context as rich as this. Sir Leicester cannot fail to think that a far worse accusation against his much loved wife is in the offing, and Bucket can scarcely misjudge his victim's fears. Even before this denouement, we note that Bucket enjoys his power over a noble family; there are hints of some subtle if unpremeditated class-revenge in the relish with which he always calls Sir Leicester 'Sir Leicester Dedlock, Bart'. The only alternative explanation would be in terms of some mingling of innocence and ignorance such as we might find in Mr Boffin; but Bucket is a shrewd and highly arrogant man. At the best, Bucket seems too carried away by the pleasures of detection to be reliably human; at the worst, his profession may be a respectable occasion for insidious ends. There are moments when it would seem as churlish to mistrust his frankness as it would be to mistrust Pickwick. Yet he enjoys the pleasures of establishing false trust, like Tulkinghorn; and he enjoys the taste of a victim's fears.

The enigma remains that Bucket may after all be what he pretends to be; that a happy outcome, with justice done and innocence vindicated, is all he desires. Put differently, one might say that Bucket wants nothing better than to exist in warm friendliness with his fellow humanity, and that the deceit which prevents this is contributed by others, not by himself. If his friendliness seems both indisputably real and ineradicably devious, may it not be akin to the friendliness of a god? Yet there are seeds here of something profoundly sinister; more sinister it may even be than Dennis the Hangman in *Barnaby Rudge*. The technique of breaking down a victim by friendliness and imaginative empathy points to one of the most frightening roles in modern literature and life. The fact is that the friendliness and imaginative empathy *would* be real if the victim were not marked out to suffer; if the victim had not risked commitments which make him once and for all, and beyond all other appeals, fair game. From Dostoievsky's Grand Inquisitors, through O'Brien in *1984* to (say) Martin Eliot in C. P. Snow's *The New Men*, the pattern has become frighteningly familiar, and Bucket has his place in a line leading to these. He is splendidly uncommitted to anything except justice; and he has the Inquisitor's love, whether acknowledged or hidden, of power.

And yet Bucket is on the side of law, and resilience, in the healthiest form they can take. If anyone is fair game, is it not Hortense? Esther Summerson trusts Bucket, which is an important indication, and Dickens approved the detective's role in actual life. So perhaps George's sufferings *are* inescapable, and Bucket's is the proper exercise of power. Yet Bucket and Tulkinghorn live and resonate in a single book.

V

I propose now to turn to the structure of *Bleak House*, and to the
place of the heroine, in particular, in this. The structure of the
novel, like that of *Wuthering Heights* (1848), is experimental, in
that two narrations are intertwined. In *Wuthering Heights*, the
narration is shared between two minor characters, sharply con-
trasted in temperament and neither 'literary', who between them
create, nonetheless, the uniquely elemental quality of that work.
Dickens's procedure is sharply different. The narration of *Bleak
House* is shared between an impersonal narrator – 'the author' if
we choose to put it like that – and Esther Summerson, the most
important character in the tale. This arrangement has given birth
to several critical oversimplifications, for which the term 'the
author' – or even 'Dickens' – to describe the impersonal narrator
must chiefly be blamed. 'Not to put too fine a point on it', as Mr
Snagsby would say, the whole book is the author's, and the
notion that Esther Summerson represents only a part of his
genius, a deliberate impoverishment for reasons of 'realism', is
oddly naïve. A number of famous novels are cast in the form of
pseudo-autobiography and narrated by people who are not
represented as novelists, let alone as novelists of genius, but
usually we accept the convention readily enough. The author
creates the required tone for his 'I' character, whether ordinary
or extraordinary, and his success is a triumph, we realise, of
creative tact. Far from being an impoverishment of natural gifts
indeed this is their proper exercise, the adaptation of material
to form and structure for particular ends. We are no more
tempted to confuse the prose of Jane Eyre with that of a real
governess than we are to confuse the painted scenery in a theatre
with Venice or Rome. (It may be worth remarking, however, as
a marginal irony that, while most readers seem to be able to
accept Jane Eyre, Nelly Dean and the notorious Governess in
The Turn of the Screw as authentic narrators, the complaint
has sometimes been made that David Copperfield is not shown
as being 'creative' enough to write.)

If ironies of any kind in this area seem largely spurious, this is presumably because the creativity or otherwise of such narrators is not a cause for concern. One way or another an exact equation between the pseudo-narrator and his book does not seem to be made, and there is no reason, given the irreducible artificiality of art, why it should. In the consideration of *Bleak House*, however, it has often been asserted that the issue comes alive for a particular reason: which is, that Esther's chapters are deliberately 'toned down' in order to contrast with the 'pure', virtuoso Dickens of the rest. Geoffrey Tillotson, in a charming epilogue to the Signet edition, has put this most forcibly:

One method used for the construction of *Bleak House* came near to imperilling Dickens's power of writing as a poet writes. He entrusted the telling of some part of the story to one of the participants in it – Esther Summerson. It is possible that he made a mistake here. In any event it was a self-denying arrangement because it is a waste to have part of the story told by a comparatively simple person when it could have been told by a complex person such as Dickens himself.

This is courteously argued, but it seems to me mistaken, and to overlook the necessary requirements and varieties of form. W. J. Harvey argued a similar case in his admirable *Character and the Novel*, where he has excellent and highly sophisticated things to say about the structure, but includes in his defence of Dickens's method such admissions as this:

Esther's narrative is plain, matter-of-fact, conscientiously plodding. Only very rarely does her style slip and allow us to glimpse Dickens guiding her pen. . . . Such moments apart, any stylistic vivacity or idiosyncrasy in Esther's prose comes from the oddities and foibles of other characters. Dickens imagines them; Esther merely reports them.

It is possible to see how such distinguished critics come to make this distinction between Esther and her author, but still to wonder whether it arises only when Esther is recalled in retrospect and not when the novel is actually being read. Esther has a tone certainly, very complex really for all its serenity, but what tone is not limiting to some degree? If we return to her chapters, we

find in them many of the most characteristically Dickensian
things we could ask. Chapter 5, for instance, is a marvel of
symbolism. It describes the first visit of the wards in Jarndyce to
Miss Flite's room, their first sight of her birds, their first meeting
with Krook and Lady Jane. The web of circumstance which
Esther does not know about already entangles her, in that she is
now under her father's roof. The prose is richly poetic, and
develops, as a subtexture to Esther's sane good humour, the
themes and images of the chapters before. To describe this as
'matter of fact' or 'prosaic' can only be a compliment to Dickens,
for preserving our sense of such qualities in Esther *despite* her
style. Later, Esther's narrative contains scenes of vintage Dickens
humour – the visit to the Bayham Badgers, the announcement
to old Mr Turveydrop and then to Mrs Jellyby of Caddy's engagement, the visitation of Mrs Guppy – where satire is beautifully controlled by Esther's humorous eye. In addition, a number
of the most famous of all Dickens's characters are created wholly
or almost wholly in Esther's chapters: Mrs Jellyby, John Jarndyce, Miss Flite, Harold Skimpole, Mr Turveydrop, Mrs Pardiggle, the Bayham Badgers, Richard Carstone, Allan Woodcourt and his mother, Mrs Guppy, Mrs Blinder, Mr Boythorn.
She also has her fair share in the creation of still further unmistakably Dickensian characters: Krook, Vholes (the best
descriptions are hers), Guppy, and Bucket himself. To suggest
that Dickens 'imagined' these characters and Esther merely
'reported' them must be an oversimplification since where, but
in 'her' prose, do they exist? Her quality of observation, moreover, is essentially creative; Skimpole and Turveydrop would not
have grown quite as they do without Esther's tone. All of this
inventiveness not only stands up excellently to the inventiveness of the impersonal narrator (whose characters include the
whole or most of Sir Leicester and Lady Dedlock, George and
Phil, the Rouncewells, the Smallweeds, Mr Chadband, Mr and
Mrs Bagnet, Mr and Mrs Snagsby, Jo, Guster, Tony Jobling,
Volumnia, Bucket, and pre-eminently Tulkinghorn), but they
stand up as belonging to the same structure and texture, the
same novel. It is worth remarking that the fifty or so main

characters in *Bleak House* have, almost without exception, their distinctive speech-rhythms, whether they belong to Esther's chapters or not. Esther also enjoys the Dickensian distinction of creating unforgettable characters with *en passant* felicity: witness Professor Dingo, whose famous last words mediated by his relict are all we have of him ('Where is Laura? Let Laura bring me my tea and toast'), and the novel's escalating children – Mrs Jellyby's, Mrs Pardiggle's, Coavinses', Mr Skimpole's, and Mr Vholes's.

Esther is able to create Dickensian characters and situations plausibly by virtue of a number of qualities, some obvious, some apparently less obvious, which she is given. She is highly obser-vant (the one quality she readily admits to), and extremely intelligent, the most intelligent good woman that Dickens drew. Her intelligence is chiefly moral and intuitive, a kind of common sense raised towards wisdom. She can 'smell out' people's moral natures by instinct (a characteristic which she shares with one or two other virtuous characters, like Little Nell, but also with one or two morally ambivalent characters like Susan Nipper and Jenny Wren, as well as with villains like Carker and Jasper, in whom the clairvoyance takes a frightening form). She is also given a high degree of self-knowledge and unusual gifts of self-sacrifice even though she lacks the experience of the world required to 'place' people of unusual types. Her instinctive sense that there is something seriously wrong with Mrs Jellyby and Mrs Pardiggle, with Harold Skimpole and old Mr Turveydrop, coexists therefore with suspended judgement, and a willingness to let them speak for themselves. In all this, Esther's tone is wholly without malice. Indeed, her morally aware but un-malicious intelligence is sufficiently a rarity to make of it, in so far as it is really Dickens's, a virtuoso display. Against her grow-ing insight into Skimpole and Turveydrop we have counter-pointed her charitable tolerance and her unfailing eye for the 'funny side'. Our own awareness of these characters, sufficiently scathing, is mediated through this distinctive view. It is modi-fied, indeed, by Esther's tone, as well as by the more normal Dickensian complexities attendant upon larger-than-life charac-ters with a talent for creating themselves.

My claim is that Esther is that rare thing in the novel, a convincing depiction of moral goodness; and what I have to say on the structure of *Bleak House* depends on this claim. But why, if this is so, is she unpopular? – as she seems to be with many students today. The deeper causes are no doubt historical, and to these I shall return. Changes in attitude towards humility and gratitude, for instance, have followed the rise of welfare services and the emancipation of women, and Esther's world is already extinct. But a few obvious strands must first be disentangled, in the area where modern readers rush towards a 'personal' response. The two most usual criticisms of Esther centre on her 'false humility' and her 'cloying sentimentality', the first in her references to herself when she is recording other people's praise of her, the second chiefly in her relationship with Ada Clare. Some readers appear to read all humility as false humility, and to forget that Uriah Heep's creator might not have shared this view. If humility can be real, how can it express itself? – how, except in terms of a whole personality, can we tell true from false? Esther does not use her humility to work upon or to embarrass other people, and her tone is eminently part of shared household ease. She does not really use it to evade self-knowledge; the passages in which she comes to accept her lost looks, for instance, are touchingly direct and frank. It arises, rather, from her unwillingness to be more central to the novel than she need be, or to see her affairs as in any way competing, in our attention, with her tale. And this is because she doesn't see herself as central; it is only we who come to see this before the end. There is no reason, after all, why Esther should think of herself as important, since she shares no romantic obsessions with the 'self'. As an illegitimate child with no particular gifts or prospects, she has been trained to regard herself chiefly as a blight. We have to remember that she is born an outcast, and that her childhood is overshadowed by the gloomy view that her birth is a misfortune and a disgrace. One of the most basic challenges in the novel is voiced by Esther's godmother: *would* it have been better if Esther had never been born? If the reader is confronted even today with complexities in such a question, it is unlikely that

Esther herself would have emerged unscathed. Then, we must recall Esther's debt to Jarndyce, without whom she would have been at best a governess, at worst part of the floating wreckage of society like Jo. Gratitude seems a natural as well as an appropriate response to Jarndyce's selfless love of her (selfless even after he has been led, by all too understandable weakness, to his one big mistake). A Victorian girl could expect no rescue through educational opportunities or welfare services, and there is no reason why Esther should have shared the mistrust of gratitude which a modern woman, attuned to education and welfare, might feel. Anything like political engagement with women's rights is wholly outside the range of her social position or, indeed, her temperament. (When Borrioboola-Gha fails, Mrs Jellyby turns her attention to 'the rights of women to sit in Parliament'. Esther's gentle scorn merely mirrors the larger scorn of Dickens and, of course, Carlyle, whom Mrs Jellyby might have been specially designed to please.) Esther pre-dates, in effect, democracy as well as socialism, and is happy enough to make the best of her lot in a tragic world.

'Happy enough': but this may still be found offensive, even when the historical imagination has done its work. Would a more spirited woman not have anticipated our modern attitude, and reacted with rebellion or despair? Esther's virtues, whether of patient suffering or domestic affection, seem curiously alien to our present time. It may be all too easy, then, to overlook that her good humour and sanity are won at the price of great courage and self-discipline, or, noticing this, to feel that the victory is not worth the price. A modern Esther might brood on the problem of her identity as of obligation, and feel a moral duty, almost, to go mad. Such a character would undeniably be interesting, and it is no accident that Dickens's most emotionally self-indulgent heroine, Florence Dombey, finds an easier path to modern hearts. Yet courage and sanity like Esther's are not despicable, and are never easily achieved in a tragic world. Esther has to confront an existence overshadowed with gloom and mystery, and beset, despite Jarndyce's kindness, with suffering; she has to endure Richard's downfall (dragging Ada with him), her own unrequited (as she thinks) love, smallpox and the loss of her looks, her guardian's proposal (a very subtle sadness), and, most terrible for one of her temperament, the knowledge that her very existence is a threat to her mother's life. All of this is not melodrama but simple reality; the notion of a 'ruined woman' was not cant in Victorian society, whatever it might be in ours. It is in this context that we have to assess Esther's habit of spreading sanity and healing in other people's misfortunes, and her rejoicing in Ada's friendship and love. Many modern readers find the tone of this relationship particularly upsetting, since tenderness and whimsy in private life are currently taboo. Esther's relationship would be 'interesting' if it were labelled lesbian and pursued into sordid fantasies or dismal obsessions, but it is somehow embarrassing as it stands. Yet Dickens preferred not to label human affections, but to sense their individual qualities – in Miss Wade destructive and rooted in hatred, in Esther constructive and rooted in love. It is unlikely that Dickens would have been surprised by the insights of modern psychology, but he would have been contemptuous of any tendency to harden human relationships towards dogmatic norms. No doubt he would have detected hypocrisy in our present-day cult of toughness, just as we detect it in his occasional sympathy with gush.

There is one further criticism often made, of the chapter where Jarndyce reveals the second Bleak House to Esther, and this stands apart from the rest. The problem arose from Dickens's original marriage of a romantic plot and tradition with the *Bleak House* material, since the use of such surprise denouements is the classic stuff of romance. A similar doubt will be felt about *deus ex machina* figures like the elder Martin Chuzzlewit, and the testing of heroines, such as Bella's two testings in *Our Mutual Friend*. It may be that these romantic devices do not, or should not, consort with psychological realism – yet Dickens belongs with Shakespeare among those who made the attempt.

I have been making a case for Esther, but I hope not forensically, since it is not a matter of trying to assert personal liking for her against opposite views. The importance of the issue penetrates to *Bleak House*'s structure, to which Esther is more central than any other heroine (Amy Dorrit may be a possible exception to this) that Dickens produced.

Before my remarks on this aspect can be completed, however, a few observations about the impersonal narration require to be made. This impersonal narration isn't 'just' Dickens, it is Dickens more than usually split between roles. The impersonal narrative does not attempt the illusion of a single character, but includes everything Dickensian that is outside Esther's range. Perhaps for this reason it gives the impression of being 'masculine', but this is the only generalised comment I would care to make. The opening chapter, one of the most magnificent things in English, starts as a stage direction, then moves, with the introduction of main verbs in paragraph three, to a hauntingly permanent sense of here and now:

> The raw afternoon is rawest, and the dense fog is densest, and the muddy streets are muddiest near the leaden-headed old obstruction, appropriate ornament for the threshold of a leaden-headed old corporation, Temple Bar. And hard by sits the Lord High Chancellor in his High Court of Chancery.
> On such an afternoon, if ever, the Lord High Chancellor ought to be sitting here – as here he is – with a foggy glory round his head, softly fenced in with crimson cloth and curtains, addressed by a large advocate with great whiskers, a little voice, and an interminable brief, and outwardly directing his contemplation to the lantern in the roof, where he can see nothing but fog. On such an afternoon some score of members of the High Court of Chancery bar ought to be – as here they are – mistily engaged in one of the ten thousand stages of an endless cause . . .

and so on. At a stroke, Dickens has performed his usual miracle of combining social realism with myth. Fog is in the imagery, in the long sentences, as it is in the endless causes brought up in Chancery, and in the Lord Chancellor's contemplation of the roof. All these things are one London afternoon, some time in early Victorian England; they are also now, when we read them; and they are always, in the always of art. Perhaps Dickens achieves this by that irresistible 'as here he is': we look up, and yes indeed, here he *is*. The 'large advocate' is not unlike the doorkeeper of the Law in Kafka's celebrated parable in *The Trial*: both seem dreamlike, permanent, undoubtedly significant; but what do they mean?

The impersonal narrative is available for poetically rich evocations, but also for very much more. The tone in which Dickens deals with the Dedlocks is tinged with irony, yet the description of Chesney Wold in the rain is incipiently tragic, and the more we see of the Dedlocks, the more satire, in its pure form at least, is forced to yield ground. In a very different vein, Dickens depicts the three clerks conspiring together in chapter 20, where the exact nuances of their shared tone – heavy jesting, shabby goodwill or pretended goodwill, incurable vulgarity – do not conflict with equally exact discriminations: Guppy's minimal decency, given his opportunism; Tony Jobling's directionless amorality; Small's family meanness just faintly tinged with amiability. There is, in addition, the side of Dickens which celebrates the Bagnets, and the side which savagely indicts society on behalf of poor Jo; the side which creates an exuberant maverick like Bucket, and the side which probes Tulkinghorn's evil and Vholes's deceit. And not least, the impersonal narrator is available for the tremendous set-piece when Krook goes off in Spontaneous Combustion: the chapter in this novel, and most of his novels have one such chapter, where under the sanction of symbolism Dickens lets his most horrendous imaginings loose.

VI

Bleak House presents us with many features reminiscent of Kafka, but its final effect is not the same. Why not? Partly – and this aspect requires particularly to be mentioned – because Dickens believes in the human will. His pessimism has been overstressed by those who mistake his satire; if he overstates for effectiveness, as all ironists must, he is not one who stumbles, in overstatement, on despair. He was highly disillusioned with particular people and particular institutions, but he still believed in the divinity of man. He did not finally despair of men working through their own corrupt institutions and just occasionally producing – from Parliament even – a triumph of enlightened common sense. By the same token, he did not despair of righting wrongs, however longstanding and intractable. If he were writing today about Negro ghettos in great American and British cities (and if he were alive today, who would stop him?) it would be more in the tone of battered liberalism than of bitter hate. His vision of suffering is not absurdist but tragic, with the particular areas of hope allowed by this.

It follows that Dickens would have expected *Bleak House* to be effective, and that he would not have been surprised by its success. He would have agreed with leading articles in *The Times* of the same period that the abuses of Chancery were curable, and that society might be forced in the end to pay for sanitation, however unwillingly, by the twin spurs of residual idealism and personal fear. He would have expected that horrors such as Tom-All-Alone's might be demolished and relegated to history, first in Britain (*pace* Mrs Jellyby), and later perhaps throughout the world. His novel is no statement of the inevitability of such evils nor does it employ them as symbols of metaphysical gloom. It is important to reflect that the specific abuses pervading *Bleak House* have in fact all been remedied or greatly alleviated, including one which Dickens would almost certainly have regarded as beyond repair. Even the fog has been banished from London, *and* by Act of Parliament. Since the Clear Air Act, there are no London Particulars any more.

The social evils depicted in *Bleak House* were solvable, and Dickens knew this in his bones. The law still has its delays, but none like Chancery; there is still disease in the world, but cholera is controlled and so is smallpox; there are still slums, but children like Jo no longer die in the streets around us every day. How could such things ever be in Christian England? This was Dickens's challenge and one source of his energy; *could* ordinary men, once really appraised of such things, allow them? He was assisted by confidence in his own power as an artist, and in the power of art generally to extend human imagination and compassion in practical ways. Humphry House did a certain amount

of harm by pointing out that some of the abuses which Dickens
wrote about had already been alleviated before he published the
novel in which they appeared. This has turned in some versions
into the notion that Dickens attacked abuses only when they
were safely past. Perhaps no one who has ever engaged in social
reform could fall into this particular error. Even specific evils –
such as the Marshalsea – carry possibilities of resurrection, while
other evils, such as the Poor Laws, required to be exposed and
attacked throughout the span of Dickens's life. It is a liberal
fallacy to imagine that social progress proceeds inevitably, and
that any victory can be supposed safe when once it is won.
Dickens's task was not to remove specific evils – not that only –
but to re-educate his readers in their own day and age. Con-
templating the proliferating evils of industrial England in a
laissez-faire climate, he was winding up human understanding
and compassion towards the welfare state. This, in turn, he
would have seen as no more than applied Christianity, the trans-
lation of the simple tenets of faith into simple deeds. Do as you
would be done by; we are all members one with another;
ask not for whom the bell tolls, it tolls for thee. The universal-
ity of these tenets raised his art also above its immediate context, since they are precisely the moral elements fitted for all
time.

In all this side of his work Dickens was motivated by tremendous energy and hopefulness, which is why we cannot stress
his affinities with Kafka to the exclusion of all else; in his own
life and creation, he never succumbed to despair. Misunder-
standings about this may be aggravated by one notable aspect of
his technique. Though he tried to arouse all that was most compassionate in his readers, he did not neglect the other spur to
action through their fears. Hence the stress upon slums as a
breeding-ground of disease, crime and political subversion; of
plagues that would reach from the foul courts of London right
to the mansions of the great. The cholera struck London in 1848,
and again when *Bleak House* was being written (it was almost
unknown there until 1832, when its appearance was greeted by
some opponents of Reform as a sign). By having his heroine

infected with smallpox, however, Dickens recognises dangers
inherent in virtue itself in our fallen world.

It seems clear to me that for these and other reasons Dickens's
novels ought to remain anchored, for the critic, in their author's
close relationship with his readers – both the Victorian audience,
to whose influence he was highly sensitive, and by only a slight
extension to his very different audience of today. Our own
society, confronted with the ghettos of Harlem and Detroit,
Brixton and Notting Hill, is not all that much better placed than
the Victorians. We can no more afford surely than the original
readers either to deny Tom-All-Alone's its social reality, or to
turn it into a symbol of some supposedly incurable spiritual
or intellectual *malaise*.

VII

Which returns me to Esther, and to her part in the novel's
success.

Esther's subversive role in the novel is that of simply existing,
and the whole structure of *Bleak House* turns on this. What
would the novel be like if she did not exist in it as a central
character, but simply as Lady Dedlock's tragic mistake? Her
godmother's fears might seem wholly justified, in that she is
her mother's curse in life and her mother's death. She is – even
more strikingly – the thread used by Tulkinghorn in the spinning of his murderous web. The fear which Lady Dedlock
succumbs to, and which Tulkinghorn feeds on, is Esther's
existence in the world. Esther's existence is unfortunate not
simply, therefore, in her godmother's gloomy religion, but in the
social realities it creates. 'It would have been far better, little
Esther, that you had had no birthday; that you had never been
born!' The novel challenges its readers with this formulation. Do
we agree with it for reasons of expediency, perhaps, or of
psychological realism, if for no other cause?

If Esther were not actually present in the novel, the moral
challenge would be present in a less striking way. But, instead, it
exists in and through her personal reality, as a centre of courage,

humour, healing and love. By her actions, she proves the continuing reality of private charity and compassion; she forms, in
company with Jarndyce, Mr Snagsby, Allan Woodcourt, George,
Mrs Blinder and the two Bagnets, a most powerful witness to
good. Though Dickens believed that such charity was not
sufficient to heal society, he would have seen it as leaven in the
lump. Esther, who has so much to lament and fear, counts her
blessings, and is a source of blessing to all whom she helps.

This is the wholly simple and wholly subversive centre of the
novel's complexity, the wood we must at all costs see for the
trees. To see it isn't easy, as Dickens no doubt realised, even
before he read (if he did) his earliest reviews. Esther is fair game
to the righteous as an inconvenient bastard, just as she is fair
game to comfortable sophisticates as a bore. But her tone is a
triumph of courage and sanity over many varieties of suffering,
and its simplicity, in context, is serene. She keeps *Bleak House*
sane and sparkling, for all its terror; for all the strong pulls
against her, even, from Dickens himself. With *Hard Times*,
Dickens plunged into his gloomiest decade, but *Bleak House*
contrives to remain, somehow, in the sun.

Esther is a gravitational pull against pessimism and defeatism,
the harbinger of domestic virtue, happiness and peace. In the
larger structure of the novel, Dickens is released by his experimental form into a delicate patterning, of Esther's tone against
the rest. The impersonal narration starts in fog and rain, rises
through dramatic evil and mystery to large climaxes, and then
returns to darkness and rain. A sombre start, and a sombre conclusion – the fall of Sir Leicester Dedlock's wife, his house, the
whole order, in many ways so admirable, for which he stands.
Through this, the heroine's narrative runs like a healing thread.
The central character in the web of mystery and evil, though she
only gradually comes to know this, she continually transmutes
evil into good. The last chapter of the novel, after the impersonal
narrator has left us in twilight, is Esther's; she is still counting
her blessings, and speaking now of happiness; seven richly
rewarding years with the man she loves. For once, Dickens
depicts virtue as active and happy; and plausibly, as well as suit-

ably, rewarded from within. Later, his virtuous people become more withdrawn again, more assimilated, like Agnes already in *David Copperfield*, to shadow and gloom.

But the world of *Bleak House*, though not irredeemable, remains tragic; it is the tragic world of Christian belief. Esther Summerson is a stranger and pilgrim, and lives like one; here she has no abiding home. It is her doing chiefly (though Allan Woodcourt's more directly) that Jo dies with the unfamiliar words of the Lord's Prayer on his lips, and Richard Carstone starts a world which sets *this* world to rights. For Dickens, this is the heart of the human mystery; as it has been for Christianity in every age until (perhaps) our own.

SELECT BIBLIOGRAPHY

THERE are several journals which regularly publish articles on Dickens, notably *The Dickensian* (published by the Dickens Fellowship in London) and three American journals – *Victorian Studies, Nineteenth Century Fiction* and *Dickens Studies*.

BOOKS

For my own selection of the best modern books on Dickens, see the select bibliography in *Dickens*, ed. A. E. Dyson, in the Modern Judgements series (Macmillan, 1968). A fuller bibliography will be found in *The Dickens Critics*, ed. George H. Ford and Lauriat Lane, Jr (Cornell U.P., 1961; O.U.P. paperback, 1968). There is also Ada Nisbet's very full bibliography with comments in *Victorian Fiction: A Guide to Research*, ed. Lionel Stevenson (Harvard U.P., 1964).

The best biography of Dickens is Edgar Johnson's *Charles Dickens: His Tragedy and Triumph*, 2 vols (Simon and Schuster, 1952; Gollancz, 1953). Edgar Johnson's critical account of *Bleak House* is reprinted here, but the biography also gives an account of Dickens's life at the time when he was writing the novel, and everyone who studies or enjoys Dickens should turn to this. The biography by Dickens's friend John Forster has been often reprinted, and is still essential reading for students.

Many of the critical books on Dickens's works as a whole have excellent chapters on *Bleak House*, or illuminating comments which can be tracked down from the index. In addition to books from which extracts have been reprinted here, I would suggest the following for particular attention (they are arranged chronologically):

G. K. Chesterton, *Charles Dickens* (Methuen, 1906). This is erratic but always stimulating; less good on *Bleak House* than on most of the other novels.

Jack Lindsay, *Charles Dickens: A Biographical and Critical Study* (Dakers, 1950). A very left-wing – indeed Marxist – Dickens. But the best of the Marxist accounts.

George H. Ford, *Dickens and his Readers: Aspects of Novel-criticism since 1836* ((Princeton U.P., 1955; Norton Library paperback, 1965). An excellent factual and descriptive account of Dickens's reputation during his lifetime and afterwards.

Philip Collins, *Dickens and Crime* (Macmillan, 1962; St Martin's Press, 1962) and *Dickens and Education* (Macmillan, 1963; St Martin's Press, 1964). Two books of great value not only to readers of Dickens but also to historians interested in his period.

Robert Garis, *The Dickens Theatre: A Reassessment of the Novels* (O.U.P., 1965). A good account of the theatrical elements in *Bleak House* and Dickens's work generally.

ARTICLES

First, I have to mention the two seminal essays on Dickens with which all his readers should be familiar – those by George Orwell and Edmund Wilson. Both contain excellent sections on *Bleak House*, but they have to be read as a whole, and are too long for inclusion here. George Orwell's essay 'Charles Dickens', written in 1939, has been reprinted several times. It will be found in his *Collected Essays* (Secker and Warburg, 1961). Edmund Wilson's 'Dickens: The Two Scrooges' is also readily available, notably in *The Wound and the Bow* (Houghton Mifflin and W. H. Allen, 1941; and also in Methuen paperbacks, 1961).

The omission which most saddens me is Morton Dauwen Zabel's '*Bleak House*: The Undivided Imagination'. Permission to reprint this could not be obtained, but fortunately it is readily accessible in *The Dickens Critics*, ed. Ford and Lane (see above). Of the many other articles concerned with or mentioning *Bleak House* the following merit special mention:

Fred W. Boege, 'Point of View in Dickens', in *Publications of the Modern Language Association of America*, LXV (1950).

Norman Friedman, 'The Shadow and the Sun: Notes toward a Reading of *Bleak House*', in *Boston University Studies in English*, III (1957).

Louis Crompton, 'Satire and Symbolism in *Bleak House*', in *Nineteenth Century Fiction*, XII (1957–8).

John Butt, '*Bleak House* Once More', in *Critical Quarterly*, I (1959).

Robert Alan Donovan, 'Structure and Idea in *Bleak House*', in *The Shaping Vision: Imagination in the English Novel from Defoe to Dickens* (1966).

Finally, I should like to remind readers that the pieces reprinted here by J. Hillis Miller and Taylor Stoehr have had to be shortened for reasons of space. J. Hillis Miller's book is one of the classics of modern criticism, and Taylor Stoehr should certainly be read by Dickensians.

NOTES ON CONTRIBUTORS

JOHN BUTT held a chair at Edinburgh at the time of his death. In addition to his well-known *Dickens at Work* written with Kathleen Tillotson (1957) his publications included *The Augustan Age* (1950). He was also working on *The Mid-Eighteenth Century*, vol. VIII of the *Oxford History of English Literature*.

C. B. COX is Professor of English at the University of Manchester and co-editor of the *Critical Quarterly*. His book *The Free Spirit* was published in 1963.

A. E. DYSON is Senior Lecturer in the School of English and American Studies in the University of East Anglia, and co-editor of the *Critical Quarterly*. His book *The Crazy Fabric* was published in 1965.

MONROE ENGEL is Professor of English at Harvard. His book *The Maturity of Dickens* was published in 1959.

W. J. HARVEY was Professor of English at the Queen's University, Belfast, at the time of his death in 1967. His book *Character and the Novel* was published in 1965.

HUMPHRY HOUSE died in 1955 at the age of forty-six, soon after he had started to edit Dickens's letters. His best-known book is *The Dickens World* (1941).

EDGAR JOHNSON is Professor of English at the City College of New York. His famous biography *Charles Dickens: His Tragedy and Triumph* was first published in 1952.

J. HILLIS MILLER is Professor of English at Yale University. His books include *Charles Dickens: The World of his Novels* (1958) and *The Disappearance of God* (1963).

MARK SPILKA is Chairman of the English Department at

Brown University, and co-editor of *Novel*. In addition to *Dickens and Kafka* (1963) he is the author of *The Love Ethic of D. H. Lawrence*.

TAYLOR STOEHR is Assistant Professor in the Department of English at Cornell University. His book *Dickens: The Dreamer's Stance* was published in 1965.

KATHLEEN TILLOTSON was Hildred Carlile Professor of English at the University of London. In addition to *Dickens at Work*, written with the late John Butt (1957), she is author of *Novels of the Eighteen-Forties* (1954).

INDEX